Representations of "Japanese Nature"

Studies in Environmental Anthropology and Ethnobiology

General Editor: **Roy Ellen**, FBA
Professor of Anthropology, University of Kent at Canterbury

Interest in environmental anthropology has grown steadily in recent years, reflecting national and international concern about the environment and developing research priorities. This major new international series, which continues a series first published by Harwood and Routledge, is a vehicle for publishing up-to-date monographs and edited works on particular issues, themes, places, or peoples that focus on the interrelationship between society, culture and environment. Relevant areas include human ecology, the perception and representation of the environment, ethno-ecological knowledge, the human dimension of biodiversity conservation and the ethnography of environmental problems. While the underlying ethos of the series will be anthropological, the approach is interdisciplinary.

Recent volumes:

Volume 34
Representations of "Japanese Nature"
A Historical Overview
Emiko Ohnuki-Tierney

Volume 33
Desert Entanglements
The Making of the Badiya by Sahrawi Refugees of Western Sahara
Gabriele Volpato

Volume 32
Fig Trees and Humans
Ficus *Ecology and Mutualisms across Cultures*
Yildiz Aumeeruddy-Thomas and Martine Hossaert-McKey

Volume 31
Sentient Ecologies
Xenophobic Imaginaries of Landscape
Edited by Alexandra Coțofană and Hikmet Kuran

Volume 30
Living on a Time Bomb
Local Negotiations of Oil Extraction in a Mexican Community
Svenja Schöneich

Volume 29
Grazing Communities
Pastoralism on the Move and Biocultural Heritage Frictions
Edited by Letizia Bindi

Volume 28
Delta Life
Exploring Dynamic Environments Where Rivers Meet the Sea
Edited by Franz Krause and Mark Harris

Volume 27
Nature Wars
Essays around a Contested Concept
Roy Ellen

Volume 26
Ecological Nostalgias
Memory, Affect and Creativity in Times of Ecological Upheavals
Edited by Olivia Angé and David Berliner

Volume 25
Birds of Passage
Hunting and Conservation in Malta
Mark-Anthony Falzon

For a full volume listing, please see the series page on our website:
http://berghahnbooks.com/series/environmental-anthropology-and-ethnobiology

Representations of "Japanese Nature"

A Historical Overview

Emiko Ohnuki-Tierney

berghahn
NEW YORK · OXFORD
www.berghahnbooks.com

First published in 2025 by
Berghahn Books
www.berghahnbooks.com

© 2025 Emiko Ohnuki-Tierney

All rights reserved. Except for the quotation of short passages for the purposes of criticism and review, no part of this book may be reproduced in any form or by any means, electronic or mechanical, including photocopying, recording, or any information storage and retrieval system now known or to be invented, without written permission of the publisher.

Library of Congress Cataloging-in-Publication Data

A C.I.P. cataloging record is available from the Library of Congress
Library of Congress Cataloging in Publication Control Number: 2024952232

British Library Cataloguing in Publication Data

A catalogue record for this book is available from the British Library

ISBN 978-1-80539-855-4 hardback
ISBN 978-1-80539-867-7 paperback
ISBN 978-1-80539-856-1 epub
ISBN 978-1-80539-857-8 web pdf

https://doi.org/10.3167/9781805398554

With love and gratitude, in memory of my parents

Ohnuki Kōzaburō and Ohnuki Taka

Contents

List of Illustrations	ix
Acknowledgments	xi

Part I. Foundation

Introduction. "Nature" in Anthropological Theories — 3

Chapter 1. Inhabitants of the Universe — 21

Part II. "Japanese Nature" by the Elite

Chapter 2. Rice Paddies with Pure Water: Birth of "Japanese Nature" in the Early Nara Period (710–794) — 47

Chapter 3. Agrarian Four Seasons to Culturally Defined Four Seasons: The Late Nara Period (710–794) and Heian Period (794–1185) — 63

Chapter 4. Rock Garden as "Japanese Nature": Medieval Period (1185–1603) — 84

Part III. "Nature" as the Symbol of the Japanese Collective Self

Chapter 5. Rice Paddies, Cherry Blossoms, and Mount Fuji as "Japanese Nature": Edo Period (1603–1867) — 103

Chapter 6. Nationalization and Militarization of "Japanese Nature": Modern Period (1868–1945) — 120

Part IV. "Nature" Consumed

Chapter 7. Domestication/Commodification of "Japanese Nature": Contemporary Period (after 1945) — 137

Chapter 8. Rice as Pure Money: Cultural Bases of Consumerism 160

Conclusion 175

References 184
Index 213

Illustrations

Figures

Figure 0.1. Catfish in "nature." Chart by the author. — 13

Figure 1.1. The oldest deity figure. Ninth century CE. Matsunoo Taisha no Shin'ei, 2011. — 25

Figure 1.2. Rice straw rope demarcating sacred space. Matsunoo Taisha no Shin'ei, 2011. Photo by the author. — 31

Figure 1.3. Fox as a sacred messenger. Inari Shrine at Fushimi. Photo by the author. — 35

Figure 1.4. Cow as a sacred messenger. Sugawara Tenmangū Jinja. Photo by the author. — 37

Figure 1.5. Monkey Performance: trainer and monkey drink together as brothers. Courtesy of Y. Azuma. — 38

Figure 4.1. The rock garden at Ryōanji Temple. Adobe Stock image. — 91

Figure 5.1. Shaping tree trunks and branches. Photo by the author. — 109

Figure 5.2. *Netsuke*: tigress with two cubs. The Walters Art Museum. — 110

Figure 6.1. *Tokkōtai* (kamikaze) plane with a cherry petal on the side. Yasukuni Shrine. Courtesy of R. Kenji Tierney. — 130

Figure 7.1. An inside dog in a "pet cart." Photo by the author. — 144

Figure 7.2. "Strict taboo for footwear." Photo by the author. — 154

Figure 7.3. Taking shoes off at the entrance to an inn. Photo by the author. — 155

Figure 7.4. Buddhist monk purifying a car. Courtesy of Carolyn Dodd. 157

Figure 8.1. "Love locks" on a bridge in Paris in 2019. Photo by the author. 166

Figure 8.2. Rice wine offertory. Heian Shrine. Photo by the author. 169

Figure 8.3. Counting of money offertory. Fushimi Inari Shrine on 4 January 2020. Courtesy of *Kyōto Shinbun*. 171

Figure 8.4. Amulet advertisement for tourism in Tokyo at subway stations. Photo by the author. 173

Tables

Table 1.1. Animal Metamorphosis into Humans During the Latter Half of Edo Period. From Nakamura 1984: 190; Ohnuki-Tierney 1987: 32–33. 34

Table 3.1. Frequency of References to Seasons on Manyōshū. From Satake et al. [2013] 2019; [2014] 2019. 65

Table 4.1. Twelve Months of the Year with Each Month Defined by a Flower and a Bird. Table based on the table composed by Shirane (2012: 65). 88

Acknowledgments

The fun and agony of any research are the unexpected questions, forcing one to search for more ethnographic and historical materials and also expanding one's theoretical understanding. When I began this work, I had no idea how much stretching I had to do into history, literature and arts, and even philosophy, in addition to anthropology. This book was the most difficult book manuscript I have undertaken.

Were it not for the incredibly fortunate blessing of the Vilas Research Professorship, this book, as well as others I wrote in the past, would not have been possible. I record my profound gratitude toward the William F. Vilas Trust Estate.

The topic of nature/culture relationship has been one of the most important and perennial topics in anthropology. I learned not only from Claude Lévi-Strauss's lifelong interest in the topic but from his brilliant insight into Japanese history and culture during the last stage of his life. His "humbleness" of reading all possible publications on Japan was simply astounding, giving me a humbling reminder about my own effort. I learned from his insistence on understanding the Other without imposing the yardstick of Western historical experience. I cherish his hand-written letters even when it became difficult for him to write.

On the opposite side of the Collège de France was the office of Pierre Bourdieu, where he listened to my interests for more than an hour, followed by offering his suggestions. He put me in touch with young scholars in his circle of research activities. His emphasis on the unconscious nature of power equality has been a most important theoretical tool to understand various types of power inequality, including the issue of representations of "nature" by cultural elite who represented "Japanese nature," which the people understood as "real nature," while the elite never intended to enforce their representations but which others willingly perceived as such.

Across the channel, Edmund Leach extended his encouragement for my work, especially on the multiple meanings of the same symbol in rituals and performances. In this work, I had to confront for the first time the profusion of "magic/superstitions" in contemporary Japan. His theory of "practical religion" turned out to be a powerful surgical knife. S. J. Tambiah's historical approach as well as his critique of social evolutionary theory gave me the theoretical model to think about the historical processes I examine in this book. Victor Turner offered me an unexpected treasure trove of intellectual stimulation and collegiality. His multivocality gave me the very foundation for the understanding of cherry blossoms that I have been writing about. I much appreciated his spontaneous phone calls.

Across the Atlantic and *the* theoretical divide, Clifford Geertz invited me to spend a year at the Institute for Advanced Study at Princeton. At lunch time those invited to the Institute made sure they sat as close as possible to where Geertz sits and engaged in fierce competition to impress him. I was not prepared for it and apparently out of it. Sensing my feeling of helplessness, he suggested that I go see a film, "Tin Men," playing in town in Princeton. It is a comedy, directed by Barry Levinson and starring Danny DeVito, about vicious confrontations and competitions between two door-to-door aluminum siding salesmen. The rivalry reaches a point of mutual self-destruction without any rationale. Geertz apparently wanted me to understand a dimension of American culture. We owe him for his monumental effort to locate cultural anthropology in the humanities. I learned from his decisive push away from functionalism in our understanding of power, as succinctly expressed in his statement, regarding Negara, that power served pomp, not pomp power.

My year at the Library of Congress, where I was appointed the Kluge Distinguished Chair of Modern Culture, gave me another learning experience from *the* librarian, James Billington. His exquisite cultural history of Russia, *The Icon and the Axe*, and meticulous attention to detail includes the use, for example, of synesthesia for understanding the liturgy of the Eastern Church. His cultural history is full of lyricism.

The two whose work became the source of encouragement for my study of Japan and its military period were Eric Wolf and Sidney Mintz. Eric Wolf's emphasis on the role of ideologies in how power works, both in small-scale societies and European nation-states, gave me the pathway to an understanding of Japan's imperial militarism. His handwritten letters when he traveled gave me such warm encouragement. Well before "global" and "everyday" became buzzwords, Sidney Mintz showed us how an anthropologist can make a unique contribution to the study of the role of the quotidian, in his case, sugar in global history. For decades, he wrote to me, encouraging me to take on Japan, a nation-state.

My incredibly fortunate career would not have been possible were it not for Jan Vansina, who was arguably the most important figure in African history. Indeed, his influence was most profound in my thinking about culture as historical processes, leading to the historicization of my study of Japanese culture. At the height of his profession, he offered a weekly reading course on theories in anthropology, despite his aversion to overly theoretical approaches in anthropology. He read every single article and book I published and offered me written comments.

James Fernandez was enormously generous in including me in the symbolic anthropology circle. His meticulous thinking in theory on metaphor and "beyond metaphor" have been most influential. Philippe Descola not only started me thinking "beyond nature and culture" but generously included me in his seminars so that I stayed in touch with the goings-on at Laboratoire d'Anthropologie Sociale, Collège de France. Michael Silverstein and Terry Turner kept mailing me a copy of their unpublished manuscripts, which I shared with the graduate students in our department. I met Don Handelman in 1982. Since then, we have been close colleagues and friends. This book falls short of truly incorporating his "forming" of "form," that is, his refusal of the static treatment of "form/structure," as articulated in his Deleuzian book *Moebius Anthropology: Essays on the Forming of Form*.

Mack Horton at the University of California, Berkeley, has been incredibly generous in helping me understand *waka* poems in *Manyōshū* of the eighth century. Haruo Shirane's *Japan and the Culture of the Four Seasons* is intimidatingly rich and detailed on the topic. I appreciate our collegial correspondences. I am deeply indebted to Miyata Noboru, whose encyclopedic knowledge of the folk culture of Japan has been an invaluable source.

All these extraordinarily fortunate professional experiences were possible because of Chester S. Chard, who supported me throughout graduate school. Working for him as a project assistant, I learned a great deal about the archaeology and prehistory of Japan. This became invaluable as I undertook the study of the Ainu and subsequently the anthropology of Japan, which involved a long period of history and prehistory.

I am profoundly appreciative of invaluable help I received at different stages of writing this book from Dr. Michael Hayata, Dr. Cody Gerhartz, Amanda Todd, and Leslie Kriesel.

On the home front, my late husband Tim tolerated me when I abandoned him several times to accept positions at the Institute for Advanced Study at Princeton and the Center for Behavioral Science at Princeton, The John W. Kluge Center at the Library of Congress, and several visiting positions, including those at Harvard, the University of Manchester, the *Ecole des Hautes Etudes en Sciences Sociales*, and the National Museum of Ethnology in Japan. Once, I told him that I had just finished my book manuscript. He asked me if I was starting the next one that evening or wait until the morning. He was known for his dry Irish humor. With his deep appreciation for the aesthetics of the quotidian, my son Alan took many marvelous photos in Japan, some of which have been used in my work. I learned from my anthropologist son Kenji's insights into Japanese culture and society.

This book is dedicated to my parents. They had gone through the 1923 Kantō earthquake, World War II, and many other calamities that the contemporary Japanese cannot even begin to understand. Through all these, they protected us from bombs, bullets, the scares of B-29s in the sky during the war, and from human malice, so that we grew up innocent of all the ills of the world. Yet, I left them, not realizing how much they would have enjoyed having me close and taking care of them in their last stage of life. I do not forgive myself for it.

Part I

Foundation

Introduction

"Nature" in Anthropological Theories

"Nature" as a concept is extremely elusive, yet it is commonly taken for granted by those who live in postindustrial societies that "pristine nature" is "out there." Using Japanese culture, I demonstrate how we often think of "representations of nature" as "pristine nature objectively out there," and I explore the factors that naturalized this view, challenging the positivist view, beginning with Plato, that "real nature" is "out there." I compare Japanese culture with other societies, including hunting-gathering and agricultural societies, on the one hand, and some western European societies, on the other.

With an understanding of culture as historical processes, this phenomenological study over a long period of Japanese culture proves that the cosmological scheme, such as the basic spatial division of the above with a positive valence and the below with a negative, does not constitute separate mental activities at higher levels but is intimately involved in the daily lives of people.

My discussion is in dialogue with debates in anthropological studies about "nature," social evolutionary theory, symbolic structure and the quotidian, representations, mimesis, and practical religion.

Anthropological Studies on Nature/Environment

The foundational work in the anthropological effort to understand the "nature" of various peoples is *Primitive Classification* by Durkheim and Mauss ([1901–2] 1963), written at the time anthropology was born in France as comparative sociology. They and many subsequent anthropologists have used the term "nature" to refer to the environment when describing peoples who themselves had/have neither a term nor a concept for "nature." Nonetheless, these anthropologists have left invaluable descriptions of these peoples' views of their environment.

Lévi-Strauss is the major figure whose Mythology series and in fact entire oeuvre is about the relationship between nature and culture, or "cooking" as the basic mode of culturalizing nature ([1949] 1969).

Approaches by anthropologists are quite diverse, leading to a very apt phrase, "Nature Wars," by Roy Ellen (2020). "Environment," also a diverse concept, complicates the question of what is "nature." Ellen ([2006] 2008: 190) opposes those who consider "nature" intrinsically "cultural." Tim Ingold (1993: 152) similarly opposes "the sterile opposition" between the "naturalistic view" of the landscape and the "culturalistic view."

While recognizing the importance of the question, I focus on representations of nature as untouched nature. People interact with their environment in reference to those beings who inhabit "nature," which is seldom perceived as an abstract space. Using examples of indigenous Australians, the Zuni, the Sioux, and the Chinese, Durkheim and Mauss describe how they perceive and conceptualize their environment. For example, among the people in the Mount Gambier area of Australia, the "crow quite naturally, by virtue of its colour, covers the rain and consequently winter, clouds, and—through these—lightning and thunder" ([1901–02] 1963: 20–21).

"Who" are allowed to be members of the universe and the stratification among them are crucial questions to ask for an understanding of a people's "nature." As detailed in chapter 1, the Japanese universe is predominantly inhabited by plants, which occupy the highest throne. Southeast Asians portray their universe in art primarily with plants, including flowers. The self-designation of both the People's Republic of China and the Republic of China starts with two characters for "The Central Flower of the Universe." In contrast, the African universe is inhabited primarily by animals. Like for the Ainu, it is *without* flowers, as Goody (1993: 1–27) points out in his first chapter, "No Flowers in Africa," in *The Culture of Flowers*.

In every culture, a large number of inhabitants, both plants and animals, are excluded from the mental stock of "nature." Many plants are written off as weeds, even though some may be a delicacy for some other peoples, as in the case of Japanese *nori*, referred to as seaweed in the West. The Japanese also associate dandelions with childhood memories of being in a field blowing the seeds to disperse them, as do Americans. As the lawn took pride of place in some societies, the plant became the most annoying enemy for those who treasure their lawn, i.e., culturally created nature, and for farmers since it may delay hay production because of its high water content. There are innumerable examples of undesirable fauna and flora excluded from "our nature."

My first anthropological work was a study of the Sakhalin Ainu, for whom, as for the Achuar of the Ecuadorian Amazon (Descola [2005] 2014), there is no separate concept or word for nature. They have an exhaustive knowledge of the beings of their environment, but their language does not have words for overall domains, such as "plants," "animals," and "nature." They select a certain number of fauna and flora to be the inhabitants of their universe. During my first fieldwork in 1965, on a fine spring day after a long winter in Hokkaido, Japan, Husko, my Ainu friend, and I stepped out of our house to collect plants in the field just outside, now full of vegetation. I immediately realized that the promontories in her mental picture of the grass field and those in mine were entirely different. My vision of the field was only flowers, nothing else catching my eyes. In contrast, Husko spotted every edible and medicinal plant whose useful parts were well developed, even those at some distance. There is no name for the whole plant in the Ainu language; rather, a distinct lexeme is given to each part of the plant—leaves and roots—that is useful. Flowers do not receive lexemes and did not have a place in Husko's mental image of the field (Ohnuki-Tierney 1974, 2021). Like the Achuar, the Ainu consider nonhuman animals similar to humans. When they meet humans, they don fur to offer the fur and the meat as their gifts to convey good wishes to humans.

Multisensory Perception of the Environment

The means of perception and understanding of the environment vary among peoples. Among European peoples, what Jay calls ocularcentrism ([1993] 1994: 40–41) began in the Renaissance as opposition to the interference of textuality preventing an unmediated vision of the divine, and it spread to nonreligious fields, leading to the celebration of Cartesian physics and turning nature into "a ventriloquist's dummy, of which man could make himself, as it were the lord and master" (Descola [2005] 2014: 61).

The Sakhalin Ainu use multiple senses, but vision is of least importance. Their perception of the environment and its inhabitants is uncannily reflected in their classification of headaches and boils. The terrestrial beings, such as bears, musk deer, dogs, and woodpeckers, are perceived auditorily (Ohnuki-Tierney 1977). For example, the bear headache is perceived by the sound that simulates the bear's heavy footsteps in the head, as opposed to the musk deer headache with the sound of lighter footsteps. The aquatic beings are perceived through thermal and tactile senses. The octopus headache simulates the tactile feeling of the suction cups of an octopus, accompanied by the chill, as opposed to the lamprey headache, which has the tactile sensation of sharp pain at one locus and accompanied by chills (for details, see Ohnuki-Tierney 1977).

Billington ([1966] 1970: 32–33) points out that at the fringe of "European civilization" in the Russian north, new church murals were becoming musical illustrations in the fourteenth century, and that the interdependence of sight, sound, and smell had been important in the liturgy of the Eastern Church. Although not about nature, this example shows the way multiple senses are used simultaneously.

Nature had been captured and represented by other means, such as music, as seen in Beethoven's Symphony no. 6 (*Pastoral*), in Flight of the Bumblebee by Nikolai Rimsky-Korsakov, or in "Song of the Flea" by Modest Mussorgsky—the list is long.

The affective dimension of nature varies widely. The Sakhalin Ainu consider its inhabitants as *pirika*, meaning "sacred and therefore beautiful." Thus, the bear is *pirika* because it is the supreme deity (Ohnuki-Tierney 1974). In Western scholarship, the discussion of nature often involves concepts of aesthetics: the "beautiful" and "sublime." The discussion of sublimity often begins with Longinus, a scholar of perhaps the first century CE, who defined it as "a kind of height and conspicuous excellence" and said its presence in speeches and writings drives people "not to persuasion, but to ecstasy" (1985: 8–9). That is, he emphasized that sublimity is not a conceptual understanding but an emotive response. Often referred to is Kant's distinction: "The Beautiful in nature is connected with the form of the object, which consists in having [definite] boundaries. The Sublime . . . is to be found in a formless object, so far as in it or by occasion of it *boundlessness* is represented, and yet its totality is also present to thought" ([1790] 2000: 101–2; [1793] 2001: 306–8). He adds: "Sublimity, therefore, does not reside in anything of nature, but *only in our mind*" ([1790] 2000: 129; my emphasis). Elsewhere, he explicitly states that it is incorrect to call any object of nature sublime, but it is correct to call many objects of nature beautiful (103). "The *beautiful* is that which pleases universally without [requiring] a concept" (67), and therefore, "*Beautiful Art is an art in so far as it seems like nature*" (187).

Some Basic Themes

There are some themes in reference to "nature" that are quite common across cultures, if not universal. Let me describe a few of them.[1]

No "Nature" as a Distinct Category

For people in small-scale societies, primarily hunting and foraging peoples, there is no "nature" as a category of their environment. Descola ([2005] 2014) points out that "nature" as a separate category does not exist among the Achuar as well as among many other groups. He describes the Achuar view of hunting: "Woolly monkeys, toucans, howler monkeys . . .

are . . . the 'complete persons,' . . . we kill them for food, but they are still relatives." The hunters establish "the bond of friendship" with particular members of these species (15). His book, *Beyond Nature and Culture*, starts with a quotation from Aristotle, who warns that "any attempt to demonstrate that nature exists would be absurd" but defines nature as "the sum total of beings" (1, 65).

The Sakhalin Ainu do not have nature as a separate category. Their "hunting" was a supreme religious activity, and less an economic value, as in the case of their treatment of the bear, the supreme deity. The deity, the bear, offers its flesh and fur as gifts to the Ainu, who, during the elaborate bear ceremony, offer their treasures as their return gift and send its soul back to the mountains, the home of the bear (Ohnuki-Tierney 1974: 16–31, 90–97; 1999).

Wild Nature to Be Conquered

In some of the large nation-states built on an agrarian economy, "wild nature" is constructed to be conquered by the king or some elite males. Pointing out how the strong symbolic connection between kingship and the hunting of oxen/bull developed and persisted, Bertelli ([1990] 2001: 114–26) tells us that Gilgamesh, the Sumerian ruler who is said to have reigned between 2900 and 2700 BCE, was called "the mighty wild bull." In Mycenaean Greece (c. 1600–1100 BCE), hunting was the source of political and military power (Hamilakis 2003).

The Greeks had various forms of hunting, with different significations for social status. Hunting with hunting dogs, called *cynegia* (dog driving), had the highest status. In Plato's utopia, young ruling-class males practiced only *cynegia* (Cartmill 1993: 31–32). Beginning in 80 CE, gladiatorial contests between Roman "hunters" and exotic animals vividly portrayed the Roman elites' attitude and activities related to hunting, an utmost show of the *conquest of wild nature* and a demonstration of masculinity. The medieval "royal hunt" starts with *the creation of wild nature*, a large royal forest near every chateau, like Château de Fontainebleau, which Francis I redeveloped starting in 1528, or Château de Versailles, where Louis XIII built a hunting lodge in 1623. In these artificially created forests, kings and other elite males hunted animals to demonstrate their power by conquering wild nature. Hunting was their supreme political activity. In Eurasia, including the Middle East, India, central Asia, and China, the royal hunt was also extremely important and continued well into later periods (Allesen 2013; Bates 2013; Cartmill 1993).

In European societies, hunting remained a privilege restricted to nobility; commoners were not allowed to be in these royal forests. Therefore, it was far from a subsistence economic activity providing a source of food, as clearly supported by the fact that people's riots took place *always* at times of grain shortage, as exemplified by the Flour War during the reign of Louis XV (Kaplan 1976a: xxvii–xxxix; 1976b: 446–47).

Countryside/Farmland as "Nature"

A universal phenomenon following urbanization, the construction of the rural-cum-natural took place in many of these societies. When cities are born, the rural is born, and urbanites often long for a connection or reconnection to "pristine nature." For them, nature is/was "there" among peoples engaged in foraging, pastoralism, and agriculture, when in fact nature does not exist either as a concept or word among these peoples. Farmland, created by a thorough destruction of nature, by clearing all the trees and other plants, becomes nature in the view of urbanites, giving birth to the symbolic opposition of nature and culture. In many post-agrarian societies, the two became antithetical concepts, each assigned with positive and negative values. The city represents culture with human achievements and, alternatively, the decadent human-altered space, while the rural represents the unspoiled pristine space or the wild or uncivilized nowhere. This development started early, reaching back to classical times (Williams 1973: 46–54). The cultural construction of the "English countryside" is well articulated by Newby (1979), Williams (1973), and others.

> To most inhabitants of urban England ... the countryside supports a serene, idyllic existence, enjoyed by blameless Arcadians happy in their communion with Nature; or alternatively it is a backward and isolated world where boredom vies with boorishness, inducing melancholia and a suspicion of incest. (Newby 1979: 13)

In the 1970s, "in contrast to the apparently unending gloomy news about conflict-ridden, strikeprone, double-digit inflation, urban, industrial England," a *real* English countryside thrived in the minds of the people, especially middle-class English mostly ignorant of agriculture, and on calendar illustrations and chocolate-box lids (Newby 1979: 14–18).

In France, Marie Antoinette built a little farm in Versailles where she could play at raising sheep. Painters both major and minor chose rural France as their motif. The "grain stack" series by Claude Monet (1840–1926) and paintings of farmers (*L'Angélus, Des glaneuses*, etc.) by Jean-François Millet (1814–75) are the most celebrated examples.

In Japan, there already was "the rural" for the urban courtiers in Kyoto during the eighth century (chapter 3). However, the discussion of the rural/urban gained force during the late early modern period in reference to modernization. The Japanese nativist scholars supported the modernization and industrialization of Japan while at the same time lamenting the decay of the quality of life in Edo (Tokyo) (Gluck 1985: 179–85). Yanagita Kunio's *Tales of Tōno* (*Tōno Monogatari*), published in 1910 (Yanagita [1968] 1981), is often cited as representative of the nostalgia for the rural at the time when Japan was rapidly industrializing. Yanagita collected the oral tradition of Tōno in present-day Iwate Prefecture during the last of the Meiji period (1868–1912). Harootunian (1988: 416,) is critical of Yanagita Kunio "re-presented" the voiceless narrative of the folk as opposed to civilization and rationality, and Orikuchi Shinobu equated orality with village simplicity.

Today, against incredibly tall skyscrapers mushrooming in Tokyo, NHK, the national television network, has a number of series featuring individual farmers informing viewers about their meaningful lives.

Pastoralism is also idealized as "a simplified life in the country" (Frye [1957] 1990: 143) and even reinforced by Christian teachings, as in a series of metaphors such as Christ the lamb, ministers as pastors, and believers as the flock. ([1957] 1990). Yet, in some European cultures, pastoralism, which required grazing land, was seen as in competition with agriculture, as noted by Braudel ([1967] 1973: 68; my emphasis), who unabashedly favored animal husbandry and meat eating, and lamented that "fields were cultivated *at the expense* of hunting-ground and extensive stock-raising. . . . [A] larger and larger number of people were *reduced to* eating vegetable foods . . . *often insipid and always monotonous*." Japan never had a pastoral economy until it was introduced on a small scale to a few places, like Hokkaido, during the Meiji period.

Nature in Foundational Myths and Religious Canons

In Greek mythology, Hercules is "Man the Hunter," and Deianira is "Woman the Tiller." In the Old Testament, God's preference is for Abel, a keeper of sheep, rather than Cain, a tiller of the ground. This differential treatment of animals and plants continued in history (Smith [1889] 1972: 269; Braudel [1967] 1973: 68; Ohnuki-Tierney 1993: 119–20).

As detailed in chapter 2, wet-rice agriculture was introduced to Japan toward the end of the ninth century BCE, giving the economic foundation for the development of a large complex society. With the establishment of the emperor system, the imperial myth-history explained how the grandson of the Sun Goddess was sent down from heaven (Takamagahara) to transform the Japanese archipelago from wilderness to a land of succulent ears of rice. The soul of rice grain was placed at the apex of the hierarchy of soul-bearing inhabitants. The emperor was endowed with the exclusive right to officiate all the rituals pertaining to rice and its growth—the role persisted throughout history up to today. The role of the emperor as the custodian of rice was not preceded by a hunting tradition. This led to the emperor being in charge of temporality. Miyata (1992) emphasizes that this role is indeed at the very foundation of the emperor's power.

In some agrarian societies, the grains are considered deities, as in the case of corn and maize, and in others they are symbols of deities. In Christianity, wheat is not God but the abode for God, as further discussed in chapter 1.

"Nature" as Representations: Theoretical Overview

By "nature," I refer to the space in people's view of their universe that humans do not occupy. My interest is how that space is represented. It is an attempt to show how representations of nature become "nature," with Japan as an example. The Japanese have been like a poster child of "people who love and live in nature." *Nihon no shizen*—Japanese nature—has become so naturalized that hardly anyone questions it—like the word nature itself. Yet, the Japanese have engaged in extensive representations of nature through literature, music, architecture, and other visual and performing arts.

In Western scholarship, Plato, an early fifth-century Athenian scholar (429?–347 BCE), first articulated the notion of *representation*—art as a false representation, mimesis—of "nature." In the well-known allegory, he introduces "men dwelling in a sort of subterranean cavern," who are allowed to see only the shadows on the wall of what passes outside. In this situation, they "would deem reality to be nothing else than the shadows of the artificial objects." When one is freed from his fetters and "compelled to stand up and lift his eyes to the light, he realizes that what he was seeing was "a cheat and an illusion" (Plato [1935] 2000: book 7, 119–23). Using the painter as an example of an artist, Plato calls him the imitator who produces "an imitation of a phantasm or of the truth," and declares that "mimetic art is far removed from the truth," presenting a minor part while claiming to reproduce the whole. For Plato, art is a failed attempt to produce truth/nature (429–33). Ever since, "nature" has been at the center of much of academic discourse, especially in philosophy, art, and anthropology.

In his very short but enormously influential article, Benjamin ([1966] 1986: 333) points out that nature creates similarities, but it is humans who possess the highest capacity for producing similarities. This capacity, according to him, is "a rudiment of the powerful compulsion in former times to become and behave like something else."

Like Plato, Benjamin uses examples from nature for his theory of mimesis. As a concrete example, Benjamin ([1982] 2002: 33) points to the introduction of arcades and the construction of panoramas as "the scenes of perfect imitation of nature," which was an "attempt to produce deceptively life-like changes in the represented nature," and which prepared the way not only for photography but for [silent] film and sound film." The arcades built during the latter half of the nineteenth century symbolized the watershed of a dramatic transformation of Western society from a culture of production to that of consumption (Benjamin [1982] 2002).

Benjamin's theory of mimesis is a significant part of his theory of modernity, in which "the decay" comes from a transformation of the mimetic faculty ([1966] 1986: 332–33). Taussig (1993: 20) considers that mass culture today "both stimulates and is predicated upon mimetic modes of perception." As this book, especially chapters 7 and 8, will show, the mimetic faculty continues to function or, in an even more intensive way, to convert the representations of nature into "true nature."[2]

Further developing Marx's proposition of the "fetishism of the commodity form," Lukács ([1923] 1971) proposed a highly influential analytical concept of *reification*—how the commodity form becomes the dominant form of objectivity in capitalistic societies. We will see in Chapters 7 and 8 the particular role Japanese religions, including "rice as pure money," have played in the passage to the naturalization of the commodity as the dominant form of objectivity.

For anthropological inquiry, the "real" or the "truth" in the sense used by Plato, the positivist, is not the concern of this book, since its starting point is how nature is culturally construed and defined, and how the culturally defined nature is represented and transmitted as real. If not regarding it as "a cheat and an illusion," we all too often assume that we know "the real" inhabitants of "the real nature," when in fact much of our knowledge comes from representations—culturally constructed images and meanings.

The realization that there is *no* "nature objectively out there" was forcefully presented by Latour ([1991] 1993: 90; 2010: 97), who wrote, "Real as Nature, narrated as Discourse, collective as Society, existential as Being: such are the quasi-objects that the moderns have caused to proliferate." According to him, this is what we, who pretend to be moderns, subscribe to. Although his argument is based heavily on the biblical tradition of the West, Rich (2021) likewise argues that "nature" has always been what humans make, although his emphasis is more on what he calls the "postnatural world."

Shirane (2012), who meticulously examined "the Japanese four seasons" during the premodern period using textual, performative, visual, and other materials, uses the term "secondary nature (*nijiteki shizen*)" to refer to the represented nature which became "a substitute for a more primary nature that was often remote from or rarely seen by the aristocrats" who lived in the city (Kyoto) (4).

My own personal experience took place when I began writing an article (Ohnuki-Tierney 1981). I drew a "real catfish," which my colleague Norman Whitten, then editor in chief of *American Ethnologist*, pointed out really did not look like a catfish. I then realized that I had never seen a "real" catfish, which the Japanese "marginalize" and hence is not sold or seen in fish stores. Yet many Japanese are familiar with visual representations of the fish and meanings assigned to it in their folklore, which include its role as the causal agent of the 1855 earthquake that destroyed a wicked society by punishing the rich and bringing a new world (Ouwehand 1964).

The importance of representations as the source of people's conception of "nature" is of paramount importance in societies where literary, visual, and auditory representations are highly developed. At times, there is a subtle "tug of war" between nature and its representation. For example, cherry blossoms are of paramount importance in all forms of representation of spring, the most cherished season. On the other hand, in ancient Japan there were only mountain cherry blossoms. Today, television follows the degree of blooming, starting from northern Okinawa, the southernmost region, as it goes up to Hokkaido in the north. It was humans and the successive governments who made Japan into the land of cherry blossoms by planting the trees all over Japan's riverbanks, school yards, military bases, and so forth. By far the most common type of cherry tree is a *someiyoshino*—a *hybrid*—that is, a type culturally altered by humans, created during the Edo period.

The above discussion of representation is only one side of the whole process, in my view. In other words, the basic question is: are these representations really "mimesis" of what is supposedly out there objectively? It is the issue of "form" versus "matter," debated by Plato and Aristotle (Rogers 1935; Shields 2020), as well the Japanese philosopher Nishida Kitarō. It is the question of whether there is some "matter" out there, which an artist or people give a "form."[3] Let me return to this topic in later chapters and the conclusion, using the examples of the rock garden, netsuke, and bonsai, which raise the possibility that in fact these representations are *not* mimesis of "objective nature" out there.

Culture as Historical Process

Since I have taken the most difficult path for research by choosing the entire prehistory and history of Japan for this project, let me explain by briefly discussing the need for a study over a long period of time.

Jan Vansina (1970: 165; 1985) has been the most prominent champion for the necessity to abolish "the zero-time fiction," emphasizing oral tradi-

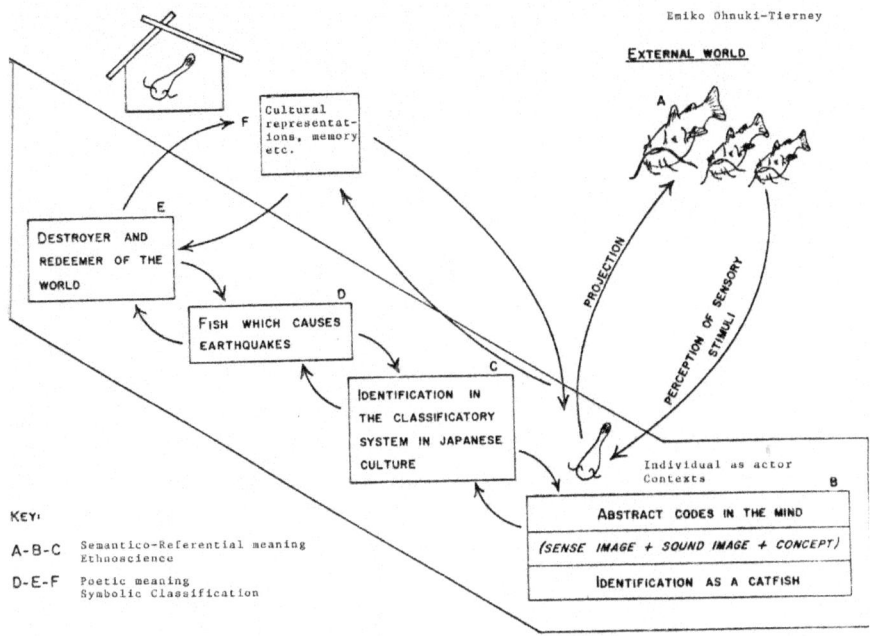

Figure 0.1. Catfish in "nature." Chart by the author.

tion as history. As I explained in my previous work, there are a number of approaches for studying culture as historical processes (Ohnuki-Tierney 1990a; 2001; 2002a; see also Hunt 1989). One major issue is the length of time chosen, depending on the problem under research. Sally Moore (1986) chose one hundred years for her study of the Chagga of Tanzania, and for his study of Western colonialism and capitalism, Sidney Mintz (1985) examined the entire modern period, during which sugar was transformed from a rare foreign luxury into a necessity for working-class British.

A tripartite scheme for historical research was proposed by Fernand Braudel, Marc Bloch, Emmanuel Le Roy Ladurie, and others of the Annales school. Braudel defined the "structure of the long run," or *longue durée*, in contrast to two shorter spans: the *conjuncture*, which covers a decade or up to a century, and the *event*, a short period of time when "surface oscillations" are most conspicuous (Braudel [1969] 1980; Furet 1972: 54–55; Le Goff 1972). Their choice is the *longue durée*, with apparent skepticism about the other two, as succinctly characterized by Paul Ricoeur (1980: 11), who forcefully stated, "History characterized by short, rapid, nervous oscillations" is "richest in humanity" although "the most dangerous." The basic assumption is that the structure remains intact for a long period of time and therefore it is worthy of study.

Culture always consists of more than one paradigm. By "paradigm" I mean the basic model or pattern of culture. Revolutions—be it French, Bolshevik, or Mao's—are all the result of an alternative paradigm coming to the fore. There was no revolution, but medieval Japan epitomizes the presence of two paradigms, with the one below trying to usurp the existing paradigm (chapter 4).

In addition to the synchronic presence of more than one paradigm, historical flow involves the rise of a new paradigm. In the literary field, Charles Baudelaire (1821–67), in his well-known essay "Peintre de la vie moderne" ("The Painter of Modern Life"), clearly defined the term *moderne* (modernity) for the first time: "By 'modernity' I mean the ephemeral, the fugitive, the contingent, the half of art whose other half is the eternal and the immutable" ([1855] 2001: 12). Baudelaire's modernity was a new paradigm that emerged at the time and assumed dominance along with another that was stable and noncontingent.

According to Marc Augé ([1992] 1995: 79), with *surmodernité* (supermodernity) we witness the emergence of "non-place" (*non-lieux*)—impersonal space—without the complete erasing of "place," with its personal connections to the individual's space. He argues that the two constitute "palimpsests." When a new paradigm emerges, it interacts with the previous ones and may eventually become dominant. Culture as historical processes is always in motion (Moore 1986)—becoming and reproducing itself even when disintegrating. It transforms itself at the core in a constant ebb and flow, with local-transnational interactions as the engine of historical change.

Studying Japanese culture and society over a long period of time enabled me to examine the relationship between the quotidian and the "lofty" cosmological scheme. My research proved that cosmology/ontology and the like are not separate mental activities at higher levels but are intimately involved in the daily lives of the people. It is not a solid structure over which surface oscillations occur. Instead, the basic symbolic axis of the above and the below has persisted, upholding the everyday behaviors of the people, *and* verse versa, while both undergo historical transformations.

In reference to the topic of nature, my research enabled me to see that nature recedes as a series of representations take over and become "nature." Along the way, I was able to explore the complexity of historical change, in which no single individual exercises power; rather, historical change takes place, in the main, while those "in power" as well as those "without power" are more or less unaware of the process—those who created representations of nature did not tell others to copy their representations, but the latter willingly accepted the representation as true "nature." With the development of capitalism, nature became commodified and reified as "nature objectively" out there. Even this process does not involve coercive pressure; people are willing participants without knowing the process involved.

While we witness the development of capitalism all over the world, Japan's case offers an example of how its penetration of societies is not uniform. From ancient times, rice was "pure money" and naturalized the financial payments to religious practitioners as legitimate. In addition, the Japanese emphasis on reward during one's lifetime, rather than after death, has become the enduring practice, "endorsing," as it were, consumerism. Both of these factors have operated for a long time, giving consumerism a long and successful history in Japan, with people being willing participants without being aware of the factors involved in the process.

About This Book

Part 1 offers the basic information about Japan, its prehistory and early history, and its cosmology. Chapter 1 describes the nascent "Japan," when the political economy based on the wet-rice agriculture introduced by Koreans was established, when the imperial court constructed the cosmogony that deified rice grains, and when rice paddies became "Japanese nature." It also established the spatial division of the above and the below, with the former assigned a positive value and the latter defined as defiled. The book describes how this symbolic structure governing cosmological space as well as daily behavior continued to be upheld through time and remains even today.

Chapter 2 examines the inhabitants of the universe and their interrelations. The relationship between deities, humans, and some nonhumans is highly complex due to the border crossings by nonhuman animals, as well as humans who can be deities. Each of them, animate or inanimate, is endowed with a soul. Most importantly, the soul remains dormant until it leaves the physical body, upon which time, if not treated properly, it inflicts punishment on the individual, who may not always be the offender, leading to the collective responsibility among members of a social group. I consider animism to be the most important belief in Japanese religiosity, in the past and today.

There is a distinct hierarchy among all beings. The Japanese universe is dominated by plants, with rice at the apex. Next are trees. The hierarchy among trees depends on whether a divine soul uses it as a temporary abode. The normative classification of nonhuman animals follows the basic cosmo-spatial principle, degrading the "four-legged" animals as the most defiled and hence taboo to eat. It is not because of the physical property of four leges but because the number of legs maximizes their contact with the ground. Yet, the same four-legged animals, such as monkeys and foxes, are the messengers to the deities. Furthermore, important religious cults developed, such as the Fuji Shinkō during the Edo period, in which the monkey played the important role as messenger for Mount Fuji. Another is the Inari Myōjin, the deity of rice grains, with the fox as the messenger with enduring strength even today.

Part 2 focuses on how "Japanese nature" was defined and represented in different periods of history. Chapter 3 starts with the poetic praises of rice plants in the *Manyōshū* during the late Nara period (710–94), which saw the initial development of the "four seasons" based on the original seasons used by the Chinese and reformulated by the Japanese. With the move of the capitol from Nara to Kyoto (Heian period), there was an efflorescence of the imperial culture, in which the imperial version of "the four seasons" became detached from the environment but was well established as "the Japanese four seasons," that is, "Japanese nature." The "imperial nature" reflected the opulence of the lives of courtiers at the palace, symbolized by butterflies, which fly above the ground, and by flowers without roots—neither touching the ground. Developing highly sophisticated aesthetics, the courtiers placed the beings of the imperial nature at center stage in their *waka* poems, such as *Kokin Wakashū*, and literary pieces, such as *The Tale of Genji*, which became important classics.

Humans too began systematic avoidance of the ground. The most important expression of this was the permission one must receive from the emperor to "go up" to the main building of the Imperial Palace for an audience, which was granted only to individuals of the highest rank. Others, called "people on the ground" (*jigenin*), including warriors, had to stay outside, kneeling with one knee on the bare ground.

The invention of footwear was the first attempt to enable people not to directly touch the ground when walking. Footwear then became the culprit and has not been allowed inside ever since, leading to the ubiquitous presence of signs declaring, "NO FOOTGEAR INSIDE." Carriages followed this development. For the emperor a special type of carriage exclusively for the emperor, called *hōren*, was used throughout history until the introduction of an automobile during the Meiji period. The ox-drawn carriage, called *gissha*, was for the courtiers who used ever more elaborate *gissha* to show off their status and wealth.

Chapter 4 discusses a most dynamic period in Japanese history, when the paradigmatic plurality came to the fore. The "lower conquering the upper (*gekokujō*)" reigned in Japanese society, as both the mentalité and the governing principle of the social structure. The most dramatic example showing the power of historical agents is Toyotomi Hideyoshi, who was born the son of a farmer of no distinction and orphaned at a young age, and who ascended to the apex of the Japanese political system as the most fearsome of the warlords. While trying to prove he too was "cultured," he became the grand patron of the tea ceremony.

At this time, the warrior class rose to the top of the social hierarchy, pushing the emperors to the background. The emperors ceased to have power over the military, which became the exclusive domain of the warriors. Cultural affairs, such as composition of *waka* and *renga* poetry and events celebrating and appreciating "nature," became the courtiers' role and preoccupation. During this period, the representation of "Japanese nature" was completed, as it were. The year came to consist of twelve months, each defined by a plant (flower or tree), a bird, and a particular activity. Even if a particular flower might not bloom during the month to which it was assigned, the constructed "nature" governed.

Meanwhile, the most fearsome and brutal of warriors had to prove that they too were cultured (*bun*), rather than simply excelling in military skills (*bu*). The development of rock gardens and tea ceremony was the result of their efforts. The ground is not to be seen—all covered with rocks and pebbles. The rock garden became the quintessential "Japanese nature." Unlike the Western landscape, the Japanese *tei'en* (landscape) is said to represent "nature." Yet, the rock gardens show how the "representations" are not mimesis of "nature"—far from it. It is neither a mimesis nor a fractal minimalism.

Part 3 focuses on uses of "Japanese nature" as the symbol of the collective self of the Japanese as they became increasingly aware of Japan as a country in the world and their sense of *cultural* nationalism developed. Chapter 5 describes the ironic outcome of the prevailing peace within the country under the shogunate—the warrior class's loss of a raison d'être and consequently their economic and political powers. The highly urbanized new capital of Edo saw the rapid rise of capitalism. Since both the courtiers and warriors were legally prohibited from engaging in commercial affairs, the merchants seized economic power and developed their plebeian culture. Through a number of venues in art and literature, they celebrated "Japan as the land of rice paddies, cherry blossoms, and Mount Fuji"—creating the enduring symbols of "Japanese nature."

Another important development during the Edo period is the efflorescence of the plebeian culture of the merchant class, which further refined the non-minimalist tradition of poems of haikai and haiku—the literary tradition with the use of 5-7-5 words—and small-scale arts of bonsai ("garden in a pot") and netsuke (toggles).

Chapter 6 points out that with the rise of *political* nationalism, "Japanese nature" became a favorite tool used by the government for various purposes, not only to strengthen nationalism but also for economic development by luring both domestic and foreign tourism. Already in 1912, the Japan Travel Bureau was established, and in 1931 the national parks were designated for the promotion of tourism, at times when devastating changes to the "natural" environment were allowed to take place in Akan in Hokkaido, Oze near Tokyo, and elsewhere. At the height of Japanese militarism, cherry trees, which had represented Japan or Japanese nature since the Heian period (794–1185), were planted in the colonies to mark that they belonged to Japan, against the wish of the South Koreans, who are now planning to replace them with their own "king cherry" (Rubin 2014). This was also the time when the military government attempted to aestheticize the murder of its own soldiers by using the metaphor of cherry blossoms, which fall after a beautiful but short time.

In part 4, chapter 7 focuses on the role of consumerism, which gained velocity in contemporary Japan, playing a powerful role in the domestication of "Japanese nature." Contemporary consumerism also takes advantage of the cosmo-spatial principle and its valences in a number of everyday practices, including purification of cars, which accumulate dirt from the defiled ground on their tires, and the promotion of pet carts so that the feet of the pets do not get soiled when they "take a walk." This mutual reinforcement between capitalism and Japanese cosmological beliefs is so naturalized that most people do not realize the real nature of current consumerism. Likewise, the government and tourist industries promote tourism by the Japanese and foreigners to appreciate "Japanese nature" when tourists are not fully cognizant of the economic motive of their promotions.

Chapter 8 is an attempt to understand contemporary Japan, described in chapter 7, where consumerism has almost a free hand, domesticating the inhabitants of "nature." Meanwhile, magic and magical thinking flourish and animism legitimizes the business prosperity of temples and shrines. At the same time, the symbolic principle of above and below with respective valances also bolsters consumerism, promoting the need to supply footwear and other commodities to facilitate and reinforce the symbolic valences. Furthermore, this principle remains the cardinal rule for the everyday life of the contemporary Japanese—from the requirements for everyday behavior, such as taking off one's shoes, to architectural structures, such as the mandatory entrance area (*genkan*).

Through a critical assessment of social evolutionary theory, which sees a unilinear path of history from primitivism, characterized by magic and irrationality, toward modernity, marked by celebrating rationality as the ultimate, I suggest that we abandon this yardstick—one based primarily on the historical experiences of Western European societies. Instead, we should look into the paramount role that "magical practices" play in *sociality* for the Japanese, who are known for an extensive practice of gift exchange. These magical practices play the role of "gifts," expressing one's concerns to a particular individual.

The ease with which temples and shrines have "cooperated" with consumerism requires some explanation. Money is equivocal in most societies and its nature—pure or impure—is determined in practice, that is, in how it is used. In the case of Japan, rice—the dominant symbol of "Japanese nature"—has been "pure money" almost throughout history. It was what the Japanese offered to the deities. Therefore, offering money to Shinto priests and Buddhist monks, for example, for the purification of cars, is not a departure for the Japanese, who have been used to offer rice and currency for religious purposes.

After a summary of major points raised in the book, the conclusion focuses on "the representation of zero"—are art and other human products always a mimesis of "matter" and other phenomena that are presumably to be copied? Or should we interpret, for example, the rock garden as human products without reference to "matter," and netsuke and bonsai *not* as miniatures but human products based on, for example, people's imagination of what a tiger, never seen by the artist, is about? To put it in reference to the Aristotle-Plato debate, should *form* without *matter* be another way to think about the problem of "representations"?

Notes

1. I use the term/concept "culture," which is more inclusive than cosmology and ontology, although the recent "ontological turn" ushered in intensive debates over these related concepts. "Ontology" has a long history in philosophy (e.g., Deleuze [1988] 1993, [1990] 1995) and has been used differently by various scholars under such terms as "differential ontology," "perspectivist ontology," "cosmological deixis," etc. Descola (2014: 271; [2005] 2014: 57–88) prefers "worlding" to differentiate his approach from ontologies, and offers a comprehensive history of "The Great Divide," including nature versus culture, in the Western scholarly tradition. Descola ([2005] 2014: 3–9, 13–17) considers that the similarity of interiorities justifies the extension of "culture" to non-humans, including "intersubjectivity to a mastery of techniques, ritualized conduct and deference to conventions" (129–30). He states: "[A]ll this does not suffice to blur the major differences that exist between the cultures presented here as examples" (31).

    Viveiros de Castro (1998: 470, 479) proposes multinaturalism—the same culture, different natures. "Ontology Is Just Another Word for Culture" is an

edited volume (Venkatesan 2010), whereas Graeber (2015) entitles his article "Radical Alterity Is Just Another Way of Saying 'Reality.'" For further discussions, see Candea (2010), Geschiere (2013: 170, 256–57), Kelly (2014), Latour (2005), Ramos (2012), and Turner ([2009] 2017: 205–43).
2. For further discussion on the topic of representation and mimesis by Erich Auerbach, Walter Benjamin, and Michael Taussig, see Ohnuki-Tierney 2015: 14–15, 210.
3. Kant ([1781] 1966: 34) identified space and time as the two forms of sensibility. Some scholars have focused on the temporal element. Handelman (2020: 291) emphasizes that all forms are moving with time, as does Deleuze ([1990] 1995: 14, 47), who discards notions such as structure, the symbolic, or the signifier.

CHAPTER 1

Inhabitants of the Universe

Inhabitants without Physical Form: The Soul and the *Kami* (Deities)

The occupants of the Japanese universe have changed historically. In addition to "humans," animals, and plants, some inhabitants with or without materiality have also been important inhabitants. Miyake (1995) offers a most comprehensive coverage of the beings in the Japanese universe. My discussion is confined to: (1) two categories of inhabitants without physical form—the soul and the *kami* (deities); (2) invisible inhabitants—ancestors and other deceased humans; and (3) animals and plants that are culturally recognized as inhabitants. Other inhabitants include *yōkai* (ghosts), which Yanagita Kunio famously pointed out deserve serious scholarly attention, and on which he published a number of articles beginning in 1931 (Yanagita [1968] 1981b: 285–438). There has been a renewed scholarly interest in *yōkai* (ghosts) in recent years.

The Soul

Crucial for the understanding of the inhabitants of the universe is the Japanese native religion of Shintoism, whose animistic premise is that every being of the universe—what we call animate and inanimate beings—has a soul. The soul as the common property of *all* beings is the basis for continuity among them, enabling a being to cross categorical boundaries and take on the identity of another category.[1]

On the other hand, there is a distinct hierarchy among the souls (Miyake ([1989] 1992: 383–86; Ohnuki-Tierney 1993: 53–57). The soul of the rice grain is the most important and powerful, occupying the highest place in the hierarchy. The emperor's symbolic power is based on his role as the exclusive custodian of the soul of rice. The imperial soul is "lodged" in an emperor and transmitted to the next upon his death. Since this ritual is a secret ritual, the notion of the imperial soul has not been well known among the folk (cf. Ohnuki-Tierney 2002a: 72–77).

The most important properties of the soul are (1) it is invisible; (2) it is immaterial; (3) its ability to "sojourn" (*yadoru*) in some object (*yorishiro*), but not permanently; (4) its departure from the body of the host signaling the death of a human or some other being; and (5) its negative power generated only when it inappropriately leaves the physical entity where it has been staying (Minzokugaku Kenkyūjo 1951: 666–67).

There are special properties of the soul of the deities. The notion of the *yorishiro*—an object where the soul of a deity sojourns, often a tree, a rock, some animal, or a human, especially a shaman (Minzokugaku Kenkyūjo 1951: 666–67)—is most important, because the *yorishiro* is the medium through which the deities express their intentions.

The notion of the soul applies even to words, especially divine words (*shingo*). Orikuchi emphasizes that the soul of a word, *kotodama*, and its invocation, *kotoage*, are paired concepts that apply only to the words in incantations and other words of communication between humans and deities (*shintaku*) (Orikuchi [1924] 1983: 92).

According to Orikuchi ([1927] 1983: 134–35; [1943] 1976; [1924] 1983: 92), the belief in the soul of a word, *kotodama*, began to develop shortly before the Nara period (646–794 CE) and was widely held by the people by the time of the *Manyōshū*, a collection of 4,516 poems composed during the four hundred years before 759 CE.[2] The power of *kotodama* is revealed with the utterance of words—the act of *kotoage* (Orikuchi [1927] 1983: 134)—in an incantation to invoke the deities and seek divine help. The *kotoage* must be done only at the most appropriate time, lest the power of the released soul bring calamity. In the *Manyōshū*, Horton locates *kotodama* in eight poems and *kotoage* in ten poems. Horton uses the characters for *kotoage* and translates it as "word lifting"; *kotodama* he translates as *mana* (a Melanesian and Polynesian term for spiritual life force) (Horton 2012: 87, 236–37, 270, 272, 302–3, 532). To show how dangerous it is to invoke the gods without good reason (236–37), he refers to a long poem by Kakinomoto-no-Hitomaro about the hazardous voyage of an envoy to Tang China at the beginning of the eighth century:

> The land of abundant rice
> of the reed plains
> Is a divine land
> where one does not invoke the gods,
> And yet
> I will invoke them!
> May your voyage be safe,

completely safe from harm, . . .
[11 lines deleted]
Yamato,
the land called Shikishima,
is a land succored
by the mana of words—
may you be safe from harm!

Ebersole (1989: 19–23) offers us the geopolitical background of the development of the concept of *kotodama* sometime before the eighth century. It was the time when massive cultural and linguistic influences of the Korean and Chinese civilizations reached Japan and were embraced by the elite. The introduction of the Chinese writing system compelled the Japanese elite to preserve its own identity, leading to the assignment of magical power to orality. Ebersole (1989: 20–21) points to a poem by Yamanoue Okura (Satake et al. [2013] 2019: 104–6) in which Yamanoue Okura expounds that Japan (*Yamato no Kuni*) is "a land of imperial deities" and "a land blessed by the spirits of words" (Satake et al. [2013] 2019: 104).

Nishida Kitarō (1870–1945), a prominent philosopher of the Kyoto School, wished to give the philosophical foundation of the ancient belief "to see the form in the formless and to hear the voice in the voiceless":

> The spectacular development of the Western civilization, which is based on the recognition of the form and its development as "good," is something we should respect and learn from. However, it seems that the foundation of the Eastern civilization, nurtured by our ancestors, lies in the belief in seeing the unseen and hearing the voiceless. Our mind [*kokoro*] yearns for this belief, and therefore I wish to offer its philosophical foundation. (Nishida 1965a: 6; my translation)

Nishida's emphasis is not on the static notion of "form." Nor is it only on the visual dimension; rather, the auditory dimension—hearing—is also involved, since he emphasizes that the world we live in is the world of actions and the world of expressions, not the world of objects or the world of consciousness (Nishida 1965b: 265–66).

Horton (2012: 272) points out that language or words as actions have been noted by various scholars. Ong ([1982] 2002: 32) stresses the importance of recognizing language as action, rather than mere countersigns of thought. In volume 2 of *The Philosophy of Symbolic Forms*, whose volume title is *Mythical Thought*, Cassirer (1955: 40) wrote: "Word and name do not designate and signify, they are and act. . . . In the mere sound of the human voice, there resides a peculiar power over things. . . . But, the mythical-magical power of language is truly manifested in articulated sound." Frazer ([1890] 1959: 238–46) also emphasizes the importance of names, rather than just words, in this regard.

In the case of Japanese ontology, not just words but the formless soul that resides in every being of the universe is the very essence of the ontology. The Ise Shrine is the architectural expression par excellence of the Japanese belief in the invisibility of power. It is by far the most important shrine in Japan, where the Sun Goddess, Amaterasu Ōmikami, resides. She is arguably the most powerful deity in the pantheon of the agrarian Japanese, providing light to the universe and warmth for the crops, especially rice.[3] The Sun Goddess is in the inner shrine, not to be seen. Isozaki (1995) emphasizes the importance of "hiding" (*kakusu*) the goddess. When visitors come to the shrine, they must invite the invisible deity by clapping their hands, talk to her as if she is there in person, and offer her items that she uses in her daily life, including foods (1995: 24).

The Shinto deities are beings of nature, and therefore there is no need to build a structure for them. Nor is there any need to physically represent them as statues. However, Buddhism, with enormous emphasis on statues, was introduced and became popular in the sixth century CE. Shinto was forced to build shrines as well as produce wooden images of deities, starting in the ninth century (Itō 2011b: 51, 84). The first actual statues of Shinto deities include three at Tōji Temple and three at Matsunoo Taisha, a Shinto shrine (figure 1.1), both made during the ninth century (early Heian period) (Kageyama [1978] 2001: 296–97; Itō 2011b: 84).

This was an epochal event. It was the first time the "nature" occupied by the Shinto deities was forced to be represented as visual forms. Nevertheless, the belief in and practice of no physical representation of deities have remained firm. Even today, at any shrine, people clap their hands to summon the deity and pray in silence in front of the invisible deity.

Buddhism came to Japan during the sixth century and had significant influence on the Japanese (LaFleur 1983: 29). The doctrine of Buddhism recognizes no sharp line or hierarchy between humans and animals. A significant influence on the Japanese is the introduction of the Buddhistic notion and practice of the memorial service *kuyō*—a memorial service for the soul of a deceased human and other beings of the universe, which led to an important belief for the Japanese that the proper treatment of the departed soul guaranteed that it would not harm the living.

The afflictions of the soul caused by improper treatment of the dead include mental illnesses and some physical illnesses without possibility of cure (Yoshida [1972] 1978). The exact nature and form of memorial service have changed through time and varied greatly from elaborate rituals for the elite at great temples during the Heian period (Fukutō 1998: 236–37) to simple impromptu rituals by the folk. The harm inflicted by neglecting this memorial service is far more general in that its neglect does not always incur the wrath of the soul of the deceased right after death.

Figure 1.1. The oldest deity figure. Ninth century CE. Matsunoo Taisha no Shin'ei, 2011.

The information from Yoshida's intensive fieldwork in Kōchi Prefecture tells that almost every case involves no direct relationship between the afflicted individual and the owner of the mistreated soul. In many cases some long-gone ancestor's soul is found to be responsible, but there is no particular link (Yoshida [1972] 1978: 112–43).

Nonetheless, the memorial service has become an important ritual for the Japanese. For example, today many municipal governments establish a certain section in their cemetery for the souls of those who left no relatives (*muen botoke*) or cannot be identified, like those washed ashore after drowning.

Not all the beings receive a memorial service when they die. Who/which receive the memorial service reveals, in an uncanny way, that not all beings of the universe are of equal importance, even though they all are believed to be endowed with a soul. Insects harmful to crops received the service after they were killed. Monkeys, whales, boars, deer, birds (pheasants, cranes, and wild geese), and some fish are well-known examples of those that do (Shirane 2012: 17–18). However, the first time in history when a memorial service was performed for each varies considerably. For example, for the monkey it was only in 1961, but since then the memorial service has received considerable attention (Asquith 1984: 41). Today memorial services are held at several primate research centers and widely reported in the mass media, as memorial services for whales are.

The so-called inanimate objects also receive memorial services. But not all. The most prominent and long-lasting example is for used sewing needles (*harikuyō*). There are enormous variations in how to memorialize "tired" needles, depending on the region. In the eastern parts of Japan (kantō), 8 February and 8 December are considered the date(s) for *harikuyō*; in the western parts (kansai), it is 8 December. The details vary, but a common practice involves putting the needles in soft food, such as tofu or furofuki daikon, or just eating these foods (Minzokugaku Kenkyūjo 1951: 482).

Also well known are the memorial services for chinaware (*setomono*). While the memorial service for the used needles is done by individuals, the memorial service for the chinaware is a collective endeavor by the retailers of chinaware. Every August, in the downtown section of Tokyo, the road from Suitengū to Ningyōchō, retailers of chinaware put up tents. A Shinto ritual is held to express appreciation for the service by the chinaware and also hope for future prosperity. The chinaware is sold at reduced prices.

While the memorial service for chinaware is not nationwide, the memorial service for dolls has a very long history and is nationwide. The doll for the *hinamatsuri* (Doll's Festival) and other dolls that the owner no longer uses are given the memorial service. Today the most frequently used method is to ask a temple that may specify times to bring the dolls and charge a fee for the service.

In Chapter 7 I describe an extension of memorial service to pets, whose ownership became a recent fashionable practice among the people in urban areas.

Kami (Deity, Deities)

The term *kami* (deities), which originated with Shinto, has been used to refer to all beings, including Buddhas, that possess power over humans, who nonetheless can also become *kami*. In Japanese religiosity the sacred and the profane do not constitute absolute oppositions. Neither superhuman nor supernatural is the right term to refer to *kami*. The Japanese assign to both deities and humans dual characters and powers: good and evil, constructive and destructive, and so forth (Ohnuki-Tierney 1987:

130–40). The concept of a "human deity" (humans becoming deities, or *hitogami*) is central in this cosmology, where humans and deities exist on a continuum (Ozawa 1987).

Kami are altogether different from God in monotheistic religions like Christianity, Judaism, and Islam. For example, two medieval warlords demanded their own apotheosis from the emperor, who alone had the power to deify humans, as detailed in chapter 4. In the case of Toyotomi Hideyoshi, Emperor Goyōzei did not offer the particular *shingō* (a title of a *kami*) requested, Shin-Hachiman, but gave another, Toyokuni Daimyōjin, chosen by Hidetada (1605–23), the second son of the most powerful shogun, Tokugawa Iyeyasu. Furthermore, Tokugawa Iyeyasu asked, or more appropriately ordered, the imperial court to strip off the divinity previously granted to Hideyoshi (Fuji'i 2011: 266–70, 337). Tokugawa Ieyasu in his will requested the imperial court to deify him as Tōshō Daigongen, and his divinity became the bulwark of shogunate power for the next 250 years (Inoue [1963] 1967: 258–59; for details, see chapter 4).

These incidents show the fluidity of the notion of *kami*, which can be created or stripped of its status by a superhuman, while a human can be a *kami*. The hierarchy of beings in the universe consists of humans, shaman-emperors, and deities in ascending order. The hierarchy is neither permanent nor linear, as demonstrated by the orders by Hideyoshi and Ieyasu to the emperors to deify them. These humans willfully bestowed upon the emperor the power to create deities. Likewise, the human architects of the imperial system during the Meiji period assigned themselves the power to create a bona fide deity out of an emperor by resurrecting the belief in the imperial soul (*kōrei*) that is transmitted from one emperor to the next, guaranteeing the continuity of what Kantorowicz ([1957] 1981) called the institutional body (for details, see Ohnuki-Tierney 2002a: 61–101). The power these warlords held seems to render the ambition of Napoleon Bonaparte to become the emperor of France innocuous. But the concept of *kami* allows neither the presence of an almighty god nor fixed boundaries between the inhabitants of the universe.

Such inversions of the hierarchy are embedded in Japanese religions, where the hierarchy of beings is neither fixed nor linear, as detailed later in this chapter. Miyata (1975: 22) reminds us of the essence of Japanese religiosity—an ordinary human can assign divinity—referring to a phrase often recited even today: "If you pray in the morning to Kan'non Deity and to Yakushi Buddha in the evening, even the head of a sardine will become a deity" (*Asa kan'non ni yū yakushi, iwashi no atama mo shinjin kara*).

These individual instances expressing the dynamic characterization of the *kami* in Japanese religiosity are paralleled by the fluidity with which the Japanese adopted Buddhism, a foreign religion. When Buddhism was introduced from India via China and Korea, it was embraced eagerly by the elites, including the imperial family. But "most people in Japan at that time [the sixth and the seventh centuries] probably thought of the Buddha as just another *kami*" (Kitagawa [1966] 1990: 136). Officially, the Japanese tried to reconcile the two religions by claiming that the *kami* are manifestations of the Buddhas and bodhisattvas, a theory known as *honchi suijaku*. With equal ease, the Tokugawa Japanese, especially the elites, adopted Neo-Confucianism with its emphasis on natural law and the Way of Heaven (Kitagawa [1966] 1990). Astonishing as it may be from the perspective of Western religions, much later in history, the Meiji government concocted "non-religious Shintō," which was to be adhered to by every Japanese subject, regardless of his or her personal "religious affiliation" (161). As I elaborated elsewhere (Ohnuki-Tierney 1984a), most Japanese today are at least nominally both Buddhist and Shintoist simultaneously and usually without personal conviction.[4]

Beyond the extreme flexibility, the above discussion of the Japanese concept of the soul and deities requires some comparison with other religions. In some agrarian societies, staple plant foods are deities, as with the case of the "Maize God" of the Mesoamerican peoples, including the classical Maya (Henderson 1981: 84–85; Taube [1983] 1985). Corn is a symbol of fertility for the Navajo (Richards [1963] 2016) and many other peoples. In many parts of Eurasia, during the Greek and Roman periods, before axial religions developed, Demeter was the Olympian goddess of agriculture, and grain and bread were depicted with sheaves of wheat, even though wheat was not a goddess. Squatriti (2024: n.p.) points out three examples that offer important aspects of wheat in Christian tradition. First, Christians "celebrated Jesus's Last Supper using whatever bread they had at hand." Second, in "his *Summation of All Theology* (published in the 1260s), Thomas Aquinas stated categorically that God was not present in sacred breads made from any grains other than wheat." Finally, for medieval Christians, "the divine presence would occur in specific types of flour, and doughs shaped in specific ways."

In other words, it is not rice itself but the soul of rice that commands the highest position in the universe. The notion of *yadoru*—the sojourn of the soul in certain objects—is similar as God in Christianity who can be present in bread.

Invisible Inhabitants: Ancestors and Other Deceased Humans

For the human inhabitants, the most important coinhabitants are ancestors. Though invisible, they are very much alive in the daily lives of humans, who, today, start their day by praying at the ancestral alcove at home and offer *gokū* (five offerings)—incense, flowers, water, food (rice), and candles. At my own home, we offered water and tea. Rice was offered when we cooked, usually not in the morning. There is a set rule for the manner in which these offerings are made for the deceased. Rice is placed in a special container, usually made of metal, so that it forms a small mound—the distinctive way for offerings to the dead—while rice and other foods for the living should never form a mound. Only on special occasions did we offer "flowers for ancestors" purchased at a flower shop. After offering these items, we gently hit the altar bell and prayed, with our fingers flexed. When relatives or others close to our family visited us, they first went to the ancestral alcove to pray and offer a box of sweets, if they brought one, as they usually did.

The contemporary Japanese use the term *sosen* (ancestors) to refer to those who are ensconced in the family altar. In our family, the most important "ancestor" was my parents' first child, who died as a child, but whom my parents could never forget. They would regularly offer pineapple slices, since it was her favorite and she asked for it with her fingers when her illness, possibly meningitis, deprived her of the ability to talk.

The ancestors are in fact living members in the daily lives of the Japanese. The decisive proof of their importance to the Japanese is that for the few days during the *bon* employers from the government all the way to small businesses give their employees days off. During the annual celebration of *bon*, usually held from 13–16 July (depending on the lunar calendar), the Japanese welcome the visit of their ancestors at their home. The most important rituals are paying a visit to the family tomb and a twin ritual of kindling a welcoming fire at the beginning of *bon* to guide the ancestors to the proper house and at the end to send them off. In the districts where communal activities are well organized, dancing, called *bon odori* (*bon* dancing), is held. (For details of *bon*, see Minzokugaku Kenkyūjo 1951: 529–31; Smith 1972: 99–104).

In some regions the beginning of *bon* is marked by *tanabata*—the star festival when people decorate bamboo branches with pieces of colored paper on which poems are written. *Tanabata* celebrates the annual romantic encounter of a male and a female star across the Milky Way (Minzokugaku Kenkyūjo 1951: 354–55).

Unlike Buddhist rituals that deal with death, the *bon* is a festival with a cheerful spirit. The ancestors are "clean"—clearly dead, in contrast to those who just died, which incurs enormous "impurity." There have been a number of interpretations in which the ancestors live on (Saigo [1967] 1984: 62–66). Overturning previous interpretations, Hirata Atsutane (1776–1843) published in 1813 *Tama-no-mihashira* (a work reprinted in 1998), in which he portrayed the world of the ancestors as almost exactly the same as this world, with mountains, forests, sky, and so on. Harootunian (1988: 152–68) offers an extensive interpretation of Hirata's concepts in reference to deities and ancestors within the broader cosmological principles of the visible/invisible.

Yanagita's posthumously published book, *Sosen no Hanashi* (Stories about ancestors, 2013) further elaborates on how the ancestors live in the mountains, look after their descendants, and visit them during the *bon* and around New Year's.

Other Inhabitants of the Japanese Universe

Plants

Rice plants occupy the apex of the hierarchy among the inhabitants of the universe.[5] Next come the trees, which are even above animals, human and nonhuman. Trees and stones become *yorishiro*, the place where the souls of deities are thought to sojourn (*yadoru*). Pine and cedar are especially important as sacred trees (*shinboku*) since they are the favorites for the souls of deities to perch on (Takashima 1975). Cypress is also important, as at the time of the renewal/rebuilding of the Ise Shrine (shinen sengū) every twenty years, over ten thousand cypresses are required (Jinja Honchō 1995). Flowers and grasses are not considered sacred.

The sacred trees are marked by *shimenawa*, a rope made of bundles of rice plants in various shapes, hung or wrapped around them (figure 1.2). Although other materials have been used, especially lately, the bundles are made of rice plants dried before bearing grains. This is done to demarcate the sacred space from the profane, marking the space forbidden to humans. The first recorded mention of this practice is in the "Ame-no-Iwayado" (Heavenly cave) episode in the *Kojiki*. After the Sun Goddess, Amaterasu, was lured out of the cave, a male deity with a strong hand pulled her out and placed a *shirikumenawa* at the cave entrance,[6] thereby making the cave a sacred place she could no longer reenter (Takeda and Nakamura [1977] 1982: 38). It has the power to prevent an evil spirit like Smallpox Deity from coming to the settlement (Ohnuki-Tierney 1993: 53)

In sharp contrast to nonhuman animals, no plant becomes an evil spirit able to possess humans. Nor does any of them cross the boundary to become humans, as nonhuman animals do.

Nonhuman Animals

The normative classification of nonhuman animals presented below is only one dimension of an enormously fluid system of classification. Boundary

Figure 1.2. Rice straw rope demarcating sacred space. Matsunoo Taisha no Shin'ei, 2011. Photo by the author.

crossings, presented in the next section, are quite frequent. The cardinal rule for nonhuman animal classification is the cosmological principle of the above and the below with respective valences—beautiful/sublime versus defiled. That is, the basis for the classification is not the number of legs an animal has but how much their morphological characteristics make them touch the ground, the most defiled space in the universe. The descending order of defilement consists of land mammals with four legs; birds with two legs; and fish with no legs and in water, rather than on the ground (for details see Harada 1993: 92–95). Thus, animals with four legs (*yotsuashi*) are the most defiled and taboo for human consumption.

There are a few explanations for the abomination of four-legged animals. An important one is that sitting down to eat is the defining quality of humans, whereas animals do not sit and eat. Despite the recent and intensive Westernization of Japanese eating habits by McDonald's and other fast food restaurants as well as standing buffets (*risshoku*), *tachigui* (eating while standing) remains a strict taboo (for further discussion, see Ohnuki-Tierney 1997). Today, many groups host a gathering over a buffet without chairs, in which case the host specifies that it is a *risshoku* gathering. Another rationale for the abomination of four-leggedness is that the character for the number four is a homonym for the character for death.

Birds walk only occasionally on two legs and mostly fly. They are thus edible. The swan swims on water and never walks on the ground. The white swan was one of the most cherished in Japanese haute cuisine, referred to as *bibutsu*, literally "beautiful things." It therefore was a choice gift item between the emperors and warlords (Fujii 2011: 34, 79). Birds were also seen to possess the same qualities prized by humans (Shirane 2012: 116–19). For example, the pheasant (*kiji* or *kigisu*) is a symbol of a mother's devotion to her child, and the swallow is the symbol of marital and familial harmony (118).

Chickens, with two legs like birds, were not eaten until the Meiji period, but roosters were used as alarm clocks. They also carried a special meaning because of their role in the *Kojiki*, with the Sun Goddess hiding in the cave (*Ame no Iwayado*, which according to some scholars means "structure"). One of the devices the deities used to lure her out was to gather roosters so that their crows signaled the arrival of the morning. This succeeded in bringing the Sun Goddess out; thereby the universe regained sunlight (see both the text and comments in Takeda and Nakamura [1977] 1982: 36–37).

Folk Classificatory Schemes

The folk created ingenious ways to subvert the normative system of classification to satisfy their dietary preferences. One method was to call meat of forbidden animals "medicinal food" (*yakuji*) (Harada 1993: 920). Another was to manipulate the counting system. As with the Chinese, the Japanese have a counting system with a very large number of lexemes, each used for a different class of nonhuman animals. *Tō* is used for counting animals larger than humans and *piki* (*hiki*) for those smaller than humans. The word *ha* (wings) is used for birds. For animals with hooves, the term *tei* is used. The word *piki* is used for fish while swimming in water, but when it becomes food, various other words, such as *bi*, *mai*, and *hon*, are used. Pillar (*hashira*) is for deities and *shu* (neck) is for poems. There are other usages and rules.[7]

This system enabled people to subvert the official classification by reassigning an animal to the edible food class. Hare with four legs was an outstanding example. Called *no'usagi* (field hares), they had been a regular part of the diet ever since the Jomon period (Kobayashi 2018: 159–164). There were many of them and they were easy to catch, and the meat was tasty. Thus, hares were counted by the term *wa* (wing) used for birds (Harada 1993: 109), placing them in the edible class of birds, rather than the term *piki*, used for counting animals smaller than humans. It was a clever device, enabling warriors and monks to enjoy eating them.[8]

Another method was to label the meat of forbidden nonhuman animals as flowers. This method was strengthened after the fifth shogun, Tokugawa Tsunayoshi, issued an ordinance in 1687 called "Shōrui Awaremi-no-rei" (Ordinance for mercy for all beings), prohibiting the killing of many animals. Borrowing from French during the Meiji period, game animals were called *jibie* (from *gibier*, "wild animal," in French). Wild boar became peony (*botan*) or mountain whale (*yamakujira*), whereas deer meat was maple (*momiji*). When chicken became a food item in the Meiji period, it was called oak leaves (*kashiwa*). Other animals enjoyed for food were dogs, wolves, foxes, and monkeys, although not officially acknowledged. During the Edo period these animals were procured on farms and brought to Edo via the Tone River by proprietors of *momonjiya* (hundred beasts stores). The two characters for *momonji* stand for one hundred wild animals, with one hundred meaning "many." Today, in Ryōgoku in Tokyo, right across the Sumida River on the eastern side, there is a *momonjiya* that was founded in 1718.[9] Today it is an upscale restaurant with quite expensive dishes, as *jibie* became enormously popular.

Boundary Crossing

If the classificatory scheme described above is quite flexible in practice for food, it is even more so in the realms of religion, folktales, and art, in which some nonhuman animals are assigned various identities through boundary crossings. I will briefly discuss two mechanisms: metamorphosis and the role of semidivine messengers.

Metamorphosis

Nakamura (1984) offers an exhaustive study of the available tales of various types, from the first written documents of *Kojiki* and *Nihongi* at the beginning of the eighth century to the end of the Edo period (1869). According to him, in the genre of *mukashibanashi* (stories of the ancient times), there are forty-two cases of humans becoming animals and ninety-two cases of animals becoming humans (Nakamura 1984: 10). These examples offer a sharp contrast to the Grimm Brothers' tales, in which hardly any animal becomes a human. Another contrast is that, in the Japanese tales, humans becoming animals—almost always birds—represents ascendency rather than degradation (11–19).

Not all animals become humans. The total number in these tales of the ancient times is largest for foxes (twenty-nine), followed by badgers, snakes, frogs, cats, and snails. Nakamura (1984: 15–16) points out that the

Table 1.1. Animal Metamorphosis into Humans During the Latter Hal of Edo Period. From Nakamura 1984: 190; Ohnuki-Tierney 1987: 32–33.

	Seventeenth and eighteenth centuries	Nineteenth century
Fox	17	43
Badger	13	29
Cat	15	5
Monkey	2	0
Cow	1	0
Snake	8	2
Birds	2	1

monkey seldom becomes a human; instead, it marries a human without changing its physical appearance. This theme of monkey-human marriage without metamorphosis continued during the medieval period (145), by which time the snake had lost its divinity (181). The changes during this period also include the demotion, as it were, of deer and wild boar from mountain deities to messengers for specific deities—deer at Kasuga Shrine, fox at Inari Shrine, monkey at Hiyoshi Shrine, and crow at Kumano Shrine (181). During the medieval period the kinds of animals involved in metamorphosis increased. Those becoming humans included badgers, mice, birds, and clams. Humans metamorphosed into horses, birds, insects, weasels, mice, and moles (182). While during the first half of the Edo period the fox, the badger, and the cat were the animals most frequently changing into humans, during the last half of the Edo period, the metamorphoses were almost exclusively by the fox and the badger (table 1.1) (225).

The complex picture of metamorphosis tells us that animism, which assigns a soul to "all" beings of the universe, does not necessarily render those beings the same or coeval in relation to humans.

Nonhuman Animals as Sacred Messengers

The complexity of the classification of nonhuman animals is immediately apparent when we note that the four-legged animals are in fact also semi-divine messengers from the deities. I offer some examples.

Fox
The fox is the messenger for the *inari*—the god of five grains. This concept was introduced from the Asian continent, likely by the Hata clan, which

Figure 1.3. Fox as a sacred messenger. Inari Shrine at Fushimi. Photo by the author.

was most active in trading with other Asian countries (Komatsu 1982: 13; Matsumae [1988] 1990a, [1988] 1990b; Minzokugaku Kenkyūjo 1951: 35–36; Yoshino 1980: 99). Of 156 cases of metamorphosis of animals into humans, the fox is the most frequent (see also Yoshida [1972] 1978: 13–16).

At the beginning of the Heian period, the *inari* cult grew rapidly, and by the middle of the period, a New Year's visit to the *inari* shrine at Fushimi in Kyoto, the headquarters of the cult, was already a tradition among the city folk (for details, see Toriiminami [1988] 1990). Even today, *inari shinkō*—belief in *inari*—remains powerful, and there are a large number of shrines throughout Japan, with the one in Fushimi as the headquarters where the annual ritual on 23 August draws enormous attention from the public and in the mass media.

The strength of the belief in the power of the fox in contemporary Japan may be illustrated by an incident involving the Haneda Airport. In 1945, the year Japan surrendered on 15 August, the United States GHQ (General Headquarters) demanded the takeover of the airport on 13 September, less than a month after the end of the war. For its expansion into an international airport, the GHQ ordered about 3,000 residents (1,200 families) in the three adjacent towns to evacuate within forty-eight hours. They had to "pack" whatever they could carry. The airport had been the site of the Anamori Inari Shrine. The expanded airport was completed in September

1947. Although the shrine itself had been moved, a red gate (*tori'i*) was left behind. In 1966, when the issue of moving the *tori'i* was rekindled, a series of air disasters took place at Haneda (Miyata 1995: 84–87). The residents voiced their interpretation: it was the *tatari* (punishment) by the fox who had been enshrined at the Anamori Inari Shrine and had been the guardian spirit of the area. As noted above, the power of a soul is demonstrated when it is inappropriately removed from the physical entity where it is lodged. Only in 1999 was the red *torii* finally moved to the present location at Bentenbashi Kōban-mae.

Deer

Kasuga Shrine (*Kasuga-taisha*), at the foot of Mount Mikasa in Nara, was established by the Fujiwara clan in 768 CE and rebuilt several times over the centuries. Deer are sacred messengers of the Shinto deities and inhabit the shrine compound and surrounding mountainous terrain. They roam freely in the shrine compound. The legend has it that the first deity (*kami*) of this shrine, Takemikazuchi, rode on the back of a white deer to the top of Mount Mikasa in 768 CE. The deer is also the messenger to the deities at the Itsukushima Shrine, dedicated to the three daughters of Susanō-no-Mikoto, the brother of the Sun Goddess, Amaterasu. Iizumi (1996) cites a poem from *Manyōshū* in which a white deer is depicted as the metamorphosed figure of the Mountain Deity.

Cow

Until Western influence reached Japan, the cow was not consumed but was used for agricultural work and considered the messenger of the Deity of Scholarship (Tenjinsama). An enormous number of shrines all over Japan feature models of cows made of stone, concrete, or metal (figure 1.4) (Minzokugaku Kenkyūjo 1951: 53–54).

Monkey

The monkey occupies a special space in relation to humans in many of the areas where it lives, and it is even elevated to a powerful deity, as in the case of Hanuman, a Hindu god.

For an understanding of the Japanese conception of "nature," how the Japanese assigned identities for the monkey offers a critical insight. The Japanese think of the monkey as the animal closest to humans because it is a social animal par excellence. Asquith (1984) reports that contemporary Japanese ethologists focus on the "society of monkeys" and their cooperation for survival by joint ownership of resources rather than the survival of the fittest, the focus of the Euro-American ethnologists.

To the monkey the Japanese have assigned various identities, from bona fide deities to mediators between humans, to laughable beasts, to clowns

Figure 1.4. Cow as a sacred messenger. Sugawara Tenmangū Jinja. Photo by the author.

who offer metaphysical commentaries on Japan and the Japanese, as detailed in my book (Ohnuki-Tierney 1987). During early historical periods, the Japanese attitude toward the monkey was positive. Sarutahiko in the eighth-century myth-histories *Kojiki* and *Nihongi* was a monkey whose role was the mediator between the deities in Takamagahara (Heaven) and humans (1987: 42–45). The monkey as a sacred mediator continued to develop throughout the medieval period. For example, according to the belief in the Mountain Deity called *Sannō Shinkō*, the monkey is the messenger to humans from various other deities, especially the Mountain Deity (Minzokugaku Kenkyūjo 1951: 240; 642–44). The monkey as a mediator is also fused with other beliefs and practices associated with mediation.[10]

The monkey performance offers invaluable insight into the Japanese conception of "nature" and the relationship between humans and non-human animals. The earliest record of the monkey performance is in *Ryōjin Hishō* (1169–79), which depicts the monkey dancing and wearing an *eboshi*, the type of hat previously worn only by men of high status, and which became a trademark for performing monkeys. This continues to be a popular street performance even today. Its basic premise is teaching the monkey bipedal posture so that the monkey walks and dances to music, songs either sung by the trainer or played on the three-stringed shamisen

Figure 1.5. Monkey Performance: trainer and monkey drink together as brothers. Courtesy of Y. Azuma.

instrument or a drum. Based on the belief that the monkey is the guardian of horses, the performance originated as a ritual in stables during which the monkey harnessed the sacred power of the Mountain Deity to heal sick horses and to maintain their general welfare. Later it was also done on the street and at the doorways of individual homes, both as entertainment and to bless humans with health and prosperity (see Oda 1980: 2). Toward the very end of the medieval period and the beginning of the early modern period, an additional role was assigned to the monkey performance: blessing a new crop of rice.

Strikingly, the monkey performance reveals what the Japanese conceptualize as unique to humans—bipedalism and a "high" cultural repertoire of music and dancing. As discussed earlier, bipedalism should not be translated as morphological features. The first requirement for the monkey to achieve bipedalism is to reduce its contact with the defiled ground. The monkey is a fierce animal capable of ripping off a finger or ripping any part of the body with its powerful forelegs and claws, making this process excruciatingly difficult for the trainer (Murasaki 1980: 148). After it has been humanized, the trainer, Tarō, and the monkey, named Jirō, drink together as brothers (figure 5). The humanized monkey will perform the most human activity of dancing to music. Dancing is an act whereby the biological body is transformed into a culturalized body, just as music is a human creation out of patterned sound (cf. Lévi-Strauss [1949] 1969).

Bipedalism in Japanese culture is thus quite different from the bipedal monkey depicted in other cultures. In both the seventeenth-century Dutch paintings by Jan Brueghel the Younger and the paintings dated to the years 1735–40 by Christophe Huet, the monkeys are bipedal, engaged in the activities of the upper class. They are satirical depictions of those who try to climb the social ladder.[11]

The Japanese monkey performance, on the other hand, also foregrounds the dividing line between humans and nonhuman animals, as the trainer highlights when the monkey fails to perform (Ohnuki-Tierney 1987: 186–94). Thus, unlike most animals in the folktales, the monkey seldom possesses humans—a role assigned to other animals such as foxes, badgers, snakes, and cats (Yoshida [1972] 1978: 13–14). For the same reason, in contrast to other animals, metamorphosis between monkey and human is much less frequent, as we saw earlier.

As the early modern period (1603–1867) progressed, the idea of the monkey as a scapegoat became dominant. It was the way to establish the difference between humans and nonhuman animals. A "human being minus three pieces of hair"—a beast lacking the essence of being human—came to be a popular reference for the monkey. Another example is a proverb: *Tōrō ga ono, enkō ga tsuki* (The axe of a praying mantis is like the moon for the monkeys). A praying mantis trying to crush the wheel of a cart with its forelegs (the axes) is portrayed as being as ridiculous as a monkey mistaking the reflection of the moon on the surface of water for the moon itself and drowning while trying to capture it. Although the proverb originated in a Chinese story called "Sōshiritsu," its prevalent use during the sixteenth century is shown by the famous painting *Enkō sokugetsu* (Monkey capturing the moon) by Hasegawa Tōhaku (1539–1610), depicting a monkey unable to tell the difference between the moon and its reflection in water.

The monkey as a scapegoat is depicted also in a well-known painting of Ōtsu-*e*, a genre of folk paintings by anonymous artists that flourished from the late seventeenth to the early eighteenth century. Its immediate message is that the monkey, which tries to subdue a catfish with an equally slippery gourd, is a fool who tries to do the impossible. During this period, the catfish was believed to be the causal agent of earthquakes (Ouwehand 1964). Therefore, the painting can be read as a monkey trying to control an earthquake. Either way, the monkey is depicted as a fool, not knowing the limits of one's power, as humans do.

It was not a coincidence that the meaning/role of the monkey as scapegoat emerged during the medieval period, when Japanese society became a caste society, especially under Hideyoshi, who codified the castes to consists of "warriors, farmers, artisans, [and] merchants (*shinōnōkōshō*)," with two "outcastes." Intermarriage of persons belonging to different castes was strictly prohibited (See Ohnuki-Tierney 1987: 75–100 for details of the history of these discriminated groups).

The meanings and identities given to the monkey thus tell us that animism, which assigns a soul to all beings of the universe, does not translate into sameness or equality among them. The Japanese hold the right to assign a place for the inhabitants of the universe.[12]

Summary and Discussion

In order to understand "Japanese nature," this chapter began with the Japanese concept of the soul. One might even say that interest in the soul of "the other" ("primitives") was one of the major foci at the time of the birth of anthropology, as exemplified in *The Golden Bough* by James Frazer, published in 1890, in which "soul" is an often invoked concept. The English translation of Lucien Lévy-Bruhl's work, *L'âme primitive*, published in 1927, is *The "Soul" of the Primitive*, in which he argued that for "primitives," the soul is the essence of all beings of the universe. This led to the idea of equality among all the beings of the universe, with its most recent resurgence being the "ontological turn" of Descola (2013) and the "perspectivism" of Eduardo Viveiros de Castro (1998). In chapter 6, "Animism Restored," in *Beyond Nature and Culture*, Descola (2013: 129; my emphasis) defines animism as "the attribution *by humans* to nonhumans of an interiority identical to their own" and states that the "similarity of interiorities justifies extending a state of 'culture' to nonhumans, together with all the attributes that implies, ranging from intersubjectivity to a mastery of techniques and including ritualized conduct and deference to conventions." The interiority or the soul has "intentionality, subjectivity, reflexivity, feelings, and the ability to express oneself and to dream" (116).

Perhaps it is fair to state that all peoples acknowledge in nonhumans some kind of interiority—call it soul or mind, for instance—but the specificity of what it comprises and how it acts varies, as Descola himself notes: "[A]ll this does not suffice to blur the major differences that exist between the cultures" (2013: 31). In *Ways of Baloma*, Mosko (2017: esp. 86–87) offers an extensive comparison between the Amerindians' and the Trobriand

Islanders' conceptions of the soul and animism: "[T]he differences between Trobriand culture and sociality and Amazonian animism amount to considerably more than just so many substantively distinct worldviews among others."

The soul, the *kami* (deities), and the ancestors show the most important Japanese ontological principle—formlessness, entities without physicality, which means neither visible nor audible. Their "presence" is known through their actions.

This leads to the important principle in how the Japanese classify the inhabitants of the universe. The basic criterion for the classification is *not* their morphology but the resultant behavioral characteristics. The four-legged animals are the most abominable because they are most in touch with the ground, the most defiled space of the universe.

Animism provides the basis for crossing normative boundaries and for metamorphosis. The four-legged animals—the most defiled—become semidivine messengers for deities, as in the case of the monkey, cow, deer, and fox, for example. Nonetheless, not all nonhuman animals metamorphose into humans, and the animals and the ways they change their identity vary depending on the period in history.

Scholarly debates over human and nonhuman animal relationships have a long history. Aristotle taught that men must use animals for their own purposes, otherwise they would be in grave danger of leading a bestial life. Also, from the time of Hesiod, the animal world was seen as the kingdom of unreason, without the ability to judge justice or injustice (Detienne and Vernant [1979] 1986: 8). The possession of reason distinguished humans from animals. In the past decades, the topic has been invigorated by the line of interpretation proposed by Jakob Johann Baron von Uexküll (2010), who stressed the subjectivity of nonhuman animals rather than how humans view them. In *The Open: Man and Animal*, Agamben (2004: 33–38) foregrounds how the "anthropological machine" of Western thought created an absolute difference, with humans above the animals and environment.

In contrast to "the Emperor the Farmer" in Japan, in many western European countries it is "the King the Hunter," for whom hunting and meat eating have had enormous importance, above all as the basis for political power. In contrast, in the Japanese universe, plants have always occupied the apex of the cosmic hierarchy. Yet in both the West and Japan, the establishment of this social/cultural hierarchy was not a natural process or strictly on utilitarian grounds. Religions have played a significant and long-lasting role in buttressing the importance of such hierarchies. The well-known story of Cain, the farmer, and Abel, the shepherd, in the Old Testament (Genesis, chapter 4) offers an explanation how Almighty

God preferred the meat offered by Abel to plant foods offered by Cain. In Japan, from the first myth histories of the *Kojiki* and *Nihongi*, in which grains, including rice, came out of the deity's body, we find overwhelming evidence that rice has held supreme economic, political, and symbolic importance.

Notes

1. There are a number of terms distinguishing various kinds of soul: *shinrei*, the soul of a deity; *ikiryō*, the soul of a living person that is out of the body and can move around freely; *shirei*, the soul of the dead; *hyōi*, possession by an animal or the soul of the dead; and *hyōrei*, possession by a soul (Komatsu 1982: 42).
2. The belief is embedded in the notion that Japan, called *Yamato-no-kuni*, is blessed with deities and flourishes with the souls of words, as clearly expressed in the beginning of the poem by Yamanoue no Okura (Horton 2012: 243–44).
3. Ukemochi no Kami, the deity in charge of food, was the guardian of the imperial family; only after the emperor system was well established did the Sun Goddess become the imperial ancestress.
4. This phenomenon has been debated by scholars. Eisenstadt (1996: 13–14) explains it in term of his scheme of axial versus non-axial religions; Kitagawa ([1966] 1990) describes it as "eclectic"; others describe it as "multilayered"; while still others see that various religions have been "fused" (for details, see Ohnuki-Tierney 1984a: 145–49).
5. Miyake (1995: 96–98) provides a list of the inhabitants.
6. *Shirikumenawa* is a rope whose ends were not cut. It was used to demarcate a sacred place during the ancient period.
7. The system originally came from China and thus their uses are similar but not identical. The Chinese also use the head (*tou*), but *pi* is used to count horses, *zhi* is for birds, *kuai* is for tofu, and *tiao* is for fish (personal communication from Dr. Zhang Muyang).
8. This insight was pointed out by R. Kenji Tierney.
9. English terms such as "pork," "beef," and "venison" are not euphemisms but originate from the time of the Norman conquest of Britain in 1066 and the conversion of French words into English.
10. An example is the *kōshin* belief and practice, with which the monkey is closely associated. The term *kōshin* refers to the fifty-seventh day or year of each sixty-day or sixty-year cycle in the Taoist calendar: the time between two temporal cycles. The oldest record of the all-night *kōshin* wake dates to 838 CE, but the practice started during the latter part of the eighth century when Taoism was introduced to Japan (Kubo 1961: 538, 540). On the night defined as *kōshin*, three worms (black, green, and white in color) believed to dwell in a person's body are said to ascend to Heaven to report to the emperor of Heaven their host's transgressions during the previous cycle (Blacker 1975:

329; Minzokugaku Kenkyūjo 1951: 196–97). This belief led to the custom of staying up all night to prevent the worms from leaving the body to report on their host. The practice on the night of *kōshin* was already popular among aristocrats during the early phase of the Heian period (794–1185) and was one of the annual events at the imperial court (Kubo 1961: 540–46; see also Iida 1983: 53–54). While remaining popular among aristocrats, the *kōshin* belief and practice diffused to warriors and to commoners, at least those of high status, during the latter half of the fifteenth century, and have spread even more widely since then (Kubo 1961: 549, 606).

A major change in the nature of the *kōshin* belief took place toward the end of the sixteenth century when it took on a religious nature as recorded in a document dating to 1595 (Kubo 1961: 585). Believers created a deity—the *kōshin* deity (*kōshin sama*)—and prayed for their protection and welfare, especially at times of illness. It was an influential deity among the commoners during the early modern period (342, 607).

Given that mediation between temporal cycles, between humans and deities, and between Heaven and earth was their primary meaning and role, during the late phase of the Muromachi period (1338–1603), the *kōshin* belief and practices became fused with various forms of belief in the monkey, including the aforementioned Saruta Biko and the Mountain Deity (Minzokugaku Kenkyūjo 1951: 196). An example appears in one of the amulets used by believers in the sacredness of Mount Fuji, which had been closely associated with the *kōshin* belief. Depicted on these amulets are Saruta Biko and more than sixty monkeys worshipping Mount Fuji at its foothills (Miyata 1975: 148). Another example is the engravings of monkeys on the stone monuments called *kōshintō* (*kōshin* monuments), which began to appear during the late Muromachi period (Kubo 1961: 586; Minzokugaku Kenkyūjo 1951: 196), although the engravings became a standard feature only during the early modern period.

11. The depiction of monkeys as bipedal is fairly common in many cultures. In the seventeenth-century Dutch paintings by Jan Brueghel the Younger, bipedal monkeys represent the upper-class Dutch who engage in the utmost stupidity of tulip mania—the craze over the recently introduced and fashionable tulips, which developed into the first futures markets in Europe and peaked in February 1637. Another example is the depictions of the monkey in aristocratic pursuits in French culture, dated to the years 1735–40, by Christophe Huet in the two salons (*la grande Singerie* and *la petite Singerie*) in the Château de Chantilly (Dannaud and Dordor 2009). At the time, social mobility/climbing was on the rise, and the aristocrats and their lifestyle were gently satirized.

12. For the Achuar of Amazonia, "language is the discriminating criterion between nature and culture," and it establishes a subtle hierarchy among the beings of the universe. "Cultural continuity" is seen in degrees of sociability, in particular marriage patterns. Hence the Achuar, who practice exogamy, condemn monkeys and dogs as "incestuous beasts" because of their sexual promiscuity (Descola [1986] 1994: 325).

Part II

"Japanese Nature" by the Elite

CHAPTER 2

Rice Paddies with Pure Water

Birth of "Japanese Nature" in the Early Nara Period (710–794)

This chapter describes the original blueprint, as it were, of "Japanese nature" as laid out by the emperors during the ancient period. It was during the ancient period that wet-rice agriculture came to Japan and laid the foundation for the political economy of the imperial system. In order to buttress the political economy, the early emperors created two cosmological themes that have become the bulwark of "Japanese cosmology," which in turn created and defined "Japanese nature."

First, the imperial cosmogony/cosmology was created to place rice with its soul at the very top of the hierarchy of the inhabitants in the universe. The basic spatial divisions and valences were set accordingly, with the above being clean and the below being defiled. Given this scheme, rice paddies were called *suiden* water paddies—with pure water without showing ground.

Second, "imperial cartography" was equally, if not more, important in creating the long-lasting cartography of the universe with the emperor in control of both the vertical (up and down) and horizontal (right and left) divisions and associated valances.

These concepts became *naturalized*, although they underwent historical transformations. Nonetheless they served as the basic principles of the Japanese cosmology and governed not only the so-called cosmological/symbolic structure but also the classification of humans and nonhuman animals, as well as the everyday behaviors of the people.

I start this chapter with the early stage of the foraging economy before it gave way to the agrarian economy in order to show how "Japanese nature" was represented by the imperial court.

Jōmon Hunting-Gathering Period (14,500–3,000 BCE)

In July 1998, potsherds were discovered at the Odaiyamamoto site in Aomori, the northern tip of the main island. Testing confirmed that they date to 16,500 years before the present (*Asahi Shinbun* morning edition, 17 April 1999; Habu 2004; Kobayashi 2008: 28–35). The potsherds at the site signaled the beginning of the "Jōmon period," ending the long Paleolithic period, which began around 35,000 BCE. It is now accepted by most Jomon scholars that pottery was invented in various parts of the Eurasian continent and was introduced to Japan, involving different populations and using different routes, some from the north and others from the south. It is now well-established that the invention of pottery antedates the beginning of agriculture (Miyao 2018).

The Jōmon subsistence economic activities consisted of hunting, fishing, and plant gathering. Miyao (2018: 7) emphasizes the importance of pottery for the cooking of fish to produce fish oil. A large number of animals and plants from the land and sea were consumed as food (for a comprehensive list, see Kobayashi 2018: 159). Bones of dogs were found at Jōmon sites, but they were not used for food, since the bones were buried in a shallow grave dug in the ground (Kobayashi 2008: 111–15). For the Jōmon people, deer and wild boar were the most important sources of food (Kobayashi 2008; Sasaki [1991] 1992: 116–60). The domestication of wild boar was practiced already during the early stage of the Jōmon (Harada 1993: 39–40; Kobayashi 2008: 117). Deer antlers were also used (Kobayashi 2008: 11–20). Other animals hunted and consumed were the brown bear in Hokkaido and black bear in Honshu and Shikoku; badger, wild goose, pheasant, duck, fox, monkey, rabbit, flying squirrel, and antelope; and whales and other sea mammals, including seals, sea lions, and fur seals (Kobayashi 2008: 111–24; Sasaki [1991] 1992: 116–24). Although a wild boar made of clay was found at a Jōmon site (Sasaki [1991] 1992: 14), there is little evidence of "big game hunting" for prey such as bears. At the sites called shell middens, shellfish and fish were consumed in abundance, as were acorns and other nuts. People had perfected a way to get rid of the bitterness of acorns (Sasaki [1991] 1992: 117–60; Watanabe 1967: 27–28).

Agricultural Period: Yayoi (800 BCE–250 CE)

The transition from the Jōmon to the Yayoi had been set at around 350 BCE for a long time, but this received wisdom was overturned by the results of carbon-14 tests and other methods at sites in western Japan (Fujio 2014).

Now it is certain that wet-rice agriculture originated in the middle of the Yangtze River and was introduced during the twenty-year period at the end of the ninth century BCE to northern Kyūshū (Kobayashi 2008: 035) by people of southern Korea, who also brought an extensive repertoire of technological skills (Rhee, Aikens, and Barnes 2021: 32–35, 41–42). It then moved eastward in three successive waves, although there may have been some differences in how the Jōmon people in different regions adopted it. The people never took up animal domestication, either for meat and/or milk consumption or ritual sacrifice (Sasaki [1991] 1992: 298–312, 340).

The introduction of wet-rice agriculture was revolutionary, as in all the other areas of the world where it developed. The yield ratio of rice far surpassed that of wheat. As Tanaka (2002: 49) emphasizes, "even in the most advanced agricultural regions of Western Europe, the ratio [of wheat] was just about ten or eleven to one in the early eighteenth century." Tanaka continues: "Even in ancient times, one grain of seed rice could produce more than one hundred grains." Bray (1986: 198) notes that the staple foods of wheat, barley, and rye all bear relatively few grains, compared with the hundred or more grains in a panicle of rice or millet. Gregory (2004: 4) also points out that of the crops grown in Japan's three agricultural zones—wheat, yam and taro, and rice—"rice is the only one of these three staples that is consumed almost exclusively by humans." Wheat is "more suited to large-scale, capital-intensive means of production," leading to large estates in England, in contrast to rice production based on family smallholding (see also Bray 1986: 199).

The Japanese adoption of rice led to state formation and social stratification without improving the lot of the common people. Collection of rice as taxes began during the Tomb period (250–646) (Watanabe [1964] 1967: 32–36). With the introduction of wet-rice agriculture, the diet of the elite and that of the common people began to be different (48–49). The diet of the aristocrats was centered on rice and adopted Chinese-style cuisine, while the commoners had hardly any access to rice and ate primarily other grains, such as millet, vegetables, and meat. That is, rice farmers more or less remained rice producers without being rice consumers (Ohnuki-Tierney 1993). Wet-rice agriculture thus set the foundation of social inequality for the rest of Japanese history. Although I use the term "rice" throughout this book, there are many kinds of rice, with some "low quality" rice—another source of inequality—existing even today (Ohnuki-Tierney 1995).

During this period, emperors and princes continued to hunt, and the activity played an important role in imperial power, although it was hardly real hunting, as done by European kings. *Fudoki*, regional histories, are excellent sources of information, including the records dated even before the volumes were published. In 713 CE Empress Genmei (r. 707–15) issued an order to compile the geographic history of each region so the imperial government could exert greater control over them. The history was to include the name of the region, its origin, oral traditions, products, and degree of fertility of the soil. Five of these survive to date. In these regional histories, there are records that did not enter the official myth-histories of *Kojiki* and *Nihongi*—perhaps they were purposely left out of those works, or they escaped deletion since many oral histories of the local elders were also included (Iizumi 1996).

On the basis of *Harima no Kuni Fudoki*, a regional history dated to 713 of the Harima district, the southwestern part of present-day Hyōgo Prefecture (Iiizumi 1996: 41–42), Iizumi describes hunting by emperors and princes during the ancient period. There were two types of hunting: the emperor shooting with a bow and arrow, and the other with him watching the whole operation from a hill, called *mitachioka* (hill where the honorable emperor stands). *Ukehigari* was a ritual to ask the deities to tell their fortune by hunting. Prince Kagosaka-no-Mikoto and Prince Oshikuma-no-Mikoto, both around 201 CE, could not become emperor because they failed in the *Ukehigari* Emperor Ingyō (b. 376, r. 410–53, dates uncertain), on the other hand, failed in hunting but tried to find the cause of his failure through divination, enabling him to be the emperor (Iizumi 1996: 42).

In an episode in the *Fudoki*, a deity comes from Izumo and sets a trap in a river in which a deer, instead of a fish, gets caught. The deity tries to eat the raw meat of the deer, but it will not go into his mouth and drops to the ground. Iizumi interprets this act as a demonstration of the power of the Deity of the Earth, appearing as a white deer, who overpowered the visiting deity, forcing him to give up his plan to seize control of the region. In other words, the success or failure of hunting, by either an emperor or a deity, was according to the will of the Deity of the Earth. Given the importance of the successful hunt for an emperor, these episodes clearly testify that the imperial power was subordinate to the power of that deity (Iiizumi 1996: 45–46, 54–55, 57).

Manyōshū, the oldest extant collection of poems, dates to the seventh and eighth centuries. Hirono (1998: 187–88) cites two poems by Kakinomoto no Hitomaro and one by Yamabe Akahito from *Manyōshū* to reconstruct imperial hunting at the time. The hunt by a prince is called *nogari*. Kakinomoto no Hitomaro describes the hunting by Karu-no-miko, which qualified him to become Emperor Monmu (r. 697–707). It had been assumed that the prince and his entourage slept in the field, but the excavation at Akino in 1995 found that they built an elaborate structure with a garden paved with stones. The hunting methods during these earlier periods were a pitfall and a device that shot off an arrow when an animal stepped on it.

Hunting continued to be undertaken by emperors and princes after the introduction of wet-rice agriculture, which became the basis for the political economy. However, they are "mock hunting" in comparison with hunting by European kings, whose capture of big game and distribution of the meat in an elaborate ritual of commensality were crucial for their political power.

State Formation: Nara Period (710–784)

According to Chinese sources, before the development of the agrarian monarchy or the Yamato state, there was quite a different monarchical system, located in either Kyūshū or central Japan. Referred to as the Yamatai federation of kingdoms, it had a different set of rituals, especially for the imperial funeral. *Gishi Wajinden*, a Chinese source, recounts that a powerful shamaness, Pimiko (Himeko or Himiko), ruled over some thirty kingdoms by controlling access to Korean iron ore, which was of vital importance for making agricultural tools and military weapons between the end of the second century and the first half of the third century. In 239 she was given the title of king (*ō*) by the Chinese monarch.

The Yamatai state was established and maintained principally by the priestly control of ceremonial power, not by the physical power of armies and material possessions (Brown [1993] 1997: 26). Citing *Gishi Wajinden*, Yoshimura (1998: 24–31) introduces Himeko as

> a king (*ō*) who was skilled in the demon's craft (*kidō*; witchcraft) and misled people into confusion. She was not married, but her younger brother helped govern the state. After becoming the king, she became not to be seen. She had a thousand servants, but only one male served meals and relayed messages. (my translation)

Yoshimura emphasizes that she became invisible to the people *after* she assumed the kingship. At that time, the kings in many areas were not to be seen. At the time of her death, a large house was built and some one hundred servants were buried with her (Saeki [1990] 1995: 986).

During the third century CE the Yamato state developed in central Japan. Scholars' opinions differ on the relation between the Yamatai and the Yamato states and between Himeko and Amaterasu (Sun Goddess). Whether the Yamatai was located in Kyūshū or Kinki remains controversial (Kitagawa [1966] 1990: 4–6; see also Brown [1993] 1997: 1–47; Sansom

1978: 29; Tsunoda and Goodrich 1968: 14–15). With greater agricultural production and closer contact with the strong Korean kingdom, the Yamato developed into a powerful state, whose rulers were buried in large tombs (*kofun*), for which the period is named the Tomb (Kofun) period (250–646). The Yamato clan rulers founded an imperial dynasty that has continued to the present. Takagi (2017) details the problems in identifying who exactly is buried in these tombs and questions the official line of unilinear descent, pointing to changes in the mode of burial—from interment to cremation and back to interment.[1] Efforts to identify the burials by contemporary scholars have met with difficulty due to the problem of getting permission from the imperial household to open some of the key tombs. What we have so far is a fluid and complex picture of the political leadership from the so-called Tomb period to the early Nara period (710–814), rather than a straight line from the establishment of the imperial system, as it has been portrayed.

Buddhism was introduced via China either 538 or 552 CE and first embraced by the aristocrats, although the native religion of Shintō persisted throughout history. The most fundamental legal "reform" took place in 645 CE. Known as the Taika Reform, it laid the foundation for the basic legal and bureaucratic system, following primarily the Chinese model.

The political, legal, sociocultural, and religious systems of the Nara (710–94) and Heian (794–1185) periods continued to be greatly influenced by China, although the move of the capitol from Nara to Kyoto itself shows significant changes in the attitude of the emperors and courtiers toward Buddhism, as detailed below. The eighth and ninth centuries were crucial periods for the Japanese political leaders to consolidate their power, for which they turned to the rice-centered ontology as the state ideology.

The Soul of Rice-cum-Deity— Cosmological Basis of Imperial Power

During this incipient period, the imperial court exerted a strenuous effort to systematically develop an agrarian cosmology and then turned it into ideology for its political purposes. The most conspicuous result was the compilation of the myth-histories of the *Kojiki* (dated to 712) (Kurano and Takeda 1958) and *Nihonshoki* (dated to 720) (Sakamoto, Ienaga, Inoue, and Ōno 1965). Both are replete with references to rice and its relationship to deities. Thus, the soul of the rice grain (*ina dama* or *ina-damashii*) is clearly identified as a *kami* (deity), called Uka no Kami. In one version of the creation myth of various grains in the *Nihonshoki* (Sakamoto, Ienaga, Inoue, and Ōno 1967: 100–102), when Ukemochi-no-kami, the deity in charge of food, turned his head toward land, *ihi* (the term for rice/meal at the time) came out of his mouth, and when he turned his head toward the sea, fish of various sizes emerged from his mouth. When the deity was slain, various foods came out of his corpse: rice born from his stomach, millet from his forehead, Deccan grass from his eyes, and wheat and beans from his anus. Although the eyes and anus were important organs (Ohnuki-Tierney 1987: 42–43), the stomach (*hara*) has always been of crucial importance in the Japanese conception of the body, and still is today (see Ohnuki-Tierney 1984a: 57–60). The soul was thought to reside there, hence the well-known cultural institution of male suicide in which a man cuts open his stomach to release his soul. Given the centrality accorded to the stomach, it is significant that in the myth-histories, rice is depicted to have been born from it—the abode of the soul and fetus—whereas other grains are born from other parts of the body. This passage clearly establishes that rice was the most important among grains.[2]

In the version in the *Kojiki* written after the Sun Goddess, Amaterasu Ōmikami, was established as the ancestral deity to the imperial family, likely after the seventh century (Matsumae 1977: 136–37), she is the mother of a grain soul called Masakatsu Akatsu Kachihaya Hiame no Oshihomimi no Mikoto (Kurano and Takeda 1958: 111, 125). Thus Emperor Jinmu, the legendary "first emperor," is the son of the grain soul (Ninigi-no-Mikoto) and the great grandson of the Sun Goddess, who sent her grandson to rule the earth. Another name for this grandson-cum-first-emperor is Amatsu Hiko Hiko Ho no Ninigi no Mikoto, meaning "rice stalks with succulent grains" (Kurano and Takeda 1958: 125). At the time of his descent, Amaterasu gives her grandson the original rice grains that she grew in the two fields in Heaven (Takamagahara) from the seeds of the five types of grains (*gokoku*) given to her by Ukemochi no Kami, the deity in charge of food (Kurano and Takeda 1958; see also Murakami 1977: 13). The grandson transforms a wilderness into a country of rice stalks with succulent ears of rice (*mizuho*) and the five grains (*gokoku*), thanks to those original seeds.

As the *Kojiki* continues, Amaterasu's grandson marries a beautiful woman who gives birth to two sons, Hoderi no Mikoto and Hoori no Mikoto. The older brother (Hoderi no Mikoto), who is also called Umi Sachi Biko (Sea-Bounty Lad), tends to the sea and engages in fishing, while the younger brother (Hoori no Mikoto), who is also called Yama Sachi Biko (Mountain-Bounty Lad), tends to the land, hunting land animals. The two brothers decide to exchange their tools and occupations for a while. The younger brother loses the fishhook while trying out fishing. The older brother insists on having it back. The younger brother's search for the fishhook leads him to the palace of the Sea Deity at the bottom of the sea, where he marries the Sea Deity's daughter. The union gives birth to the first and legendary emperor, Jinmu, said to have been enthroned in 660 CE, when he changed his name to Kamuyama Itohare Biko no Mikoto (Kurano and Takeda 1958: 135–47).

In this creation myth, then, it is the younger brother, that is, the deity in charge of the land instead of the sea, who becomes the progenitor of the imperial line. Although the younger brother, the father of the first emperor, is described as a hunter, his alternative name, Amatsu Hiko Hiko Hohotemi no Mikoto means "a male child of the Sun Goddess and lord of rice stalks with numerous ears" (Kurano and Takeda 1958: 135). Thus, the struggle between sea and land ends with the latter's victory. On the other hand, the story reveals that the ultimate celebration of rice agriculture, expressed in his alternative name, must have constituted a gradual process, since the son of the Sun Goddess also is described as a hunter.

Although there are a number of different versions in these myth-histories (Matsumae 1977), these well-known examples are not about the creation of the universe but about the transformation of wilderness (*ashihara no nakatsu no kuni*) into a land of abundant rice at the command of, according to the *Kojiki*, the Sun Goddess, whose descendants, the emperors, rule the country by officiating at the rice harvest rituals (Saigō [1967] 1984: 15–29; Kawasoe [1978] 1980: 86).

A Few Ounces of Divinity: Ontological Justification for an Agrarian Polity

The notions that each rice grain has a soul (*inadama*) and that rice is alive in the husk are fundamental to the meanings assigned to rice in Japanese culture and in most other cultures that use rice as a "staple food." Husking, for example, was traditionally done a short while before consumption to prevent rice from losing its soul; husked rice soon becomes lifeless rice, that is, "old rice" (*komai*).[3]

I suggest that the soul of the rice grain is not simply equivalent to a deity but should be identified more specifically as the *nigimitama*, the positive power of divine purity. While most deities have dual—positive/creative and negative/destructive—qualities and powers, the Deity of the Rice Paddy has only the *nigimitama*, or peaceful soul. In fact, drought or flood, which destroys rice paddies, is an act of the Mizu no Kami (Water Deity) rather than an expression of the *aramitama* (violent spirit) of the Deity of the Rice Paddy. Yangita (1951a: 357–60) equates the *inadama* with the Soshin (Ancestral Deity), who in turn is the Ta no Kami (Deity of the Rice Paddy).

Human lives wane unless the positive principle replenishes their energy. Therefore, humans and their communities must rejuvenate themselves by harnessing the positive (*nigitama*) power of the deities. This can be accomplished in two ways: by performing a ritual or through the consumption of food. Through the consumption of rice, the Japanese internalize the divine power, which then becomes part of the human body and its growth. Alternatively, humans can harness the divine power of rice by performing rituals celebrating each stage of its growth cycle—the planting of rice seeds, the planting of seedlings, and harvesting. Soliciting supernatural power to ensure a good harvest relied on the performance of these rituals by the magico-religious leaders, namely, shamans-cum-political leaders, including the emperors.

Thus, the annual harvest ritual served to legitimate a local political leader, ensure the leader's rebirth, and rejuvenate his power (Murakami 1977: 4–6). For this reason, many scholars consider the emperor first and foremost as the officiant in rituals for the soul of rice (*inadama no shusaisha*), who ensures the blessings of the deities for the new rice crop on behalf of the people (e.g., Akasaka 1988; Hora 1979, 1984; Inoue 1984; Miyata 1989, 1988: 190–94; Murakami 1977, 1986; Okada 1970; Yamaori 1978). The emphasis on the religious-ritualistic nature of Japanese kingship, even by Marxist scholars like Murakami, deemphasizes its exclusively political and economic aspect.

The combined religious, political, and economic nature of these agrarian rituals of early leaders, including emperors, is clearly expressed in the concept *matsurigoto*, which was the conceptual basis of the political system, called *ritsuryō-sei*, at the time (cf. Kitagawa 1990: 138–89). Advancing the interpretation by Mitsuya Shigematsu and Andō Seiji, Orikuchi (1975a: 160–61; 1975b: 175–77; [1947] 1983: 275–77) proposes that the early use of the term *matsuri*, which in contemporary Japanese means festivals or ceremonies, meant *osukuni no matsurigoto*. Written in three characters representing "to eat," "country," and "polity," it denotes the country where food for the deities is made. In other words, food and food consumption were the most essential part of the polity at the time, and rice started to represent food in general.[4]

Although other rituals were added in different historical periods, especially at the time of the Meiji "restoration" of the imperial system at the end of the nineteenth century, the core imperial rituals officiated by the emperor all relate to rice harvesting: *niinamesai*, *ōnamesai* (*daijōsai*), and *kannamesai*.[5] The annual harvest ritual of *niinamesai* becomes the *ōnamesai* at the accession of a new emperor and is the last of three accession rituals, following the *senso* (including *kenji togyo*) and the accession ritual (*sokui no rei*). These are all rice harvest rituals and share many essential elements (for details, see Ohnuki-Tierney 1994: 46–51).

Transformation of the Cosmology

In this process of establishing an agrarian ontology, significant changes to the belief system based on the hunting-gathering political economy of the Jōmon period had to be made. Perhaps most important was the beliefs and symbolic meanings assigned to the mountains where the hunting took place. Although there are vast differences across the regions (Minzokugaku Kenkyūjo 1951: 642–44), the Mountain Deity (gender varies depending on the region) is arguably the most important deity in the Japanese pantheon. Iinuma offers a detailed account of the transformation of the Mountain Deity from a fearsome deity with a contentious relationship to humans (2001:11) during the period of the hunting-gathering economy to the protector of the villagers (21–26). The transformation took several centuries. In the agrarian cosmology, the Mountain Deity descends to the rice paddies on a cherry petal and becomes the Deity of Rice Paddies, whom the people send back to the mountains in the fall with their harvest ritual (see also Kobayashi 2008: 198–99; Minzokugaku Kenkyūjo 1951: 358; Miyata 1993; Ohnuki-Tierney 2002a: 29; Sakurai 1976; M. Suzuki 1991: 6–9).

Imperial Ordinance for the Prohibition of Meat Eating

The other method to promote agriculture was to discourage meat eating. According to *Nihonshoki*, on 10 April 675 CE, Emperor Tenmu issued an ordinance to enforce the performance of two rituals, perhaps the first national rituals, to ensure the promotion of rice agriculture—one for the Deity of Wind and the other for the Deity in Charge of Water in rice paddies.

On 17 April, seven days later, the emperor issued another important ordinance against meat eating (Sakamoto et al. 1967: 418). It prohibited the eating of five beasts: cows, horses, dogs, chickens, and monkeys. The list excludes deer and wild boars, the most important game animals. Deer had been an important source of meat ever since the Jōmon period, and the hides and antlers were treasured. As noted, deer were considered to have some superhuman powers and to be messengers from the deities.

During the same period, the forty-volume *Kōninshiki* (completed in 830), lays out what constitutes impurity (*kegare; shokue*). They were impurity accompanying deaths of humans and childbirth; deaths of the six beasts and their births; eating of the meat of these beasts; and mourning. The six beasts are horses, cows, sheep, dogs, wild boar, and chicken (for details of earlier developments of the notion of defilement, see Ide and Ushiyama 2016).

The official reason for the prohibition was the Buddhist doctrine of mercy for all living beings. Although nominally against meat eating, in fact the ordinance prohibits killing of these animals in order to protect agriculture (Harada 1993: 67, 70–71). Cows and horses are useful for agriculture, and the others are domesticated animals. The monkey had been a semideified animal.

The classification and accompanying negative values assigned to meat were upheld foremost by the elite. At the three-day banquet for offering medicine to the emperor at the beginning of the year, deer and wild boar meat were replaced by birds at the end of the Heian period (Watanabe [1964] 1967: 75), while meat was consumed by the rest of the population, especially the lower-class warriors and farmers, in the medieval period and later (Harada 1993: esp. 91–99).

Harada (1993: 63–76) introduces a number of scholars who argue that the Buddhist teaching was utilized to justify the prohibition of meat eating, but the ordinance was in fact to protect the agricultural/rice crop. These ordinances testify that the state control of agriculture, especially rice production, started quite early. Later in history, the ammunition for state intervention was supplied by the nativist scholars of the seventeenth through nineteenth centuries. Placing Hirata Atsutane (1776–1843) in the broad context of the nativist movement, Harootunian (1988) details how agricultural work was reconstituted and valorized as a practice of the "ancient way" and became the ideological/symbolic weapon to enforce the exclusive emphasis on agriculture, when the wheel of modernization was turning rapidly toward industrialization and other economic activities.

The official diet of the Japanese since then has consisted of fish, birds, and vegetables. The prohibition against meat eating was removed in 1871 when the Emperor Meiji announced the adoption of a meat diet at the Imperial Palace (Harada 1993:17). At the time of the funeral for the Shōwa emperor in 1989, the guests from all over the world were given a choice between Japanese and Western cuisine (personal communication from the late Prince Mikasa).

The 1942 Food Control Act (*Shokuryō Kanrihō*), which regulated food production and distribution, and the rationing system (*haikyū*) during World War II, brought rice to islands and remote regions where only "miscellaneous grains" had been grown (Tsuboi [1982] 1984: 68). State control has continued even to the present, with rice as almost the exclusive focus. Today, rice farmers are often paid to leave fields fallow to prevent overproduction (Ohnuki-Tierney 1995), since the Japanese consume far less rice than before with increased emphasis on side dishes.

Spatial Orientation in Ancient Cosmogony

The Above and the Below

Already in the eighth-century myth-histories *Kojiki* and *Nihonshoki*, the spatial orientation and the values assigned to the cosmological spaces are clearly established. Takamagahara (The Plain of High Heaven) is the space occupied by the most important deities, headed by the Sun Goddess. Ashihara-no-Nakatsu-Kuni is situated in the middle and is what we call Japan today. Yomi-no-Kuni, the space for the dead, is often referred to as the underground. Saigō ([1967] 1984: 49, 63–65) emphatically and convincingly argues that the vision of the universe at the time was that the *nakatsu-no-kuni*, that is, Japan, was surrounded by sea and *yomi-no-kuni* was located at the very end/edge of the ocean. While the High Heaven is beautiful and divine, the space for the dead is defiled (*kegare*) by the deceased bodies.

Nishiyachi (2009) points out that in *Nihonshoki*, the first "official history" of Japan commissioned by the imperial court and compiled in 720 CE, Takamagahara (The Plain of High Heaven), does not appear, while it frequently appears in *Kojiki*. He explains that *Nihonshoki* was to establish imperial rule over the people and therefore it started with Ninigi-no-mikoto, sent by the Amaterasu to be in charge of *toyoashihara-mizuho-no-kuni* (Japan, the land of abundant rice)—that is, Japan—rather than having the deities in Takamagahara.

Water Field (suiden) *vs. Land Field* (rikuden)

The land where mortals live is divided into wet land and dry land, as explicitly described in *Nihonshoki*: "Rice was born of the stomach.... Millet, Deccan grass, wheat, and beans belong to dry land, while rice belongs to wet land" (Sakamoto et al. 1967: 102). The water field, where rice is grown, is always covered with "beautiful" water so that one does not see the ground. Under the Taika Great Reforms of 645 the "water land" and its product of rice were regulated through ritual performance and a tax system. The dry land where "miscellaneous crops" were cultivated (Kameta [1993] 1996), however, was also regulated by the government.

The "Up" and "Down"

If the *Kojiki* narrated how the Japanese universe was created and laid out the spatial divisions and their respective valences, its concrete visualization, including its valences, firmly anchored to the imperial system, took place when the palaces Heizeikyō (Heijōkyō) (710–84) and Heiankyō (794–1869) were built. In both, the seat for the emperors was located in the center of the northern city limits, and Suzaku Avenue (Suzaku-ōji), the main thoroughfare extending from the palace down through the center of the city, divided the city into the Right (Ukyō-ku) and Left Capitals (Sakyō-ku). Quite significant to the main theme of this book is that to go north is expressed as *agaru*—to go up. This is not a vertical or forward motion of the feet; rather, *agaru* means to go toward the direction where the emperor resides. Conversely, one goes down, *sagaru*, when one goes south. Furthermore, the city's dichotomy, right and left, is from the point of view of the imperial seat, resulting in the opposite of the right and left for the actual locations. Thus, Sakyō-ku—the left district of Kyoto—is on the left as viewed by the emperor, but in fact is situated on the right. The addresses in Kyoto are indeed unique with many other "oddities." But the citizens resisted changes by defying the 1962 ordinance for addresses, in which the government tried to change older systems of addresses in some cities to the new uniform system. It is quite significant that this cosmological/imperial cartography was translated into the everyday lives of the folk, in addition to every person walking up and down, to and from the capital.

The Chinese characters for "up/above" (*jō*) and "down/below" (*ge/ka*) are used as a part of a large number of words. For example, *jōhin* means refined, high class, whereas *gehinn* means low class, vulgar. *Jōza* is the seating close to the most important person in the room, whereas *geza* is the opposite. The word *jōryū* means the upper class. The word *kasō* means the lower class.

Summary

Rather than the king personally hunting wild animals in the royal forest as the demonstration of his conquest of "nature," the emperors and empresses of Japan built their power through the expansion of rice fields, for which their shamanistic ability to guarantee good yield was crucial. It meant, first of all, that the ruler became in charge of temporality, that is, the seasonal calendar in relation to the growth of rice plants. As Orikuchi ([1943]1976: 364–67) and Miyata (1992: 83–84) emphasize, the fundamental importance for the imperial temporality was cyclical time—always returning to the beginning.[6]

Having become the keeper of rice crops, the imperial court had to establish agrarian supremacy, which involved an intricate tug of war between plants and animals whose meanings and roles were assigned in different historical periods, resulting in a highly complex representation of "natures."

This chapter has pointed out that during the ancient period, wet-rice agriculture came to Japan and laid the solid foundation for a highly stratified society. The imperial cosmogony/cosmology was created to provide the conceptual justification for this stratification, giving pride of place to rice, in which the soul of a deity resides. The basic spatial divisions and valences were also set, with the above being clean and the below being impure. Given this scheme, rice paddies were called *suiden* water paddies—with pure water without showing the ground.

The "imperial cartography" was equally important in creating the long-lasting cartography of the universe, with the emperor in control of both the vertical (up and down) and horizontal (right and left) divisions and associated valances.

That a political regime requires conceptual/symbolic backing is spectacularly visible in the case of the German Nazi regime, which sought its origin in the Roman Empire and used the emblems of the Roman eagle and wheat (for details, see Ohnuki-Tierney 2015).

Notes

1. According to Macé (1985), there was a sharp break in the funeral ritual for emperors during the early eighth century. When the Empress Genmyō (r. 707–15) died in 721, his body was cremated and buried one week after the funeral. This contrasts sharply with the funeral for the previous emperor, the Emperor Monmu (r. 697–707). After his death, the mourning of the *mogari* was performed for six months before his body was buried (Macé 1985)—a period much shorter than the one for Emperor Bitatsu (r. 572–85) and for Empress Saimei, which lasted more than 5 years (r. 642–54) (Yoshioka 1992: 810). The *mogari* is the elaborate mourning practice that lasts for a long period, often several months to several years, during which a special hut is built for the corpse. There is virtually no description of how the corpse was kept, but it seems to have been left to decay (Macé 1985: 58). Funeral attendants (*asobibe*) entered the mourning hut with weapons to symbolically fight against the death. These attendants, described in the *Ryō no Shūge*, a late ninth-century work chronicling earlier events, were shamans who sang "the songs of the dead" during their possession trance and also played music during the funeral rites (Akima 1972). The *mogari* mourning involved "sacrifice" of horses and, possibly, humans (Macé 1982: 611–13; for the *mogari*, see also Yamaori 1990a, 1990b).
2. For the *Kojiki*, see Kurano and Takeda, 1958; for the *Nihonshoki* book 1, nos. 6 and 7, see Sakamoto et al. 1965 and 1967. *Uka no Kami* is called *Ukano Mitama* (*uka* = *uke* = grain; *kami* = deity; *mitama* = soul of a deity). In another version in

the *Nihonshoki*, the deity was born when Izanami and Izanagi, the creators of the Japanese universe, fainted from starvation immediately after the creation of *ōyashima no kuni* (Sakamoto et al. 1967, book 1, no. 1, p. 90; see also Itoh 1979: 162–63). In a version in the *Kojiki*, the rice-deity is an offspring of Susano-o, the brother of the Sun Goddess and a notorious *enfant terrible*. In any case, the deity of the soul of rice grain is closely linked to the origin of the Japanese universe.

3. Most contemporary Japanese would not hold as their personal belief that rice has a soul or that it is alive in the husk. But even today rice farmers store their rice unhusked and husk only small amounts as needed. Urban Japanese (women) buy relatively small amounts of rice at local stores that they can trust to supply them with rice that has been husked only a few days before delivery. Similarly, the Japanese pay special attention to the new crop of rice—each fall at harvest time, many Japanese place special orders for the new crop of rice, or *shinmai* (*shin* = fresh, new; *mai* = rice). Conversely, the sale of *komai* (old rice) by the government, purchased from farmers during years of overproduction and stored, has been a central issue in attacks on the government's rice policy (Hasegawa 1987). In contemporary Japan, the terms *komai* (old rice) and *shinmai* (new rice) are used without reference to the soul. Contemporary Japanese phrase their preference for newly husked rice and their aversion to old rice in terms of taste rather than the soul of rice—new-crop rice is tasty while old rice is not palatable. In a thoroughly secularized form, the Japanese continue to view rice not as a lifeless object but as a special food that has life and provides a special source of energy.

4. Orikuchi further suggests that this notion involved the people's obedience to the order issued by the deity (Orikuchi 1975b: 178–79). This meant that the central government collected the new crop of rice from various parts of the country for offerings. The religious act of following the orders of the deity who gave rice seeds to humans and offering the deity their harvest in return involved the political act of collecting the rice crop from the people. The head of the nation, then, had an obligation to oversee the growth of rice. Most scholars accept his insight regarding *matsurigoto* and the concept of soul in ancient Japan. However, his inference of the Japanese emperor system as an absolute monarchy and his other nationalistic interpretations are rejected by most scholars.

5. Until the latter part of the seventh century, the *niinamesai* and *ōnamesai* were identical. Although there are different interpretations of the term *niiname*, the predominant view is that it means the tasting of new crops (*name* = to taste; *nii* = new). Orikuchi (1975b: 180–81) suggests that the term *ōname* derives from *nihe no imi* (*nihe* = *nie* = offering to a deity; *no* = possessive case; *imi* = taboo), which refers to the taboo observed by the officiant of the ritual (the emperor) in the period before the *ōnamesai*. The *kannamesai* is a ritual in which a new crop of rice is offered to the Ise Shrine, rather than at the Imperial Palace itself (Orikuchi 1975b: 183).

Another accession ritual, introduced from China and independent of the *ōnamesai*, was performed early on. At the accession of Emperor Kanmu (r.

781–806) in the eighth century, this accession ritual of Chinese origin was formalized as the accession ceremony (Murakami 1977: 21). Consequently, the *ōnamesai* has come to be seen as a ceremony (*saiten*) rather than a political event. The earliest form of the ōnamesai included the rite of *senso* (*kenji togyo*), during which the three imperial treasures, the mirror, the sword and the *magatama* jewel, were handed to the new emperor. These three items have been found in tombs of apparent aristocrats of the Yayoi period, indicating that these items were symbols for royalty or political leaders. This rite, called *senso* (*kenji togyo*), became independent of the ōnamesai. Thus, since the beginning of the Heian period the imperial accession has involved three separate rituals: *senso* (*kenji togyo*); *sokui no rei*; and *ōnamesai*. Of these, the *senso* is held immediately after the death of an emperor so that the three symbols of kingship are handed to the new emperor without any lapse of time. The timing is also related to the fact that, unlike China and Korea where the new emperor's accession took place right after the death of an emperor, the Japanese aversion to the impurity associated with death required that the accession ritual be held after the imperial funeral in which the impurity created by the previous emperor's death was ritually removed; only then could a new emperor be enthroned (Inoue 1984). Despite these changes, since the time of the Emperor Tenmu in the mid-seventh century, the *ōnamesai* has been essential for the accession of a new emperor (Murakami 1977: 21–22), so much so that some shōguns made financial contributions to ensure its performance by the emperor.

For further details of the imperial rituals, see Ohnuki-Tierney (1993: 45–51). See also Inoue 1984; Miura 1988; Murakami 1977; Nihiname Kenkyūkai 1955; Sakurai 1988; Tanaka 1988; Ueda 1988; Yamamoto, Satō and staff 1988: 224–31; and Yokota 1988. For descriptions of the imperial rituals in English, see Ebersole 1989; Ellwood 1973; Holtom (1928) 1972; and Mayer 1991.

6. Anthropology has a distinguished history of "Time Reckoning," starting with Mauss ([1950] 1979) and followed by Leach ([1953] 1961, [1955] 1961) and others. My use of the term temporality follows this tradition, rather than *Zeit* in *Being and Time* of Heidegger ([1927] 2008).

CHAPTER 3

Agrarian Four Seasons to Culturally Defined Four Seasons
The Late Nara Period (710–794) and Heian Period (794–1185)

In China, the concept *shizen* is attributed to Lao Tzu, a legendary Chinese philosopher of the sixth century BCE (although there are some controversies about when he lived). The Chinese word was introduced to Japan and used to mean "the state without human hand / intentional intervention." Nakanishi (1995) emphasizes that in *Manyōshū*, the eighth-century anthology of poems, it appears only once, as an adjective meaning "state without human intervention." It came to be used as a noun only later in history and refers to the billions of beings of the universe. That is, "beings" of the universe, but not an abstract concept like "nature" in Western thought. The meanings and uses of *shizen* became even more complex when the Dutch and British concepts of nature were introduced during the Edo period. Nevertheless, the Japanese never espoused the Western view of nature, which humans must "conquer."

Watsuji ([1935] 1967: 1) proposed the concept of *fūdosei* (natural property of wind and soil), whose focal point is the existence of human beings. By "human beings," he refers to the dual nature of a human—an individual who is at the same time a member of society, not an atomized individual (14–15). Watsuji explains that he became interested in *fūdosei* when he read Heidegger's *Being and Time* while visiting Berlin. He then realized the critical limitation of Heidegger's concept of *Dasein*, which addresses only the individual. In Watsuji's view, only by considering the dual nature of the individual can we arrive at an understanding of both the temporality and the spatiality of human existence (2, 14–23).[1] He thus sees *fūdosei* as both a historical and spatial concept, with humans at the center rather than the "natural environment," leading to self-understanding.

Translating the term *fūdo* as "milieu," Berque (1994) has written extensively on the concept in relation to a similar idea used by Jakob von Uexküll ([1934] 1956). Berque (1994: 93) defines "milieu" as "the relationship of a society with space and nature."

The term *fūdo* consists of two characters, "wind" and "ground." The *Fudoki* is a chronicle of "the wind and the ground." This genre of work was first commissioned in 713 by Empress Genmei, who issued an ordinance to each regional government to report the names of districts and townships, the land's fertility, and the region's myths, legends, and folktales, as well as the presence of "silver, lead, grasses, trees, birds, animals, fish, [and] insects." The purpose was to centralize and solidify the power of the court at this early stage of the development of the imperial system (Cranston 1993: 469-471; Uegaki [1991] 1996).

Fūdo suggests a lived environment qua nature, rather than "nature" out there, away from "culture." The importance of the wind in Japanese culture is evident: a dictionary lists ninety-one words that start with "wind" and twenty-nine words with "wind" as the second character (Nagasawa 1990: 134–36). Among them are *fūdo* (condition of the local environment); *fūshi* (satire); *fūmi* (flavor); *fūzoku* (customs); *fūryū* (refined taste); *fūshū* (customs); and *fūkei* (scenery). There are at least fifty words whose first character is "ground" (*do/tsuchi*), with various meanings, positive and negative.

The notion of *fūdo* indicates that the Japanese folk lived in "nature," which they did not consider as a separate category/sphere. While *fūdo* remains central to the Japanese notion of nature, the culturally defined "four seasons" as nature began to develop, based on rice agriculture during the Nara period and later without direct reference to agriculture.

Contemporary Japanese perhaps most frequently use the term *shizen* to refer to nature, without questioning its meaning, assuming that somehow *shizen* without human intervention is separate, out there. The term *ten'nen* is used in opposition to "cultured," as in the case of pearls. Today it is most frequently used to specify that something is not "farmed," as with fish and other products artificially grown. The term *kankyō* is neutral and means "environment"; it appears most often in the context of environmental pollution and hazards.

The Nara Period (710–794)

During the Nara period, the Chinese were the dominant Other, and their presence prompted the Japanese elites to eagerly adopt and absorb the Han and Tang "high civilization," although not in toto, as described be-

Table 3.1. Frequency of References to Seasons on Manyōshū. From Satake et al. [2013] 2019; [2014] 2019.

	Vol. 8	Vol. 10
Spring	47	125
Summer	46	59
Autumn	125	316
Winter	28	39

low. This influence in turn compelled them to come to terms with their own sense of identity as distinct from that of the Chinese (Kawasoe [1978] 1980: 253–54; Ohnuki-Tierney 2002a: 54–55; 2015: 50; Pollack 1986).

Japan's oldest collection of poems, the *Manyōshū*, dated primarily to the seventh and eighth centuries, tells a different story from the culture of the elites during the subsequent Heian period. There are 4,500 poems in twenty volumes, and the social status of the poets varies, including emperors, aristocrats, low-ranking officials, imperial border guards (*sakimori*), street performers, farmers, and unknown authors of folk songs. More than 2,100 *waka* poems are by unknown authors, unlike later imperial collections of poems that were predominantly by courtiers and other aristocrats.

The basic concepts about seasons were introduced from China, where the key characters for temporality originated: seasons (*kisetsu*); four seasons (*shiki*); and spring, summer, fall, winter (*haru, natsu, aki, fuyu*). The poems in *Manyōshū*, the oldest collection of Japanese *waka* poems of the eighth century, are full of references to seasons (*ki*), but the Japanese poets did not copy the Chinese exactly. They chose different inhabitants of the universe to represent each season and gave them different meanings.

Volumes 8 and 10 contain poems with references to seasons (Satake et al. [2013] 2019: 321; [2014] 2019: 107). The frequency with which they are mentioned shows that autumn is by far the most important (table 3.1).

Each season is defined by certain flowers. Of the 166 plant species appearing in the roughly 4,500 *Manyō* poems (Nakao 1986: 108), the flowers with the highest frequency of appearance are: (1) bush clover—141 poems; (2) plum blossoms—118 poems; (3) cherry blossoms—42 poems; (4) flowers (grains) of rice plant—29 poems; and (5) lotus—4 poems. The numbers vary slightly depending on how they are counted.[2] Every poem in *Manyōshū* is numbered; below I use the numbers assigned to each poem.

Bush clover claims the highest frequency. At that time, there was no kanji character for bush clover, *hagi*, and the *Manyō* people invented one.

It consists of the character for grass (*kusakanmuri*) above and the character for autumn (*aki*) below (Yamada and Nakajima 1995: 427). Its earliest appearance in literature is in the aforementioned regional history *Harima no Kuni Fudoki* of 713 (427). Bush clover is a "bush" with a large number of branches on which tiny reddish flowers with a purple tinge bloom. The plant is an important source of food for cows and horses; its leaves were used for tea, its roots as medicine for women, and the bark for making rope (426).

Of the 141 poems that refer to bush clover, 81 use "autumn bush clover." The flower became the quintessential symbol of autumn, and in a large number of poems it is coupled with other symbols, including those for buck and geese (Yamada and Nakashima 1995: 435–38). The buck grows its antlers and mates during autumn. Its mating calls are often chosen by poets to express their longing for their love. Geese (*kari*) migrate from Siberia in September to stay in Japan until March. Referred to as "the first geese" (*hatsukari*), their migration signals the arrival of autumn (poem #1566).

The disproportionately large number of references to autumn and bush clover in these poems in fact tells us something more—the importance of the rice harvest for the *Manyō* people. The blooming of the bush clover flower is symbolically aligned with the harvesting of the earliest rice crops. Although the association is clearly expressed in only three poems, they leave no doubt about how the *Manyō* people saw this event as the sign to harvest the early crop (*wase*). I cite two poems (my translations):

> I will never get tired of the bush clover, which covers in red the temporary hut built for the autumn harvest. (#2100) (Satake et al. [2013] 2019: 176–77)

> Young women are now passing by [presumably to go to the rice field]. It must be the time for the harvesting of the early rice. Bush clovers are blooming. (#2117) (Satake et al. [2014] 2019: 180)

The importance of bush clover is shown also by the fact that at the time the use of the term *hanami* (flower viewing) was restricted to this plant (e.g., #2103) and plum blossoms, and not cherry blossoms, which nonetheless rank third in frequency of appearance.

During the late Nara period cherry blossoms had not gained the kind of stature within the flower kingdom that they would after the capitol was moved to Kyoto in 794, when they became the most important flower for the Japanese. As agrarian cosmology developed, the Mountain Deity descended to become the Deity of Rice Paddies. Cherry blossom season (spring) is the time for farmers to plant rice seedlings. The blossoms foretell the nature of the rice harvest in the fall—abundant blossoms mean a good harvest. There are a number of rituals and beliefs that establish symbolic equivalence between cherry blossoms and rice plants (for details, see Ohnuki-Tierney 2002a: 27–32).

These three significant plants—bush clover, cherry blossoms, and rice, references to which total 212—all relate to the rice harvest, and geese descend on the rice fields for gleaning, a joyful sign that the harvest has been successfully completed. In the *Manyō* poems with references to rice plants, the majority are about *wase*, the earliest "blooming," that is, the earliest harvest yielding grain. The other two most frequent references are to *nakate*, blooming in the middle period, and *okute*, the latest blooming.

Significantly, the aesthetic in these poems is quite different from the one in later times. Plants with practical uses—rice, wheat, and others—are considered beautiful (Nakao 1986: 107). Bush clover is "beautiful" because it represents "beautiful" ripe grains of rice. Citing four poems (#1532, 2100, 3677, 4315), Yamada and Nakajima (1995: 427–28, 434–35) point out that there is no mention at all of the color (*iro*) of bush clover in the *Man'yōshū*, and that the term *niou* (fragrant) describes the beauty of the red blossoms.

The appreciation of plum blossoms was due to the continued influence of Chinese culture on the court elite, although there is no question that plum blossoms were appreciated as the first flowers to bloom in the spring, before the cherry blossoms. The lotus is the most important flower for Buddhism, as the symbol of the birth of Gautama Buddha. The oldest lotus seed in the world, dated to two to three thousand years before the present, was found in Japan in 1951 and named Ōga Hasu, after the discoverer, Dr. Ōga Ichirō of the University of Tokyo (Watanabe 1994: 19).

The lotus has been called either *hasu* or *hachisu* (beehive), which its central receptacle with seeds resembles. The stylized lotus flower motif with petals and seeds in a circle at the center is called the "lotus design" (*rengemon*). Although the original idea was from China, in Japan "their decoration is too uniformly distinctive to be Chinese, too stylized and floral" (Griffiths [2009] 2010: 155). The earliest appearance of this motif is found on a bronze mirror, dated to 250 AD during the early Tomb period. Roof tiles (*noki kawara*) with the lotus design, dated to the seventh century AD, have also been found. During this period the Heizei Palace and other important imperial buildings must have had roof-end tiles with the lotus design. Those at the Shōsōin, the eighth-century treasure house of Tōdaiji Temple in Nara, are well known.

The lotus flower is nearly absent in *waka* poems. Even in *Manyōshū*, it appears only four times. In later collections of poems—*Konkinshū*, *Shin-Konkinshū*, and some others—the lotus is nearly, if not completely, absent. This does not mean, however, that it was not important for the Japanese. With the introduction of Buddhism, the flower came to represent the purity of the body and mind, as it floats above the murky waters of material attachments and physical desire. It was *the* flower of the afterlife/paradise (Sakamoto 1977: 52–53). As Buddhism became less popular during the Edo period, the association of the lotus with Buddhism made the flower less popular (Watanabe 1994: 23).

Despite its acknowledged beauty, the lotus never became a symbol of the collective identity of the Japanese, unlike in Egypt and India, where it is the national flower. Cherry blossoms and bush clover were more important, accompanying the rice plant at the beginning of its growth and at harvest time, whereas gorgeous lotus flowers bloom during the summer.

From the very beginning, for lotus its utilitarian value has dominated for the Japanese, who used its leaves, seeds, and especially the root, called *renkon* (Sakamoto 1977: 51–59). The root became a treasured item, for example, to offer to the imperial court, as recorded in the mid-Heian *Engishiki*, a fifty-volume record of laws and customs commissioned by Emperor Daigo; one province offered 560 roots to the imperial kitchen (Kameda 1994: 548). It is an essential item of *washoku* (Japanese cuisine) even today, when its cultivation is enormously labor intensive—some seven times more so than raising rice (Yoshida 2017).

The moon is an almost universal symbol of nature, with the "harvest moon" most frequently highlighted in celebrations, rituals, and literature. In the *Manyōshū*, the moon appears frequently: in spring—7 poems; in summer—13 poems; in autumn—28 poems; and in winter—6 poems. There are 208 poems in which it appears without reference to a particular season, testifying that the moon was not culturally assigned exclusively to autumn, as happened in later times. The ritual of the celebration of the moon, known as *jūgoya*, began only during the Heian period. We can assume that the autumn moon in the poems is the moon at the time of the autumnal equinox, when the dusk-till-dawn moonlight helps farmers to work in the fields. Although the Moon Festival is the second most important festival in China and is also celebrated in Korea, it originated as an agrarian ritual in each country, rather than in a specific place from which it diffused.

That the Japanese did not simply copy Chinese civilization has been pointed out by a number of scholars. The meaning assigned to the goose as a messenger in Chinese poetry is different from the goose in Japanese poetry, where its meaning is extended to include that it brings "a chill to leaves and changes their color" (Horton 2012: 325–26). According to Horton, orioles and kingfishers, present in Chinese Six Dynasties poems, are avoided and the monkey is nearly absent in Japanese poetry. In Chinese and Japanese travel and love poetry, "it is difficult, finally, to isolate specific examples of borrowing on the level of diction." McCullough (1985:

139–40) finds that peach blossoms and swallows, the markers of the Chinese image of spring, are absent in the *Manyōshū*. The Chinese poets write about the heat, lotuses, and ponds, whereas the *Manyōshū* poets write of trees, flowering shrubs, and birds indigenous to Japan. She concludes that "mid-Nara poets were viewing the seasons at least partly in terms of their own surroundings and tastes" (139).

In China, according to Horton (2012: 321–23), the metaphorical connection of evanescence and sadness with autumn goes back at least to *Chu ci* (*Songs of the South*), an anthology of the poems collected in the second century CE by Wang Yi. It came late to Japan, where colored leaves were celebrated, and thus was absent in *Kojiki*, *Nihongi*, and the earlier part of *Manyōshū* (Tatsumi 1993: 481–98; see also McCullough 1985: 151). An excellent example of how autumn was preferred to spring is the poem by Princess Nukata (630?–690?), wife of Emperor Tenmu, about how in the spring even though birds begin to sing and flowers begin to bloom, the hillsides grow so thick that she cannot go pick the flowers. She prefers autumn, when she can pick leaves of various colors, and concludes, "it is the autumn hills for me!"

There is little doubt that "the Japanese seasons" during the Nara period were specifically the agrarian seasons, based on the stages of growth of rice plants. For the *Manyō* Japanese, autumn was the most joyful season in the year, when people rejoiced in the harvest of rice; this is shown by the disproportionate number of *Manyō* poems for autumn, far outnumbering even those for spring. Thus, 50.8 percent of the poems in volume 8 and 58.6 percent of the poems in volume 10 are about autumn (Inagaki [1994] 1999: 25–26). This shows that during the Nara period the people, including the elite, lived in a close relationship with the agrarian growth cycle.

Horton (2012: 323) notes how autumn connotations foreshadowed the following period, becoming progressively darker in the *Manyō* poems and carrying an "overtone of being apart from one's lover in the gathering cold and dark." There are a large number of poems with sad and melancholy tones; however, in all, the poets are crying out for the lovers from whom they are separated. It is for this reason that bucks appear in these poems: their cry for their mate expresses the sad anguish the poet feels for his lover when they cannot be together.

The Heian Period (794–1185)

If the Nara period celebrated rice as the abode of deities, the Heian equivalent was cherry blossoms, the spring counterpart of rice. In agrarian cosmology, the powerful Mountain Deity descends on a cherry petal in the spring to become the Deity of Rice Paddies (Miyata 1994b: 41–60). Unlike the *Manyōshū* poets, Heian literary authors were far removed from rice and rice paddies. As for spatial division and associated values, this period saw the most articulate rules for the elite about not touching the defiled ground, reflecting the high development of the class structure.

During the Nara period cherry trees grew only in the mountains (*yamazakura*). In the eighth-century *Manyōshū*, references to cherry blossoms appear in poems by unknown poets and poets from rural Japan, indicating the importance of the flowers among these people at a time when the aristocrats in the capital still embraced the imported aesthetics of plum blossoms (Saitō 1977: 41–45; Wakamori 1975: 172–73).[3] In the eighth through ninth centuries, however, the elite gradually turned more toward the Japanese aesthetics of cherry blossoms, which became the most important metaphor of the collective identity of the Japanese throughout subsequent history (Ohnuki-Tierney 2002a).

The imperial palace was moved to Kyoto in 794 by Emperor Kanmu (r. 737–806). The new palace, referred to as Heiankyō, became the residence of the emperors until they moved to Tokyo at the time of the Meiji "restoration" in 1868. In the Heian period (794–1185), imperial power reached its zenith. During those thirty years of peace, the elite achieved the height of efflorescence of high culture—in literature, music, architecture, sculpture, paintings, calligraphy, sword making, and lacquerware with gold and silver designs. The Japanese, who had no writing system, adopted the Chinese characters en masse during the latter half of the fourth century (Brown [1993] 1997: 30–31), even though the Japanese language came from different stock and thus was far from compatible. They invented two types of kana syllabi in order to accommodate the superimposition of the Chinese kanji. Men used the characters; women used the kana and produced literature of unsurpassed quality—novels, poems, tales, diaries, and essays, including *The Tale of Genji* by Murasaki Shikibu. During this period, the Japanese elite, who had adopted Chinese civilization wholesale during the preceding Nara period, began to establish their "Japanese culture" (*kokufū bunka*). The ninth century saw significant changes in their attitude toward the Chinese, including the discontinuation in 894 of the official envoys to Tang China, which had started in 630, although a strong influence of Chinese civilization continued.[4]

One of the key reasons for Emperor Kanmu and the imperial court to move the capitol from Heizeikyō (Heijōkyō) (Nara) to Heiankyō (Kyoto) was to get rid of Nara Buddhism and curtail the power of the monks. For example, Dōkyō (700–772), a Zen monk favored by Empress Kōken, was carried around in a *hōren*, the type of carriage used exclusively for emperors, with a phoenix—the imperial emblem—on top (Sakurai 2011:

72). He thought he could become an emperor. In order to counter Nara Buddhism's encroaching power, Emperor Kanmu (737–806) and Emperor Saga (786–842) welcomed and protected different sects of Buddhism. In the early Heian period, Kūkai brought the Shingonshū sect and Saichō brought Tendaishū from China and introduced them in Japan. Both sects espoused Esoteric Buddhism (*mikkyō*), which emphasized the incantation of sutras (*kajikitō*) as a guarantee of rewards in this world—*gensei rieki*—not in the afterlife.

In the quest for those rewards, *kanzeon bosatsu*, abbreviated as *kan'non* (a female bodhisattva of compassion), became the most sought-after Buddha to pray to. Originally from Tibetan Buddhism, this female Buddha stood for mercy and salvation for all beings. Her statue, usually on metal lotus petals, stood at many temples, including those of Shingonshū and Tendaishū and others regardless of their sectarian affiliation.

This new doctrine was enthusiastically embraced by the aristocrats. The two temples most favored were Hase Kan'non at Hasedera in Nara and Ishiyamadera in Ōtsu City in Shiga Prefecture. Both were known as "temples of flowers"—Hase for hydrangea and Ishiyama for peonies. They were not very close to Kyoto for the aristocrats to visit either on foot or in an ox-drawn carriage (*gissha*), taking four to five days. That pilgrimage is described in the classic literature, such as *Makura no Sōshi* and *Sarashina Nikki*, as well as in some chapters of *The Tale of Genji*, such as Ukibune and Tamakazura. The rewards in this world granted by Kan'non included easy childbirth, avoidance of evil spirits, a good match in marriage, and good fortune as a reward for good behavior. For example, in Tamakazura, a chapter in *The Tale of Genji*, perhaps the most famous manifestation of the mercy of Kan'non, Genji is united with Tamagazura, daughter of his former lover Yūgao, through the mercy of the goddess at Hase Kan'non (Murasaki Shikibu [1000] 2020a: 11–125).

The chrysanthemum was introduced from China during the Nara period. It appears in *Kaifūsō* (Nostalgic Recollections of Literature), dated to 751, but not in *Manyōshū*. Its reappreciation in poems took place only after the revival of the Chrysanthemum banquet in 1814 during the reign of Emperor Saga (786–842, r. 809–23). The Heian elite, especially women, treasured the dew on the petals, which they collected with cotton. They applied the cotton soaked in dew to their face and body in the belief that it guaranteed longevity. Since the time of Emperor Uta (r. 887–97), the Chrysanthemum Festival on 9 September (Shirane 2012: 159–60) has been an annual event at the Imperial Palace.

Retired Emperor Gotoba was particularly fond of the chrysanthemum, and it eventually became the imperial crest, although there was no legal codification until 1889. Nor was there a strict rule as to the number of petals and forms. Only in 1889 did the Meiji government formally adopt it and specify the number (sixteen) and the form of the petals. These rules were nominally abolished in 1947 (Katō [1984] 1996). According to the late Prince Mikasa, the sixteen-petal crest was used only by the emperor, forbidden even to his brothers, like Prince Mikasa (personal communication). The chrysanthemum emblem continues to be used on the Japanese passport and on the doors of overseas embassies of Japan.

The imperial replacement of plum trees with cherry trees took some time, even though today the cherry tree on the left and the *tachibana* (mandarin orange) on the right in front of the palace are often assumed to have been there since the relocation to Heian (Kyoto). The original plum tree was planted by Emperor Kanmu in 794. The main section of the palace (*daidairi*), together with the trees, was destroyed by numerous fires.[5] A plum tree continued to be used and only in the mid-ninth century was it permanently replaced by a cherry tree (Hanawa 1929: 374).[6]

In 813, Emperor Saga (r. 809–23) held the first imperial viewing of cherry blossoms, called "the feast of the flowers" (*hana-no-en*), according to *Teiō Hennenki* (Kuroita and Kokushi Taikei Henshūkai 1965b: 183). The annual ritual of cherry blossom viewing at the imperial palace came to represent the elegance of the high culture at the court and was portrayed in many literary pieces, such as *The Tale of Genji*, and in visual artworks. This practice, with changes in form and nature through time, continued until the early 1930s (Nihon Hōsō Kyōkai 1988).[7]

During the Heian period, the elite began to intensively use the temporal scheme of the four seasons and twelve months, each defined and represented by a specific flower and a bird. *Kokinshū* (*Collection of Poems Ancient and Modern*), a twenty-volume anthology of *waka* poems likely compiled in 905, was the first imperial anthology. Unlike in *Manyōshū*, the poems selected are all by the courtiers. The poems are grouped according to the four seasons. The tone of most is decisively melancholy and sad, with the word *kanashi* (sad) often appearing. In volume 4, there are ten poems with bush clover (poems 198 and 216 to 224), often referred to as the flower wife (*hanazuma*), that is, the wife of a buck (Saeki [1981] 2020: 66), since they bloom when bucks cry for their mate. There are a number of poems with a buck. Neither symbol is used with a direct reference to rice harvesting.

In this regard there is a well-known passage in *Makura no Sōshi* by Sei Shōnagon (966–1025) (Seishō Nagon 1002: 185–86, section 95), the mid-Heian period novelist-poet who served Sadako, wife of the Emperor Ichijō. This passage vividly tells us how removed the courtiers were from the countryside, let alone "nature," even though the palace was within present-day Kyoto and not far from the "countryside." In one of her very rare trips outside the palace compound, Murasaki Shikibu with three others headed for Matsugasaki in Sakyōku of Kyoto City. On their way, they decided to stop over at the mountain villa of Takashina Akinori, Sadako's uncle on the maternal side. Akinori showed them a rice stalk, which they had never seen before and thought an apt symbol of the unsophisticated countryside (*inaka*). Several young women from the neighborhood, "who did not look dirty," were gathered to demonstrate the threshing process.

Since the elites were already consuming processed white rice during the previous Nara period, this episode shows how removed these courtiers were from the rural. The universal process whereby the countryside is borne through urbanization, discussed in chapter 5, took place in Japan well before the urbanization of the Edo period in the seventeenth century.

The more the concept of the four seasons developed, the farther away these seasons became from "nature." That they were now culturally determined also explains why in the poems of this period the moon is confined to the autumn and associated with melancholy (cf. Shirane 2012: 40–41), as if there were no moon the rest of the year. The "four seasons" even governed the daily life of the elite—what to wear and what to eat. Most of the women characters in *The Tale of Genji* are named after natural objects or phenomena, often flowers, like paulownia, heart vine, lavender, and moonlight.

One might even suggest that, in a cybernetic fashion, the culturally defined seasons became the source for further development of the idea of "nature's" four seasons. The courtiers' lives centered on the palace and its highly sophisticated cultural activities. They seldom ventured out, especially to the rural areas, although the urban area of Kyoto is surrounded by nearby farmlands. Therefore, the references to preparing a rice field (second month) and harvesting (ninth month) in a collection of poems entitled *Yoshinobushū* (ca. 979), which defines each of the twelve months (Shirane 2012: 64–65), perhaps did not derive from actual observations by the poets.

It may be for this reason that the auditory aesthetics developed by the elites related to "nature" through the singing of birds, insect cries, the cries of a buck, and so on. Birds, which were clean since they mostly fly above the ground (see chapter 2), were cherished because of their songs/cries, and some also as a source of food. The penchant for auditory appreciation of nature extended to the highly developed hobby of listening to the "singing" of insects. It was introduced from China and first developed by the court elite but also enjoyed by the folk. Poetic appreciation of the sound of insects appeared already in *Manyōshū*. However, it was the aristocrats of the Heian period who began catching grasshoppers (*kirigirisu*, the older name for *kōrogi*, whose genus name is *Gampsocleis*), bell crickets, and pine crickets and placing them in a small bamboo cage to enjoy at their residence. At times they held a banquet to listen to their "singing," as described in the chapter on the bell cricket in *The Tale of Genji*. A caged cricket even became a type of gift to the emperor to be used in the popular contest (*utawase*) for the best poems referring to the sounds of insects (Umeya 2005; see also Murasaki Shikibu [1000] 2019: essay #50). Auditory aesthetic sensibility involved appreciation of the sound of water running in streams and the sound of wind traveling through trees.

Although no auditory dimension is involved, the butterfly (*kochō/kotefu*), considered to be the carrier of the soul and able to live without touching the ground, occupied a significant symbolic space in "imperial nature" as the major motif in visual representations of the Imperial Palace. In a chapter entitled "Butterfly" in *The Tale of Genji*, there is a description of the court dance music (*bugaku*) called "butterfly," in which eight young girls (*menowarawa*) dance wearing a costume of butterfly wings on their back (Yamagishi 1959: 399). The butterfly dance music was performed paired with another dance, called "birds," a ritual of offering flowers to Buddha. During "birds" performances, cherry blossoms are placed in a silver vase, whereas during the "butterfly" dance kerria blossoms (*yamabuki*) are placed in a golden vessel (Murasaki Shikibu [1000] 2020b: 180). The "butterfly" dance is described in this passage of *The Tale of Genji* as a Buddhist ritual, although it was performed in other circumstances, and the number of dancers may have been four. Some were young boys. After World War II, the Ise Shrine—the most important of all Shinto shrines—adopted both the "bird" and the "butterfly" dance music into its regular repertoire during its annual events, although they were described as a Buddhist ritual in *The Tale of Genji* (Jingū Shichō n.d.).

Ironically, the lives of these aristocrats were both shaped and constrained by the four seasons they helped to develop. In a section entitled "Wearing the Seasons," Shirane (2012: 58–63) offers a comprehensive interpretation of the roles and meanings of the designs and colors of the twelve-layered kimono (*jūni hitoe*), which he sees as the most dramatic demonstration of the seasonal association mandated in the composition of *waka* poems. The term *jūni hitoe* is a latter-day invention during the Edo period to refer to the elegant and opulent life at the Heian court, but there were many variations in the attire used by the Heian court ladies and not all had twelve layers (Suzuki [1986] 1994: 294). Nonetheless, the Heian court ladies were "governed" by strict codes for the designs and colors that regulated how to "wear" the seasons, as defined by the Heian culture, and not by "nature."

Likewise, *waka* poetry had to conform to topical conventions—to the beings and phenomena of "nature" as well as topics classified by season, regardless of whether they actually belonged to such strictly divided seasons. The classification of these "natural phenomena" sometimes differs, however, between the anthologies (Shirane 2012: 25–112).

What occurred then is a development of culturally defined nature divided into four seasons, with each season and month well detailed. This became a combination of "the Japanese four seasons" and "Japanese nature," becoming a straitjacket, as it were, forcing these elites to conform to and replicate it in their attire, rituals, and *waka* poems. It was not "the real nature" but the culturally construed "nature." This nature arose out of the confined area in Kyoto, the seat of the imperial court, whose fauna and flora are quite distinct from those in other regions, since the ecosystems of Japan, which stretches from subtropical to subarctic, have always been quite diverse (Nakano and Kobayashi 1967: 182–91).

These seasons provided the basis for the efflorescence of literature, music, paintings, various rituals, and other cultural activities. The Japanese style of painting, called *Yamato-e*, developed during the latter half of the ninth century to break free of the tradition dominated by the Chinese style of painting, *kanga*. *Yamato-e*, also called *kachōga* (paintings of flowers and birds), focused on the depiction of the four seasons represented by flowers, birds, and other features of nature for each season.[8]

That the *waka* poems during this period were decisively melancholier than those in the Nara period and often full of sorrow which was likely not a lament over the withering of nature but a projection of sorrow in life. *Monono-aware*, said to be the most important theme in Japanese ethos at the time, is pathos over the rise and subsequent decline of human life, as exemplified in Hikaru Genji, the main character in *The Tale of Genji*, who enjoyed center stage at the imperial court, only to be banished. "Nature" offered the medium to express feelings. That is why autumn, the time of joy for the *Manyō* poets, became the time of sorrow for the Heian aristocratic poets.

The aesthetic developed around the imperial court during the Heian period is often referred to as *miyabi*. The term is used as the opposite of "the rural" to describe the aesthetic sensibilities developed by the elites in Kyoto—urbane and sophisticated. Some have argued that the infrequency of the term in the literature of the time indicates its lack of importance. Others believe that it was taken for granted, so there was no need to use the actual term.

The importance of *miyabi* as the aesthetic during the Heian period was emphasized by the early modern (*kinsei*) nativists, such as Kamo-no-Mabuchi (1697–1769) and Motoori Norinaga (1730–1801). The latter placed *miyabi* as the root (*kiban*) of *monono-aware* (pathos) (Imanishi 1994). Mostow emphasizes that the term is not found in traditional or medieval aesthetic discourse. It was "pressed into service by literary historians only in the 1940s" and was closely related to the development of cultural nationalism centered on the emperor system (1999: 70, 74–75).

This seemingly elegant and luxurious life without any worldly concerns was in fact highly constrained by many behavioral rules based on the tightly controlled ranking system. Originally introduced from China and Korea, it was instituted in Japan as early as 604 CE. It was enacted into law by the Taika Great Reforms of 645 and underwent changes several times. During the Heian period, the system consisted of twelve ranks with strict rules about clothing and behavior (Akita 2002: 16–17; Mayuzumi 1982). For clothing, the rules specified the color, with purple at the top; the type of material, with silk the most important; and the type of weaving (fine details on silk in Itō 1992; on color in Maeda 1980), all according to the courtier's rank. A hat (*kanmuri*) made of silk of the color for a specific rank marked each individual. The aristocrats lived in mansions in the architectural style called *shindenzukuri*, about which we have only written descriptions because not a single structure survived fire and war. The buildings were "rectangular, single-story, [with] post-and-beam plank floors *elevated several feet above the ground on posts*" (McCullough 1999: 143; my emphasis).

Of the behavioral rules, the most important was the permission granted by the emperor to go up (*shōden*) to the *denjōma* in Seiryōden, the main building of the palace, for an audience. It was allowed only to individuals of the highest rank. In Japan, where the humidity is very high, the houses of the upper class and well-to-do had and still have the first floor above the ground. At the palace this served an important function, allowing the emperors to demonstrate their power by restricting who could come up to the building. The privileged individuals were referred to as *denjōbito* (*denjō* person), *unkyaku* (person of the cloud), and so forth. This permission was of particular importance to warlords, who had been deemed of low status and thus had to stay outside and kneel with one knee on the ground. They were *jigenin*, people on the ground, that is, those not allowed to go up. Who could become *denjōbito* depended on the system of ranking, which underwent changes through time (Hashimoto 1985).

This cardinal behavioral rule set by the ranking system is a conspicuous expression of the basic cosmological spatial orientation that gives the negative valence to "the below," as opposed to the above.

The invention of footwear was the first attempt to enable humans not to directly touch the ground. Carriages followed this development, transporting people without touching the ground by walking. But not everyone had the same access to the privilege, creating a fascinating history of stratification whose rationale stemmed from the same cosmological principle of defiled "below," which had been naturalized.

Footwear: As Akita (2002: 14) details, *Gishiwajinden*—the earliest Chinese record of the Japanese, dated somewhere between 280 and 289—

states that "all" Japanese were barefooted, although Akita notes that it does not spell out if "all" included the upper-class Japanese. According to the Chinese document *Zuisho Wakokuden* (Wada and Ishihara [628] 1985), toward the end of the Tomb period (late sixth to the beginning of the seventh century) the elite were wearing footgear, likely in their daily life by the middle of the Tomb period, but the folk went barefoot (Akita 2002: 1–2, 18). During the Nara period *waraji* (straw sandals) was introduced from China. By the middle of the Heian, the folk were wearing *waraji* and *zōri*, two types of straw slippers (35).[9]

Carriages: If footgear was the first device to enable people to detach themselves from the "dirt," carriages served the purpose even better, not only for physical transportation above the ground but also as a visual demonstration of the rider's status. The *hōren* is a type of *koshi* strictly for the emperors, empresses, and a few others. The emperors never used any other vehicle, not even an ox-driven cart, discussed below, until the automobile was introduced to Japan in the Meiji period (Sakurai 2011: 97–98), although some shoguns in later years used it. The *koshi* is carried by men, usually two to four, but eighteen for Shogun Ashikaga Yoshimitsu (27). There were many types, with strict rules for their uses according to the rider's rank.

The very first appearance of the *koshi* in writing is in *Nihonshoki*, in which the legendary first emperor, Jinmu, rode in 630 BCE. But the historical authenticity of the event and even the existence of the emperor himself are uncertain. There is another reference to the use of *koshi* by the wife of Tenmu (r. 672–86), who became Empress Jitō (r. 686–97). In *Manyōshū*, there is a reference, dated Wadō 3 (710 CE), to Empress Genmei (707–15), who stopped her *koshi* to rest en route from Nara to Kyoto when the capitol was being moved (Sakurai 2011: 2–6, 97).

For the high-ranking nobles, their carriage was the *gissha*, with two wooden wheels and drawn by an ox. Most important, like *koshi*, *gissha* were conspicuous markers of status and wealth. The nobles rode in their carriage through the city in slow promenade, drawn by oxen and accompanied by a large number of attendants. As with the *koshi*, strict rules governed the use of various types of *gissha*, depending on their rank and the occasion. The nobles began to compete by using elaborate and expensive materials for the carriage. The two best-known literary works of the Heian period—*The Tale of Genji* and *A Tale of Flowering Fortunes*—offer a number of descriptions. The following description, from *A Tale of Flowering Fortunes*, captures the frenzy.

> When the long-awaited day arrived, the Acting Consort's carriage and the others were so gorgeous that I could not possibly describe them. Some were thatched with cypress bark; others had been constructed to resemble Chinese ships, and the sleeves of the ladies and everything else followed the Chinese style. Gold and silver lacquer adorned the paneled entrances and exits. As

the procession moved along, the total effect of so much magnificence, of so many mountain ranges, overflowing seas, and inlaid designs—the total effect, quite simply, dazzled the eyes of the spectators and paralyzed their powers of discrimination. (McCullough and McCullough 1980: 336–37)

Often there was traffic congestion or a skirmish over space for spectators at times such as the Kamo festival, as described in *The Tale of Genji* (Yamagishi 1958: 320–21), so much so that an ordinance to control the excess was issued, as in 894 (Suzuki 1984: 156–58).

Lives of the Folk and Rewards in This World (*Gensei Ri'eki*)

While the elite left enough literary and visual evidence to inform us about their lives, there is far less material to rely on for understanding of the lives of the folk during this period. One window, however, is folktales, which usually have a moral message that must have been accepted or meaningful to the people at that time.[10] The moral message is usually the "reward in this world," which was espoused by the elite for whom the reward included fulfillment in romantic love. For the folk, it is wealth, as portrayed in the folktales. Dating these tales is difficult, since some themes in a tale may have originated earlier than others. The dating is usually set to the time when the story was written down.

An example is the oldest folktale by an unknown author, "The Tale of the Bamboo Cutter," which dates from the latter half of the ninth century to the first half of the tenth century (Sakakura 1970). It is about a humble bamboo cutter who one day noticed a bamboo with a mysterious shiny spot. As he cut the stalk, a tiny baby emerged. He took her home. Since he and his wife did not have a child, they decided to raise her as their own daughter. After that, every day the bamboo cutter found a gold nugget in one of the bamboos he was cutting. He became very wealthy. The tiny girl grew up to be a stunningly beautiful woman within three years. Many nobles ardently courted her, but to no avail, since as a test to prove their worth to win her she gave each an impossible task. When the emperor courted her, she did not give him a hard task but refused his proposal with the explanation that she did not belong to this world. The third year after she was found, she began crying as the full moon in August neared and told the bamboo cutter that she was not from the world of humans but belonged to the moon. She told them how sad she was to leave them behind without taking care of them, and that she did not long to go back to the moon even though the people there were pure and beautiful and did not get old. At midnight on 15 August, the atmosphere near the house became brighter than daylight. The celestial beings came down from the sky on a cloud, which hovered about 1.5 meters above the ground (Sakakura 1970: 51). The leader explained that since the princess had committed some minor offense and the bamboo cutter had done good deeds, they had sent her to reward him with the gold for a short period of time. But that time was up, and she must return to the moon. The awestruck parents and the emperor had all prepared to fight these celestial beings, who easily overcame them. They told her to leave the defiled place with defiled food. As they were ready to take her away, she wrote a letter to her parents, telling them to read it when they missed her. She also wrote a letter to the emperor and gave it to his guard with a small portion of medicine for immortality, which the celestial beings had brought in a box. The celestial being swiftly put on her *hagoromo* (a celestial robe made of bird feathers and very light and beautiful) and took her away in a carriage that appeared above the roof of the house.

The setting is clearly after the imperial system was established. The nobles who courted her were given impossible tasks, maybe those from the Fujiwara clan, who were threatening to seize political power from the emperors. At any rate, the story is set in the time, either Nara or early Heian, when the emperor system had been well established.

The story involves important themes in Japanese cosmology that bear direct relevance to the central theme of this book. It articulates the spatial division of the universe with the "above" and the "below," assigning the former high value as opposed to the "below," deemed defiled. It thus parallels the cosmogony and cosmology of the *Kojiki* and the *Nihongi* of the early seventh century. The hallowed inside of bamboo is considered to be *yorishiro*, where the souls of the deities (*shinrei*) often stay. The baboo cutter's kindness is rewarded by wealth.

Summary

Whereas chapter 2 laid out the "imperial cartography," in which the spatial divisions and their respective valences were laid out, this chapter saw the development of "the Japanese four seasons" based on the agrarian calendar during the Nara period, which then developed into the elite's *culturally* defined "four seasons" during the subsequent Heian period.

A remarkable finding from the *Manyōshū* poems is that the affective dimension of the human perception and conception of "nature" is in fact "culturally" defined. "Autumn in nature" is not innately associated with sadness, evanescence, and other related feelings. For the Nara period poets, autumn was the most joyful time of the year, with the rice harvest. When the poets express sadness in their poems for autumn, it is not because the fall signals the end of growth of many plants but because of loneliness without their loved ones; they use the metaphor of a buck crying for his mate. For the Heian elites, "the Japanese four seasons" began to be understood within a constructed framework, regardless of what actually happens in "nature." This framework had visual, auditory, and affective dimensions, including a color scheme derived from the colors of flowers.

The development during the Heian period further solidified the spatial valence in the original cosmogony. "Nature" for the Heian aristocrats was represented by flowers, birds, and butterflies—all not touching the ground—while the elite themselves lived in raised dwellings and moved about in carriages so that they never touched the ground.

Similar themes appear in folktales, reinforcing the positive value assigned to "the above," where the celestial beings reside, while the mortals live in the defiled "below." Good behavior is rewarded by wealth and other material gains for a good life on earth. Most importantly, beings of nature serve as interlocutors.

Because it has been relegated to everyday activities, the importance of the persistent development of the spatial valence of defilement assigned to the ground has not been well recognized, whereas the other category of defilement, *kegare*, has received enormous attention by the Japanese and by scholars of Japanese culture.

In this chapter, we saw how two significant principles that govern "Japanese nature" were developed—culturally defined "nature" divided into four seasons and twelve months, and the avoidance of the ground as defiled. In the following chapters we will examine how these principles governing "Japanese nature" were upheld as Japan underwent historical changes of great magnitude.

Notes

1. Watsuji develops the relationship of the individual to society further in his book on ethics ([1937, 1942] 1962; [1949] 1962). A number of scholars have warned that this notion leads to the sacrifice of the individual to society, that is, to the Japanese imperial state. Bernier (2006) offers an exhaustive analysis of Watsuji's philosophy with a focus on this issue.
2. The numbers for plum blossoms and cherry blossoms are from Nakao (1986: 109). Both Yamada and Nakajima (1995: 427) and Saitō ([1979] 1985: 42) find flowers of bush clover in 141 poems. Saitō (1979: 42) lists plum blossoms (118 poems) and cherry blossoms (44 poems).
3. Wakamori (1975: 172–73) and Saitō (1977: 41–45) reject the agrarian association of the flower and regard cherry blossoms as the symbol of kingship and urban aristocrats.

4. Since 630, the envoy to Tang China (*kentōshi*) had been sent to acquire knowledge of Tang civilization and the international political situation. Before the termination of this practice, some five to six hundred people crossed the sea, even though the round trip took two to three years. Sugawara-no-Michizane ordered its discontinuation in 894, given the high casualty rate during these voyages and the internal turmoil in China, although it was undoubtedly part of the picture in the ninth century, when the unquestionable admiration of Tang China by the Japanese was going through reassessment (Inoue [1963a] 1967: 105–6).

    Profound adoration for Chinese civilization continued. Composition of poems in Chinese characters (*kanbun*) remained an important cultural institution. For example the *Tale of Genji* chapter on cherry blossom viewing (*Hana-no-en*) is immediately followed by the composition of poems in Chinese characters. And *The Tale of Flowering Fortunes* (*Eiga Monogatari*) of the late Heian period describes this practice: "The winding-water banquet, a pastime introduced from China and popular in the ninth century, involved reciting poems in Chinese and drinking from floating wine cups" (McCullough and McCullough 1980: 841, 843). During the Heian period, the Chinese practice of chrysanthemum viewing (*chōyō no sechi'e*) was introduced. While viewing chrysanthemums, the emperor's body was wiped with "chrysanthemum cotton," the center part of the flower, wet with chrysanthemum dew. This annual event remained an important imperial ritual, held on 9 September of the lunar calendar, often accompanied by recitation of poems in Chinese (Fujioka 1956: 120; Niunoya 1993: 619–23).

5. Fires occurred in the years 960, 976, 980, 982, 999, 1001, 1005, 1014, 1018, 1039, 1042, 1048, 1058, 1082, 1219, and 1227.

6. None of the available sources in Japanese offers a conclusive history of the cherry tree in front of the palace. According to *Kojidan* (Kuroita 1965c: 113; see also Shimura's [1980] translation in contemporary Japanese, and Minamoto-no-Akikane 1965), it was originally a plum tree that was planted at the time of Emperor Kanmu's relocation of Japan's capitol from Nara to Kyoto in 794. According to the *Teiō Hennenki* (Kuroita 1965b: 183), Emperor Saga, who held the first imperial cherry blossom viewing, also had a cherry tree planted in front of the main building. However, other passages contradict this description. According to a later section in the *Teiō Hennenki* (Kuroita 1965b: 247) and the *Kojidan* (Kuroita 1965c: 113), the original plum tree planted at the time of the construction of the Imperial Palace in Kyoto died during the Jōwa period (834–48). According to *Nihon Kiryaku* (Kuroita 1965a: 371) and *Shoku-Nihon Kōki* (Kuroita 1965a: 371), in 845, when Emperor Ninmyō held a banquet at the *shishinden* (main building), he adorned the hair of the crown prince and his attendants with plum blossoms. In addition, both *Nihon Kiryaku* (Kuroita 1965a: 371) and *Shoku Nihon Kōki* (Kuroita 1966: 176, 206) refer to plum blossoms in the palace during Emperor Ninmyō's reign (833–50).

    Some consider that it was Emperor Ninmyō who promoted the aesthetics of cherry blossoms (Kuroita 1966: 176, 206). Yet the references during his reign were primarily to plum blossoms. After 850 and the end of his reign, references to cherry blossoms started to appear in various records. Thus, *Nihon Kiryaku* (Kuroita 1965a: 386, 389) refers to a beautiful cherry tree in 850 and again in 852—both at a manor of prominent court officials (*daijin*), not at the palace itself.

Definite proof of the presence of a cherry tree is in *Kinpishō* by Emperor Juntoku, written between 1219 and 1222 (Hanawa 1929: 374), which states that a cherry tree in front of the *shishinden* withered during the Jōgan era (859–77) but was entrusted to Sakanoue no Takimori, who carefully restored the tree.

The presence of a cherry tree in front of the main building at the time of the first imperial cherry blossoms viewing is dated to 813 in *Teiō Hennenki*. Yet other records contradict this information. There are two other available dates: in 845 the tree in front of the *shishinden* was a plum tree, and a cherry tree had replaced it sometime between 859 and 877, suggesting that the plum tree was replaced by a cherry tree sometime between 845 and 859. One of the major sources of misreading is a pair of similar passages in *Kojidan* (Kuroita 1965c: 113) and *Teiō Hennenki* (Kuroita 1965b: 247), which describe how a plum tree was planted at the time of Emperor Kanmu's moving of the capital to Kyoto and how it withered during the Jōwa period. The description is followed by a statement that Emperor Ninmyō "planted again." Some interpret this to mean that the emperor planted a cherry tree. Yet a close reading of the text in Chinese testifies beyond doubt that what the emperor planted was another plum tree. Kubota (1990) guesses that the plum tree was replaced by a cherry tree toward the end of Emperor Ninmyō's reign in 850, whereas Nakamura (1982) places the time during the Seiwa period (858–76). Imae (1993) places the date between 845 and 874. Ponsonby-Fane's estimate of 960 seems to stem from a misreading of the text (1956: 63).

This cherry tree, however, was burned in the fire of 960 at the palace. At the time of its reconstruction in 965 (Fujioka 1956: 116), a cherry tree, originally a mountain cherry at Yoshino that had been transplanted in the garden of Prince Shigeaki, was transplanted on the left-hand side in front of the *shishinden*, as recorded in the *Kojidan* (Kuroita 1965c: 113), the *Teiō Hennenki* (Kuroita 1965b: 247), and the *Kinpishō* by the Juntoku Emperor (1219–22) (Hanawa 1929: 368). See also Tsumura ([1917] 1970: 82). For a detailed history of the replacement of a plum tree with a cherry tree, see Ohnuki-Tierney 2002a: 348–49.

7. A cherry tree on the left-hand (east) side and a citrus tree (*tachibana*) on the right-hand (west) side in front of the South Garden of the main building have been part of the image of the Imperial Palace for many Japanese. The two symbolize the two divisions of the imperial guards. The image has become familiar even to children through the Dolls' Festival on 3 March, observed by having at home a replica of the imperial court with the emperor and the empress, together with the paired plants, on wooden shelves covered with red cloth.

8. For *Yamato-e*, see Shinbo 1982 and Shirane 2012. Although most of the paintings were not preserved, they were resurrected by painters in later periods who produced the genre of painting called *shiki kachōzu* (paintings of flowers and birds for four seasons), which originated as a genre of paintings in China.

The well-known painters include Genshin (1476–1559), Kanō Tokuei (1543–90), and Itō Jakuchū (1716–1800) (see Shimizu 2012). As succinctly indicated in the title of the genre, flowers and birds symbolized court life.
9. In a catalogue of paintings of Mount Fuji, six depict a nobleman on horseback with his barefooted servants (Torii 1998: 9). Four of them were products of the Edo period, one dated to the Kamakura period, and the other dated to the Muromachi period, although some are illustrations of scroll paintings, such as *Tale of Ise (Ise monogatari)* of the early Heian period. Thus, one cannot be certain whether or not barefooted servants are the artists' projection of what they thought was the practice of early historical periods.
10. I use the term "folktale" for all, but many scholars distinguish various types of tales. These tales, almost always without author or attributed to the one who wrote them down, have an enormous range of variations, as similar tales are found in many parts of Japan. Seki (1978) offers details.

CHAPTER 4

Rock Garden as "Japanese Nature"
Medieval Period (1185–1603)

As Kitagawa (1990: 140) points out, "Never before or after in the history of Japan did the monarchy reach such a zenith as in the eighth century." Like most ancient regimes, the "Ancient Imperial System," *Kodai Ōchō*, began to lose its political power, which was seized by warriors. The imperial court became less and less able to uphold law and preserve order with the use of armed authority. It ceased to make even the most important political decisions, including the selection of the successors to the throne (Varley 1990: 455). Court became primarily a place for elaborate rituals and banquets, and entertainment like horse racing, which involved shooting while on top of a running horse, followed by an elaborate banquet given by those who lost the contest (Mezaki 1969: 121). The sovereigns during the tenth century became the protectors of learning and promoters of the performing arts and great literary undertakings, such as composing and reading *waka* poetry (Mezaki 1969: 120; Sansom 1958:148).

This division between the warriors in charge of military affairs and the emperors in charge of "culture" lasted until the promulgation of the Constitution of Imperial Japan in 1889, in which the emperor was suddenly assigned to be the commander-in-chief of the army and navy (Hora 1979, 1984; Ohnuki-Tierney 2020a: 69–79). However, even today, the new year starts with the imperial family members composing poems and reciting them, now broadcast and televised.

This chapter focuses on two themes: how the social structure became unhinged, yielding multiple structures, and how "nature" underwent transformations during this period.

Social Structure Unhinged

Attempts to overturn the existing social structure began as early as the late 1100s. Japan, once a comparatively peaceful country under the emperor, turned into a country under two competing North and South Emperors during the period labeled as Nanbokuchō (1336–92), followed by the "Age of Warriors," marked by cyclical conquests among the warlords (*bushō*) (Varley 1990: 447). This period (1477–1573) is characterized by the mentalité of *gekokujō*: the lower conquering the upper, especially in the sociopolitical structure.

With the height of its development during the Muromachi period, this mentalité, based on the dualistic cosmology of yin-yang and the five elements, did not recognize the absolute supremacy of any particular element in the universe. It gave rise to a genre called the literature of the *gekokujō*, which enjoyed much popularity among the common people (Satake [1967] 1970; Sugiura 1965). In society at large, *gekokujō* made it possible for a person of low social status to surpass someone above him, with Toyotomi Hideyoshi, who in 1590 succeeded in uniting Japan for the first time (described below), as the supreme example. Needless to say, the concept alone was not the sole causal factor for the upheavals and other drastic changes in society, as cautioned by such scholars as Ruch (1997: 541–43) and Sansom (1958: 234–63). Scholars (e.g., Kuroda 1972) argue that Japanese society went through a profound change during this period, becoming controlled by the military elite, who had conquered those above—the nobles. Warriors, called *busha* or *bushi*, had been disdained as people only a step above murderers, even though their executions were ordered by the nobles. With the introduction of Pure Land Buddhism, killing became a sin for which the guilty would go to hell after their death (Murai 2004: 3–4).

The hegemony of the shogunate was not without feeble resistance. In 1221, Emperor Gotoba (1180–1239) unsuccessfully tried to defeat the shogunate and restore the imperial system. He was forced into exile on Oki Island. Later attempts, such as by Emperor Godaigo (1288–1339), who in 1331 tried to restore imperial rule in the Kemmu restoration (1333–36), also failed. He too was sent in 1332 to Oki Island, where he died.

After losing financial and political power, individual emperors strove to hang on to their own status by preserving the "institutional body" in Kantorowicz's sense ([1957] 1981), for which the performance of vital rituals was crucial. As return gifts for financial contributions from warlords, the emperors gave them various ranks (Fuji'i 2011: 48–49)—the only "capital" they had the exclusive right to sell. The practice of sale of ranks (*baikan*) had been going on for some time (Tokinoya [1990] 1995), but it became the primary means when the emperors needed financial help. For example, Emperor Ōgimachi (1517–93) could not even finance the performance of his own accession ritual and had to ask a powerful feudal lord, Mōri Motonari, to arrange financial help from a number of daimyō, to whom the emperor gave various ranks. Other occasions included when the Imperial Palace needed repair or even reconstruction after parts of it burned down, which frequently happened since the palace was close to the city of Kyoto and burning embers from the fires in the city would land on palace structures. Exhaustively detailed records (Fujii 2011) tell us about the negotiations between three emperors—Ōgimachi (1517–93), Goyōzei (1571–1617), and Gomizuo (1596–1680)—and three warlords, referred to as *tenkabito* (ruler of the universe): Oda Nobunaga (1534–82), Toyotomi Hideyoshi (1536–98), and Tokugawa Iyeyasu (1542–1616). The records give the exact time and context of the negotiations as well as each item involved in these "exchanges." Both the warlords and the emperors were lively and quite tough-minded negotiators. These negotiations took place between 1565 and 1616 (the first and the last dates), toward the end of the turbulent period.

As briefly described in chapter 2, the concern of the warlords was the *shingō* (divine title)—the title as kami—given posthumously to individuals of high rank, including emperors, courtiers and, later, warlords. Each had specific qualifications and they were ranked. The right to grant apotheosis was held exclusively by the emperor. Before his death on 18 August 1598, Hideyoshi made it clear that he hoped to be deified as *Shin*-Hachiman—"New" Hachiman (Fujii 2011: 266–70). As the Shinto Deity of Warriors that had absorbed Buddhism and Daoism, Hachiman was the most powerful deity of war, with a long history of being worshiped by many well-known warlords (Inagaki [1990] 1996) and a large number of branch shrines all over Japan. In order not to discourage the warriors fighting in Korea under Hideyoshi's plan to colonize that country, his death was not publicly announced until January 1599, and his corpse was kept in his Fushimi Castle. With the public announcement of his death, the petition for deification was sent to Emperor Goyōzei. The emperor gave Hideyoshi a *shingō*, not Shin-Hachiman, his choice, but Toyokuni Daimyōjin. This was decided by Hidetada (1605–23), the third son of Iyeyasu (Fujii 2011: 266–67). Fujii (337) suspects that this was revenge on the part of the emperor, whom Hideyoshi gave a hard time about his wish to abdicate (261–64). Hideyoshi's family built a shrine, Toyokuni Shrine, in Kyoto and buried his body there.

Hideyoshi's "posthumous life" continued to be turbulent. Tokugawa Iyeyasu, who usurped him, stripped his title as a deity and moved Hideyoshi's tomb to Daibutsuden temple compound, where he had a Buddhist ritual performed. This put the final stop to Hideyoshi becoming a Shinto deity; instead, he became only a Buddha. The emperor was not involved in this process (Fujii 2011: 311–12).

Likewise, Tokugawa Iyeyasu wished in his will to be *gongen* (an incarnated deity) after his death. Despite opposition and reservations on the part of courtiers, monks, and others, this Shinto title was approved by Emperor Gomizuo—an apparent concession to the powerful Bakufu, headed by Tokugawa Hidetada, the third son of Iyeyasu (Fujii 2011: 333–37).

In other words, the power play over the dead warlords illustrates how the power of emperors—nominally at the apex of social stratification with the exclusive right over the apotheosis of humans—was circumscribed in practice. On the other hand, even the warlords did not have complete control of their destiny after death.

In general, these four centuries are regarded as the darkest premodern period in Japanese history. The fact that the country was governed by various warriors has also colored the view of the period as a time without "culture." My view is different. Although it is seldom pointed out, what we now call the "Japanese aesthetic" in fact was developed during this period. The tea ceremony, the flower arrangement, the rock garden, noh theater, and the *shoinzukuri* architectural pattern all are based on this aesthetic.

Transformations of "Nature"

"Nature" of Yūgen, Sabi, and Wabi Aesthetics

It was the period when the aesthetic of *yūgen, sabi,* and *wabi* was developed. It came to represent "the Japanese aesthetic," which continued to be expressed through "nature." Varley points out that the Heian literary figures focused on "the more conventionally regarded beauties of 'nature,' such as spring's blossoms and autumn's leaves" (Varley 1990: 454). By the beginning of the medieval period, the people began to feel affinity with the Buddhistic doctrine of *mappō*, the degeneracy of the latter days (518), that is, the weakening of Buddhism at the last stage as a great era ends. The mood of the time was best expressed in the poems in *Shinkokinshū*, the eighth imperial anthology, completed in 1205 with the selection by Fujiwara no Teika and others. It was commissioned by Emperor Gotoba (1180–1239) after his abdication of the throne but before he was exiled to Oki Island in the Sea of Japan by the Kamakura Bakufu. Two aesthetic values developed in the *Shinkokinshū* were *yūgen* (mystery and depth) and *sabi* (loneliness); while *wabi* (the plain and humble) was developed by the tea ceremony slightly later. In the following *waka* poem by Saigyō (1118–90), the *sabi* aesthetic of the desolate and lonely was developed through the metaphor of weathered and withered nature, with a shrike rising from a marsh in autumn at dusk.

> Even one who has renounced
> His worldly feelings
> Knows of the pathos of life.
> A shrike rises from the marsh;
> Autumn at dusk.
> (*Shinkokinshū*, vol. 4, no. 362; Fujiwara no Teika [1929] 2020)

The other is by Fujiwara no Teika:

> As I look about,
> I see neither cherry blossoms
> Nor crimson leaves.
> A straw-thatched hut by the bay
> At evening the Autumn.
> (*Shinkokinshū*, vol. 4, no. 363; Fujiwara no Teika [1929] 2020)

It is commonly assumed that Zen played a dominant role in developing these aesthetic values. Varley (1990: 466–67) strongly challenges this view and holds that medieval culture is a product of an aesthetic longing for or a nostalgic vision of the courtier past, and that aesthetic values had their roots in the Heian culture, or even that of the earlier period. They paralleled the values of Zen, rather than Zen providing the blueprint.

The tradition of "four seasons" did continue, with significant changes. For example, Fujiwara no Teika (Sadai'e) (1162–1241) proposed in *Jūnikagetsu Kachōwaka* (Poems on Flowers and Birds of the Twelve Months) (compiled in 1216–33 and published in 1241) that each month be defined by one flower and one bird, as in table 4.1

Table 4.1. Twelve Months of the Year with Each Month Defined by a Flower and a Bird. Table based on the table composed by Shirane (2012: 65).

	Flower/Plant	*Bird*
1st month	Willow	Bush warbler
2nd month	Cherry blossom	Pheasant
3rd month	Wisteria	Skylark
4th month	Deutzia flower	Small cuckoo
5th month	Mandarin orange	Marsh hen
6th month	Pink (Dianthus)	Cormorant
7th month	Yellow valerian	Magpie
8th month	Bush clover	First wild geese
9th month	Pampas grass	Quail
10th month	Late chrysanthemum	Crane
11th month	Loquat	Plover
12th month	Early plum blossom	Waterfowl

No nonhuman mammals are involved, even though spring is the season for both plants and animals to reproduce. Several of the flowers are either dainty and small (Deutzia flower, pink [dianthus], bush clover) or not at their prime (early plum blossoms, late chrysanthemum). Or they are even "lonely" plants like miscanthus grass. They are not the flowers to represent the vigor of life. Most of the birds are small, and known and even cherished by the Japanese primarily for their songs rather than their physical looks, testifying to the continuation of the importance of auditory aesthetics.

This scheme is a remarkable contrast to the "nature" of *Manyōshū* poets, demonstrating how the visual, auditory and emotive dimensions of nature are nature as represented by the poets. For the *Manyōshū* poets, autumn was the most important and the most joyful season, with bush clover symbolizing the rice harvest and the arrival of geese to glean the rice fields. In the *Shinkokinwakashū*, bush clover appears only in 12 of the 1,978 poems, although geese appear in 35 poems (Sasaki [1929] 2020). The lesser cuckoo appears in 47 poems and the nightingale in 8 poems, with the pine cricket appearing in 9.

Most significant is how the emotive dimension of symbolism had changed by the time of *Shinkokinwakashū*. Tatsumi (1993: 481–98) states that sadness was introduced from China while it was absent in the *Kojiki, Nihongi*, and the earlier part of *Manyōshū*. Identifying the Chinese influence regarding sadness in *Manyōshū*, Horton (2012: 322–29) alerts us to the "spring and autumn debate" by pointing to the poem by Princess Nukata (630?–690?), wife of Emperor Tenmu, in which the princess declares autumn as her definite choice over spring. Her reason is that, even though birds begin to sing and flowers begin to bloom in the spring, the plants on the hills grow so thickly that she cannot go pick the flowers. She prefers autumn, when she can pick leaves of various colors, and concludes, "It is the autumn hills for me!"

"Nature" of Karesansui (Rock Garden)

During the Heian and Kamakura periods, the manors of the aristocrats followed the architectural style called *shindenzukuri*. The *moya*, or main room of the main residence (*shinden*), was surrounded by a secondary roofed veranda, or *hisashi*. Across the court from the *moya* was the garden with a pond, forming the enclosure's southern limit. A constructed mountain, trees, and rocks combined in a landscape represented the "western paradise" of the Amida Buddha. This is a construction of "nature" par excellence.

During the middle of the Muromachi period (1338–1573), a contrasting "simplest" architectural style called *shoinzukuri* was developed for the upper-class warriors, in sharp contrast to the *shindenzukuri* of the courtiers of the previous period. Its rock garden, called *karesansui* (literally formed from the words for "withered," "mountain," and "water"), located vast nature in a very small space. The most frequently chosen representative of "the rock garden" is the one at the Rinzai Zen temple Ryōanji (figure 4.1). Built in 1450 at the request of Hosokawa Katsumoto (1430–73), the temple has been destroyed a number of times. Its garden, where there is nothing but white pebbles and fifteen rocks of various sizes that symbolize the vast ocean (Iyenaga [1959] 1970: 152), remained relatively unscathed. There is no stream or pond, leaving ample space for viewers to form their own interpretations of the "empty" space and the rocks. There are no plants except moss at the base of the rocks. This "garden" has *no ground or dirt* either. The soil is covered with white pebbles, symbolizing the sea, raked to simulate waves.[1] Famously, no matter where one sits in front of the garden, one can never see all fifteen rocks, showing how memory and imagination should always participate in one's perception, as Hall ([1966] 1969: 153) most perceptively describes. Hoa (2015: 163) points out that the small size of the garden makes visitors envision the vast universe and stirs deep emotion, in contrast to the typical French garden, which fulfills the demand for rationality.

Although utter silence, other than the sound of wind through trees, is the essential part of the experience, the wooden floor on which to sit and view the garden is constructed so that as one walks on it, it creates the song of a nightingale—another example of the importance of the auditory aesthetic and construction/representation of "nature."

It is highly significant that this garden was built by Hosokawa Katsumoto, one of the most powerful warlords, who was responsible for Ōnin-no-ran (1467–77), a civil war involving fierce battles among many warlords, and who was responsible for ushering in the long period of cyclical conquests (1477–1573).

Tea Ceremony (*Chanoyu*)

The tea ceremony, as developed and practiced during this period, shares two important characteristics with the rock garden—a minimalist philosophy and a practice embedded "in nature."

The history of the tea ceremony is highly complex. Its *wabi* aesthetic has received so much attention in and outside of Japan that the important roles that the tea ceremony played in the political and economic land-

Figure 4.1. The rock garden at Ryōanji Temple. Adobe Stock image.

scape at the time have been overshadowed. Probably during the eighth century, but definitely by the ninth century, it was introduced from China when the elite was thoroughly enchanted by Tang civilization (Kumakura [1990] 1995: 30–35). However, after the middle of the Heian period, or since around 900 CE, when the elite began to assert its own Japanese cultural identity, the tea ceremony more or less disappeared from center stage and even records of it became scarce. After roughly three hundred years, Myōan Eisai (also pronounced Yōsai), who lived from 1141 to 1215 and stayed in China studying Zen Buddhism for a number of years, revived the tea ceremony around 1200 CE. This Zen monk founded the Rinzai sect of *Japanese* Buddhism.

The tea ceremony's efflorescence, however, was much later, during the medieval period, when it was developed in Sakai, an autonomous city surrounded by four moats (*kangōshūraku*), governed by the merchants. During the Muromachi period (1338–1573), Sakai, located near Ōsaka and facing the Ōsaka Bay, prospered as a commercial/business center with lucrative trade with Ming China. Its economic power was recognized by the most powerful warlords at the time, Oda Nobunaga and Toyotomi Hideyoshi. Of particular importance for them was that Sakai merchants supplied weaponry (Berry 1982: 79).

Oda Nobunaga, the first of the three most powerful warlords, introduced the tea ceremony to the political arena. The tea ceremony aesthetic was what the warlords needed to show that they were not barbarians who excelled only in military skills (*bu*), but that they also had cultural sophistication (*bun*). In 1573, Nobunaga designated five masters as *chatō* (head of tea ceremony) and made the tea ceremony the ritual of the warrior class, thereby accruing political power to the ceremony, which in turn gave dignity to the warriors (Kumakura [1990] 1995: 175–76).

Despite its origin in China, during the Muromachi period the tea ceremony was developed into a distinct "Japanese tradition" of *wabi cha* by Murata Jukō (1422/1423–1502); it emphasized simplicity rather than show, equating its basic philosophy with Zen Buddhism. The ritual changed from *shoin no cha* (tea in a study) to *sōan no cha* (tea in a grass hut). For utensils, instead of Chinese wares (*karamono*), Kōrai teacups (*Kōrai chawan*)—the daily utensils of Korea, where the tea ceremony never developed—were sought after (Varley 1990: 497). Ironically, although *wabi cha* was based on a philosophy that rejects materialism, the tea articles became outrageously expensive and conversations during the tea ceremony centered on their prices (Kumakura [1990] 1995: 164–65; Varley 1990: 497–98).

Toyotomi Hideyoshi enthusiastically embraced the whole complex of the tea ceremony, which had gained economic and political power. He knew his own political power must be buttressed by demonstrating his "cultural sophistication." He became a strong patron of Sen-no-Rikyū, who had been chosen by Nobunaga as one of the five masters. Under Hideyoshi's patronage, Sen-no-Rikyū rose to the apex of the sociopolitical power structure, arguably overtaking Hideyoshi, who was of lower social status when their relationship started (Kumakura [1990] 1995: 191). Rikyū's personal assessment of the value of a teacup, for example, was its final value; hence he became the most powerful mover and shaker in this whole aesthetic/economic/political structure. The relationship between the two had never been without tension.

Hideyoshi knew that his humble origin was well known among the folk, as clearly shown by a pamphlet posted in the streets of Kyoto in 1591 (Elison 1981: 244).

Masse towa	The end of the world
Bechiniwa araji	Is nothing but this:
Kinoshitano	Watching the Monkey Regent
Saru Kampaku Miru ni Tsuketemo	Under the tree

In contrast, Rikyū, although he came from Sakai, enjoyed unequivocal respect for his cultural sophistication.

The final showdown came in "the second month of 1591" (Berry 1982: 224), when Hideyoshi ordered Rikyū to commit suicide. In 1589 the renovation of Daitokuji Temple in Kyoto was completed. It was the fiftieth year after the day Rikyū's father passed away, when he was only nineteen years old. To commemorate his father, Rikyū paid to replace the gate with *rōmon*, a two-story gate. He then put atop the gate a wooden statue of himself with a cane and wearing *sedda*, a type of shoe made from bamboo with a leather sole that he was said to have invented.

Although no proven reason for Hideyoshi's action is available, there are a number of speculations, with the wooden statue the most cited. This statue of Rikyū stood above the entrance to the temple, under which the emperors, imperial emissaries, Hideyoshi himself, and other high-ranking people would be passing. Whether this disrespectful position was the true reason or not, the focus on the footgear as the source of blasphemy is highly important. Making footgear of all types, tanning and making leather goods, were occupations of discriminated social groups, since all these items touch the defiled ground (Ohnuki-Tierney 1987: 91). The *sedda* worn by the statue of Rikyū had leather soles. Moreover, the manufacturing of leather goods was discriminated against because it involves the killing of animals—one of the sins identified in the *Kōninshiki* discussed in the introduction.

Hideyoshi used a new system of *gekokujō* (lower conquering the upper) to rise to the apex of political power. Yet he ordered Rikyū's suicide using then-legal social stratification that had been set prior to the nonformalized *gekokujō*: it gave Hideyoshi the power to do so, and perhaps also the negative valence of dirt in Japanese symbolic system helped to justify his action.

There is no record of the intention of Hideyoshi and there are a number of interpretations of the incident (Berry 1982: 224–25; 1994: 242–43, 280–84; Kumakura [1990] 1995: 239–55; 2007: 19–22; Varley 1990: 499). However, for the investigation in this book, it is quite significant that Hideyoshi's excuse for ordering Rikyū's suicide was seen as legitimate, that is, acceptable to the people at the time. In other words, feet and footwear that touched the ground, or were supposed to touch the ground, were so defiling that Sen no Rikyū's placement of his statue was so blasphemous as to deserve a death sentence.

Kumakura ([1990] 1995: 248) considers this event to signal the end of *gekokujō* social mobility. If the episode demonstrates the strong continuity of the negative valence assigned to the ground and its role in social stratification, there is further evidence for the same—an extraordinary measure taken to prevent emperors walking on the ground, as shown for Emperor Gomizuo. No matter how much military and political power warriors achieved, the warlords recognized that they were seen as barbarians. Thus, the best means to enhance their status was to arrange for their daughters to marry the emperors. One of the most famous examples is the marriage of Tokugawa Kazuko, the daughter of the second shogun, Hidetada, to Emperor Gomizuo (1596–1680). Nijō Castle in Kyoto was built by the first shogun, Tokugawa Ieyasu, who in 1603 held a celebration upon receiving the title of Sei'i Taishōgun, conferred by Emperor Goyouzei—the beginning of the Tokugawa Bakufu (shogunate). When there were important performances of noh drama or readings of *waka* poems, Emperor Gomizuo and his wife, Kazuko, visited the castle. To facilitate these visits (*gyōkō*), Hidetada added two buildings so that the emperor would not have to walk on the ground to move from the entrance to the building where the performance was held (Kunaichō Kyōto Jimusho 2019).

Another device for the nobles to avoid touching the ground that likely developed in the fifteenth century was the covering of the ground of temples and shrines with pebbles and stones, which is ubiquitous today. Ise Shrine, arguably the most important shrine, where the Sun Goddess is enshrined, began its purification of the compound first by getting rid of dogs in 1453. This was followed by the prohibition of laundering and other defiling activities upstream of the Isuzu River, which runs through the compound. The effort was completed by covering the compound with white pebbles from the riverbed of the Isuzu, which began in 1463 (Sakurai 1986: 110–11) and continues to the present. All the important shrines and temples, including Meiji Jingū in Tokyo and a number of shrines and temples in Kyoto, including Ginkakuji, Shimogamojinja, and Tenryūji, have their ground covered with pebbles.

Noh and *Kyōgen*

Noh and *kyōgen*, two genres of performing arts, were developed during the Muromachi period, although they are independent in origin, contrary to a widespread misconception of a common origin (see Hayashiya 1981; Matsumoto 1981). *Noh* was developed by the warrior class, who gained power over the emperors during a long and bitter struggle in the Nanbokuchō period (1336–92), and it reflects the perspectives on life of the new elite in Japanese society (Matsumoto 1981: 192). *Kyōgen*, on the other hand, was the product of and therefore reflects the views of the lowly warriors and farmers, who were finally freed from the old regime but still under the newly created ruling class.

Both *noh* and *kyōgen*, therefore, were the products of people who had risen several notches above their ascribed status at one or at various times. Yet the two differ radically in terms of philosophical premise. *Noh* represents the "great tradition," especially those traditions related to institutionalized Buddhism at the time, and, like aristocratic poetry and the tea ceremony, embodies the aesthetics of *yūgen*. Conversely, *kyōgen*, typically set amid the daily life of farmers, is often full of anti-establishment satirical commentaries voiced from below (Hayashiya 1981: 204–6; Koyama

1960: 13). Therefore, many pieces of *kyōgen* include characters who are basically tricksters or clowns, such as Tarōkaja, the lord's servant, who appears in many of the plays. Tarōkaja is a servant, but through his comical behavior he controls his master and is free to mock him and the social structure he represents. Similarly, other heroes in *kyōgen* achieve fame and fortune through their own abilities, including wisdom, courage, quick thinking, cunning, and even violence (Satake [1967] 1970: 110).²

The Monkey Performance: Toppling of the Normative Stratification of the Universe

If the *gekokujō* that rocked medieval society was a conspicuous expression of the mentalité of the time, the monkey performance was a subtle but devastating critique of the stratification of the inhabitants of the Japanese universe (for details, see Ohnuki-Tierney 1987: 75–100).

Based on the belief that the monkey is the guardian of horses, the monkey performance originated as a ritual at stables during which the monkey harnessed the sacred power of the Mountain Deity to heal sick horses and to maintain their general welfare. It was an important ritual at the imperial court, as well as for both warriors and farmers during the medieval period. During the early modern period, its importance for them diminished, although it became an important ritual held at the shogun's palace. Later it was performed on the street and at the doorways of individual homes, for both entertainment and religious reasons. Whether at stables or on the street, the dance performance of the monkey, a messenger from the powerful Mountain Deity, symbolized the deity's visit to the people in order to bless them with health and prosperity (cf. Oda 1980: 2). While the *Ryōjin Hishō* (1169–79) is possibly the earliest description of the monkey performance, several sources dated to the mid-thirteenth century testify to its full development by that time.

As portrayed by Mori Sosen (1747–1821), in the traditional monkey performance the monkey wears an *eboshi*, the headgear for the aristocrats. By the Muromachi period, the monkey had become typecast as a beast trying to imitate humans (for historical changes in the meanings of the monkey, see Ohnuki-Tierney 1987: 41–74). This led to a proverb, "saru no eboshi," (a hat for nobles worn by a monkey), that refers to the behavior of people who pretend to belong above their station in life, just as the monkey tries to look like a bipedal human.

Being a trainer for the monkey performance was one of the occupations allowed for members of a socially discriminated group called *hisabetsu burakumin* (discriminated people of the settlement), who engaged in non-agrarian occupations that dealt with culturally defined "dirt," including deaths of human and nonhuman animals, as well as making footwear and tatami mats that people's feet touched. Anything to do with animals was also "their" occupation (for details, see Ohnuki-Tierney 1987: 75–100).

Utsubozaru (Quiver monkey), a comic *kyōgen* play, is thought to be a product of the Muromachi period (1392–1603) (Yanagita [1920] 1982: 339). It is an uncanny portrayal of the highly fluid social and cosmological structures of the medieval period. Most importantly, its message is that the four-legged beast, the beast of all beasts, which touches the defiled ground twice as much as those with two legs, can usurp the throne that humans occupy as their exclusive right.

The story of *Utsubozaru* starts with a *daimyō* (feudal lord) announcing in the morning to his servant Tarōkaja that he plans to go hunting. As they set out, they immediately encounter a monkey trainer with his monkey. The lord is impressed with the beautiful fur of the monkey and decides to ask the trainer for the monkey in order to cover his quiver with its hide. The trainer begs the lord to spare the monkey since it is his only livelihood. The lord then asks to borrow the monkey, and the trainer again begs for it to be spared. The lord, becoming enraged, decides to shoot both the trainer and the monkey with one arrow. But the trainer points out that if the monkey is shot, the scar from the shot will ruin the hide. He then volunteers to batter the monkey with a stick; he knows how to kill a monkey with one stroke. In tears, he begs forgiveness from the monkey for what he is about to do and keeps stalling. The lord and his servant become impatient and order the trainer to take immediate action. As the trainer is about to strike, the monkey snatches the stick and starts to perform the action of rowing a boat, which he has been trained to perform since he was a baby. The trainer, breaking into tears, laments, "It is a sad fate for a creature when it cannot tell that its life is in immediate danger." Observing this scene, the lord too breaks into tears, and the two—the trainer and the lord—cry in unison. He tells the trainer not to hit the monkey any longer. Overjoyed, the trainer has the monkey perform a dance in gratitude for the lord's mercy. As the monkey starts to dance, the lord, impressed by its dance, offers his fan as a gift. As the monkey continues to dance, the lord joins it in dancing and offers even his sword and his jacket. *Utsubozaru* ends with the lord's servant begging the monkey to stop dancing so that his master will also stop dancing. (This synopsis is based on Nomura [1953] 1968: 158–66; see also Ohnuki-Tierney 1987: 170–79).

The play begins with the lord viewing both the monkey and the trainer as animals; the lord's threat to kill the monkey and the trainer with one arrow reveals his equation of the two. In the dominant ideology of the Japanese at the time, individuals of the discriminated group and monkeys were assigned the same meaning—they were nonhumans. At the beginning of the play, the trainer also views the monkey as an animal that cannot even tell when its own death is approaching—in contrast to humans, like the trainer himself and the lord, it cannot understand language, the epitome of culture. Yet, despite the identification of the monkey as a lowly beast, the very reason for the lord's wish to acquire the monkey's hide is his acknowledgment of its supernatural power: if placed on the quiver, the hide will protect his horse from illnesses and injuries.

As the story progresses, the monkey upstages both the trainer and the lord, in one sense, while in another sense, the monkey and the trainer jointly trick the lord. This is done through the power of culturalization exhibited by the monkey. Thus, during the performance, the monkey transforms its identity from that of a "beast" to that of an artist who employs its body in the rhythmically controlled movements of the art of dance.

Additionally, the monkey and the trainer transform the lord into a peaceful lord who enjoys dancing. This reveals that the lord, who regarded the trainer and the monkey as beings of "nature," was in fact a being of nature himself—savage, without appreciation of culture—at the beginning of the play. In short, at the end of the play, we learn that the lord in fact has been analogous to a wild beast who has to be domesticated through the monkey's power of culturalization. As noted earlier, warriors had been deemed as only a step above murderers. Thus, the play is a satirical commentary on warriors.

The play is also a satirical commentary on the sociopolitical structure of Japanese society. It starts when a lord accompanied by his servant, Tarōkaja, encounters the monkey and its trainer. Although each pair constitutes a master/subordinate relationship, the four are hierarchically ranked within the broader context of the Japanese universe: the lord, the servant, the trainer, and the monkey. Thus, at the outset we have three pairs of hierarchically ordered individuals: the lord and his servant; the trainer and the monkey; and the lord and the trainer. The play ends, however, with the monkey upstaging everyone and taking command of the Japanese universe, which includes the sacred, namely, the Monkey Deity and the three hierarchically placed humans. First, the animal proves to the humans that it has power over them, just as the Japanese deities do. Second, the monkey, which starts out at the bottom of the hierarchy and is an easy victim of the power of the lord, controls the whole scene at the end; neither the trainer nor Tarōkaja can terminate the magnetic spell cast over the lord by the monkey's dancing. Tarōkaja is forced to beg the monkey to stop. As the ritual time progresses during the play, the normal hierarchy becomes completely inverted. The "four-legged beast" upstages all others and claims the highest status.

The play also makes a more profound commentary about existential instability. The inverted structure at the end of *Utsubozaru* forces the spectators to contemplate the fragility of the hierarchy taken to be so important in their society. The monkey, who represents the discriminated social group, is therefore the trickster in the play. He tricks the spectators, unaware of how the play will unfold, so that at the end they find themselves contemplating, albeit vaguely, the fragility of existence.

Thus the play forces spectators to contemplate their assumptions about cosmology and society—implicitly urging them to question the universe in which humans claim unique superiority over nonhuman animals and in which the warrior class holds absolute power over the rest of the population. The spectators are forced to recognize, although perhaps not in an articulate manner, that this structure of the universe can easily be toppled.

Folktales

Some of the best-known tales date to the last phase of the Muromachi period (1336–1573). The tale of "Hanasaka Jiji'i" (The old man who made the old cherry tree blossom) is about a kindhearted old couple who lived next to a greedy old couple prone to losing their temper (Seki 1978a: 207–28). The tale is from the end of the Muromachi period or the beginning of Edo period (1603–1868). The kind couple finds an injured puppy and raises it as if it were their child. One day, the kind old man goes to his field with his dog, which begins barking: "Dig this place, dig this place." The old man digs at the spot and finds gold coins (*ōban koban*). The couple is very happy and shares the gold coins with their neighbors. Envious of the riches of the neighbor couple, the greedy old couple borrows the dog and orders it to find treasure. The dog points to a spot from which only junk, such as giant snakes, frogs, and centipedes, comes out.

Enraged, the greedy man kills the dog. The good couple grieves and buries it under a tree. One night, the dog appears in the kind old man's dream and tells him to chop down the tree and make a mortar from it. When the couple makes the mortar and pounds rice in it, the rice turns into gold. The neighbor borrows the mortar, but the rice turns into foul-smelling things. In a rage, the wicked couple smashes and burns the mortar. The kind, grieving couple ask for the ashes of the mortar in order to commemorate their dog. The dog appears again in the kind old man's dream and asks him to scatter the ashes on the withered cherry tree. When he does, the tree blooms with beautiful blossoms. A feudal lord happens to pass by, marvels at the blossoms, and gives the kind old man many gifts. The neighbor tries to do the same, but the ashes blow into the lord's eyes, leading to severe punishment. This story gave birth to the well-known proverb "blossoms on a withered tree," which means even after some major loss in life one can prosper again.

This tale tells how "nature," symbolized by the cherry tree, is the source of rewards for good deeds in this world—the theme of "the reward in this world" that appeared in Buddhism during the Heian period. However, the story adds another dimension—punishment of the wicked, adding "a good guys versus bad guys" theme to the folktales of the period. This is so also in other tales of this period, such as "Shitakiri Suzume" (Sparrow whose tongue is cut off) (Seki 1978b: 229–49), dated to the early Kamakura period (1185–1333), and "Bunbuku Chagama" (Racoon kettle) (Seki 1981: 113–19).

Summary

The medieval "nature," as constructed by the warriors, turned out to be almost the opposite of the "nature" of the Heian aristocrats, which was quite different from the agrarian "nature" of the previous Nara period. Devoid of flowers and birds, the *karesansui* (rock garden) is a minimalist creation, whose interpretation depends on the viewer's memory and imagination. These warlords created the next "Japanese nature" with rocks and pebbles, with no ground allowed to show.

This basic aesthetic and philosophy were shared by the *wabi cha*, the tea ceremony developed during this period, which was based on the rejection of materiality and emphasized proximity to nature. Other artistic and architectural developments of this time shared these aesthetic and philosophical tenets. In *noh* drama, even the movements are minimized with a sparse stage setting. *Suibokuga* is a style of painting using only a brush with black ink. *Shoinzukuri* architecture, as noted earlier, is an architecture emphasizing simplicity.

This was the most turbulent period of Japanese premodern history. On the one hand, the sociocultural/political structures were completely overturned, only to have the previous structure restored or even fortified. Yet, the very basic cosmological principle developed during the ancient period—the negative valence of dirt/ground—stayed and was used by historical actors, like Hideyoshi. The ground of the rock garden and of most important shrines and temples was covered with pebbles so that no dirt/ground could be seen or contacted. Hideyoshi's command for Rikyū's suicide rested likely on the same negative valence regarding footwear. Most significantly, the warriors who took the economic, social, and political powers from the imperial court never challenged the cardinal importance of the right to go up to the Imperial Palace, a physical height that symbolized the very structure of the ranking system.

Notes

1. According to Shirahata (2012: 149–56), when the garden was created, only a thin layer of white pebbles covered the ground; it was not thick enough to draw waves with a rake, as in later years.
2. *Kyōgen's* perspectives are certainly not completely proletarian, as some Marxist scholars have understood. As LaFleur (1983) argues, *kyōgen* ridicules not only "the above" but also "the below" who could not rise above the lowly status ascribed to them. It is abundantly seasoned with black humor in which those who are not clever enough to succeed during the late medieval period and rise above those ranked higher are lampooned (Satake [1967] 1970: 110). Targets include the coward, the sucker, country hicks, the physically handicapped, and those in trouble. Even the aged and the naively pious are ruthlessly ridiculed. For example, in one well-known *kyōgen*, Saru Zatō, a monkey trainer, talks to the beautiful wife of a blind man into leaving the latter and joining the trainer; he gives the woman his monkey as a substitute for her husband (Nonomura and Ando 1974). The cleverness of the trainer is acclaimed, and the blind man is the target of ridicule. The trainer, a member of a special status group, is praised not because he challenges the establishment but because of his "cleverness" in fooling the blind.

PART III

"Nature" as the Symbol of the Japanese Collective Self

CHAPTER 5

Rice Paddies, Cherry Blossoms, and Mount Fuji as "Japanese Nature"
Edo Period (1603–1867)

The medieval period was not only marked by the internal vertigo of the *gekokujō* but also had to come to terms with the encroachment of the "West," signaled by the arrival of the Portuguese in 1541. Both the emperors and the warlords chose to exclude them and their influence, including Christianity. The Ōgimachi Emperor ordered in 1565 and again in 1569 that priests be expelled from Kyoto and persecuted converts. Tokugawa Iyeyasu, who became the Seii Taihōgun (commander in chief of the expeditionary force against the barbarians) in 1601, issued a prohibition of the teaching of Christianity in 1612 and again in 1614. Tokugawa Iyeyasu chose to seclude Japan, which then became at least officially closed to the outside world—known as *sakoku*—until 1868, when the Meiji period began.

This invisible wall then became a reminder of the most threatening Other, present just outside the wall, against which the Japanese had to fortify their own collective sense of self. We see vigorous developments of cultural nationalism, whose architects were the members of the merchant class, which gained power during this period.

When Tokugawa Iyeyasu became the shōgun, he prohibited military conflicts between regional feudal lords, removing the barriers between the territories of the feudal lords. Tōkaidō and Kisokaidō—two major roads to Edo—connected shogunate in Edo with the rest of the nation, or, more appropriately, enabled the Bakufu to exercise control over the entire nation. The whole population, from the top to the bottom of society, was strictly governed by minute rules of daily behavior. Japan became a giant panopticon, as it were.

The three monkeys' relief "see no evil, hear no evil, speak no evil" at Nikkō Tōshōgū—the mausoleum for Iyeyasu—is usually considered quite an appropriate expression of the self-mockery of the people. The mausoleum was constructed in 1617 at the order of Iyeyasu's second son, Tokugawa Hidetada, the second shōgun, two years after Iyeyasu's death. The relief is said to be the creation of the legendary wood-carving artist Hidari Jingorō, who installed it himself since the authorities were not checking the details of the construction. It was placed above the entrance to the horse stable because the monkey was the guardian deity of horses.

During this period of roughly two and a half centuries (1603–1868) when Japan enjoyed peace within and avoided threats from the outside world, cities grew up, leading to full-scale urbanization and a market economy. Urbanization did not simply destroy "nature" to build cities but also led to the ever-expansive consumer culture. Manufacturing, service industries, and productive agriculture developed. The basis of the extreme consumerism we witness today (see chapter 7) was firmly established during this period (Francks 2009: 8–9).

The architects of this development were the members of the merchant class. With domestic peace and no external wars, ironically the warrior class lost its raison d'être and economic power, yet, like the courtiers, they were prohibited from engaging in commercial activities. The merchant class gained enormous economic power, leading to the efflorescence of their plebeian culture—Kabuki theater; their own style of *senryū* poetry, which addresses daily life; haikai, poems with the four seasons as their topic; *shamisen* music, rather than the aristocratic *koto*; and, above all, the woodblock prints, *ukiyo'e*. They all broke away from the elite traditions. Among the diverse themes of woodblock prints were three major groups of individuals who achieved "star" status—Kabuki actors, sumo wrestlers, and geisha—even though all three groups in reality belonged to the "minority." Woodblock prints, *ukiyo'e*, became the proof of travel to Edo, the equivalent of visiting New York or Paris today; the country folk brought them back home as *omiyage*, gifts from travel. Under the label *ukiyo'e*—prints of the floating world—they depicted the world of fantasy, out of reach for almost all Japanese, and precisely because it gave the country people a vicarious sense of pleasure. They developed a culture that privileged the body and designated "drinking and eating as objects of pleasure rather than necessities to maintain collective work" (Harootunian 1988: 172).

If society was developing into a rich plebeian culture as the Edo period progressed, the external wall securing "feudal society" had become more vulnerable to the forces of Western colonization that were raging all over the world. While the Bakufu was still trying to digest the Ōshio rebellion, in August 1837 the *Morrison*, an American vessel, tried to enter Japan, and the news of Great Britain winning over China reached the Japanese (Bolitho [1989] 1996: 124–26). The two Opium Wars (1839–41 and 1856–60) raised the alarm about Western colonization of East Asia in unambiguous terms. Commodore Matthew Perry came in 1853 and again in 1854 and succeeded in opening Japan. For many, the Ansei commercial treaties of 1858 with five Western nations, including the United States, were "a humiliating assault upon Japan's sovereignty," as Ogata Kōan lamented (Najita 1998: 239; see also Ohnuki-Tierney 2002a: 67). These external threats led to the development of cultural nationalism, reflected in Japanese cultural activities.

The development of plebeian culture, cultural nationalism, and extensive urbanization became combined forces bringing changes in the representation of "the Japanese nature."

Plebeian Schemes of Temporality

With the rise of plebeian culture, the Edo period saw alternative types of temporality—both of which were developed by the folk. They were the *saijiki* (almanac) and what I call "rice temporality."

The Saijiki *(List of Terms for Seasons)*

The practice of almanac using the seasonal words came originally from China. *Nihon Saijiki* (Japanese almanac) by Kaibara Ekken, published in 1688, is said to have inaugurated the Japanese tradition of *saijiki*, a list of *kigo* (terms for seasons) used in haiku and related forms of poetry. An entry in a *saijiki* usually includes a description of the *kigo* itself, a list of similar or related words, and some examples of haiku that include that *kigo*. Instead of "the Japanese four seasons" of the courtiers of the previous periods, *saijiki* became widely embraced by the folk through the development of a genre of poems called haikai, which evolved into haiku, focused on the seasons. In later periods, it was not confined to haikai; instead, it became, and has remained ever since, a necessary practice for letter writing and other types of greetings. These writings must begin with a reference to weather, flowers, birds, and other markers of the season, and end with another reference to a season (see also Shirane 2012: 213).

The term *shun* (being in season) has been an extremely important concept ever since. It is a concept not only for fish—the right time for consumption—which became the most important food in Edo and in the surrounding areas, but for plants and other foods too.

A major factor driving fundamental changes in the Japanese relationship to the environment was the move of the capitol from Kyoto to Tokyo. In contrast to Kyoto, surrounded by mountains and with no direct access to the sea, Edo and nearby cities were next to Tokyo Bay, leading to the Pacific Ocean. While the courtiers in Kyoto were primarily vegetarians, those in Edo and other cities with access to waterways made fish the central part of their diet. *Ryōri Monogatari* (Stories about cooking), published anonymously in 1643, lists 144 species of fish, primarily from the sea but also from rivers, 18 birds, and 7 animals. The author is unknown, but judging from the work's use of *kamigata kotoba* (western dialect), she/he must have been from western Japan. Since the Japanese place enormous importance on *shun* (being in season), during the Edo period they developed a conception of the seasons that differed greatly from the "Japanese four seasons" established in the *waka* poems of previous periods by those living in Kyoto and consuming primarily plant foods. The *saijiki* seasons were far more interactive, as it were, with "real nature" than the culturalized seasons had been in the previous period.

This new development of food culture was widely disseminated through the medium of haikai poems, which no longer adhered to the aristocratic taste of looking down on food as a "base" topic—a topic avoided in the *waka* tradition of the elite in the previous periods (for details on food and haikai, see Shirane 2012: 181–85; see also Najita [1991] 1997).

The most widespread media for referring to the four seasons were letters and other greetings, all of which had to start and end with a "proper reference" to the season. This continues as a strong tradition even today.

"Rice Temporality" and Its "Nationalization"

During the Edo period, with intensive and extensive urbanization, more Japanese were removed from the production of rice. Contrary to this reality, various artists during this period chose rice, its growth, and associated rituals as a motif in their art. An example is *Hyakunin Isshu Uba ga Etoki* (Pictures of one hundred poems by one hundred poets, with explanations by the wet nurse) by Katsushika Hokusai (1760–1849). This volume consists of illustrations of the well-known collection of one hundred poems, each by a different poet (*Hyakunin Isshu*), completed in 1235 by Fujiwara no Teika (1162–1241). Hokusai interpreted the poems as if a wet nurse were showing them to a child during the mid-eighteenth century. The most common motif by far, found in twenty-six prints, relates to rice and rice agriculture.[1] Some have sheaves of rice stalks in the scene, others are more focused on the production of rice. The stages of the growth of rice are well represented—flooded rice paddies (#19), winnowing of rice

(#71), and rice harvesting (#39). Farmers in the field are depicted (#14). Featured also are rituals and daily activities involving rice: a sheaf of harvested rice on top of a pole with people underneath in a scene from the Gion festival in Kyoto (#22); a scene of the full-moon ritual (*jūgoya*) celebrated with rice wine (in the print) and rice cakes (not included in the print) (#68); making rice wine (#78); and pounding rice to make rice cakes (#79) (the print numbers are Morse's and appear at the top of the page opposite the print).[2]

Andō (Utagawa) Hiroshige (1797–1858) created another series of woodblock prints, *Tōkaidō Gojū-San-Tsugi* (Fifty-three stations along the Tōkaidō), in which similar motifs of harvested rice fields, flooded rice paddies, bundles of rice (*komedawara*), and rice sheaves appear (Gotō 1975). The prints in *Kiso Kaidō Rokujū-Kyū-Tsugi* (Sixty-nine stations along the Kiso Road) (Gotō 1976), which contains prints by both Hiroshige and Keisai Eisen (1790–?), include similar motifs.

Another movement in visual arts during the Edo period was the development of *shiki kōsakuzu* (agrarian four seasons), paintings on folding screens depicting the cycle of growth of rice plants in each of the seasons. They became the motif of paintings by many well-known artists, such as Kusumi Morikage (1688–1704), Kanō Eiō Fujiwara Katsunobu (1731–1805), and Kanō Harukawain Osanobu (1796–1846).

The intense urbanization during the Edo period reinvented agrarian Japan with a vengeance, as it were, and reconstructed rice and rice agriculture as "Japanese nature," the symbolic foundation for the autochthony of *all* Japanese. At the most obvious level, they signal *four seasons* of the year. Flooded rice fields, like rice-planting songs, are the most familiar signs of spring or early summer. Rice harvesting scenes, including sheaves of rice stalks—the most frequently used motif—represent fall and its joyful harvest, but also the end of the growing season. What is striking from the perspective of representation is that these cycles of rice growth have become the markers of the seasons for all Japanese. For urbanites, fishermen, and all others who are not rice growers, life became marked by rice and its growth. In other words, the four seasons as codified by the elite during previous periods by flowers and birds were "replaced" by the growth stages of rice.

The degree to which agrarianism successfully penetrated the thoughts of the elites as well as the everyday life of the common folk is evident in various forms of popular culture. For example, the following haiku poems by Kobayashi Issa (1763–1827) illustrate that rice planting songs became a familiar symbol of spring, even for those far removed from farming, and that people felt uncomfortable or at least were made to feel they were not "working," in contrast to rice farmers:

> While taking a nap   *Motainaya*
> I listen to the rice planting song   *Hiruneshite kiku*
> How impious I feel   *Taue uta*
> (Kobayashi Issa 1929: 508; my translation)

> While taking a nap   *Tanohito o*
> In my heart I worship   *Kokoro de ogamu*
> Those in the rice field   *Hirune kana*
> (Kobayashi Issa 1929: 473; my translation)

The sayings dated to this time also illustrate the sacredness of rice, and some are still familiar to contemporary Japanese. For example, if one steps on a rice grain, one's leg is said to become warped. In another, a person will go blind if he/she leaves even a single grain of rice left in a rice bowl. Agrarian productivity received primary emphasis, and hard work on the farm not only became virtuous but was assigned an aesthetic value by the government and by the elites.

Culturalization of "Nature"

Major efforts at "shaping nature" developed during this period. The gardens of European palaces and other grand estates are thoroughly culturalized, almost always showing off, as it were, the creative talent of the gardeners. In contrast, Japanese gardens, although just as completely reshaped by humans, assiduously "hide" the signs of intervention by human hands, which work on every root, limb, and tree trunk (figure 5.1). The tradition of cutting the branches (*sashiki*) had begun already during the Nara period, and the craft of grafting (*tsugiki*) started during the Heian period among the elites. By the Kamakura period the practice had spread to farmers (Hida 2002: 148–54). Today, one can see the carefully reshaped trees in every temple, in shrines and castles, in the imperial palaces in Kyoto and Tokyo, and in individual homes.

Sakuteiki, by an unidentified author of the Heian period, is the oldest manual for landscaping and has been considered highly influential for the landscaping of upper-class manors during the Heian and subsequent periods. However, it was during the Edo period that the most well-known masters of the craft arose. Some were officially appointed by shoguns, such as Kobori Enshū (1579–1647), the best known *sakuteishi*, that is, *sakutei* artist (Kumakura 2007). He is known for perfecting the landscaping technique called *shakkei* (borrowed scenery). It is the technique of using the natural background, such as mountains, trees, and bodies of water, in the composition of a garden, thereby blurring the boundaries between the human-made and "nature."

Figure 5.1. Shaping tree trunks and branches. Photo by the author.

Along with the "minimalist" traditions of the rock garden and the tea ceremony, bonsai and *hakoniwa* were other important artistic developments that represented "nature." Bonsai is not the product of genetic engineering but careful cultivation of a plant as a tiny tree in a vase. Originating in China, where it was called *pun-sai*, with the earliest reference dated to 704, it was introduced to Japan during the late Heian period. It was initially a hobby among monks and warriors but it flourished and spread to the common people by the beginning of the Edo period, when it was so popular that it became one of the main themes of woodblock prints by Utagawa Toyokuni and Torii Kiyonaga, for example (Furugaki [1991] 1996; Iwasa 1976). Today, all sorts of people, but especially older ones who have time and financial means, enjoy bonsai as a hobby, and a large number of exhibitions by amateurs are held.

The tiny garden, called *hakoniwa* (boxed garden), also became popular. Dirt and sand are put into a shallow box, and miniature human figures, a bridge, a house, trees, and bushes are placed to simulate the landscape of

Figure 5.2. *Netsuke*: tigress with two cubs. The Walters Art Museum.

a manor or a rock garden. The *hakoniwa* was also a product of the merchant culture during the Edo period and lasted through the Meiji and Taishō periods with decreasing popularity.

Netsuke is another iconic artistic development of the Edo period. Netsuke, usually made from ivory or wood, is a toggle to hold small items, such as a tobacco pouch, from the sash of a men's kimono, which does not have pockets. These toggles became popular during the seventeenth century and throughout the Edo period (Arakawa 1983). They are tiny "representations" of the beings of the universe familiar to people, in a real or imaginary sense. They are not static objects but are engaged in some "activity" familiar to the people at the time. An example is a monkey holding a peach, a symbol of hope for a long life (Ministry of Foreign Affairs 2015: 5). As the being of the universe closest to humans, the monkey had long been depicted in paintings, sculptures, folktales, proverbs, and many other media (Ohnuki-Tierney 1987). While people are also represented, the Thunder God, the tiger, and other beings that are not native fauna and flora are equally common. A tigress with two cubs (figure 5.2) by the mid-nineteenth century artist Miyasaka Hakui tells us a story of the fierce determination of the tigress to protect her offspring, as shown in the piercing bright eyes of the inlays. This netsuke is made of ivory with shell inlay and its size is 2.2 x 4.2 x 3.7 cm. Mothers' determination and dedication to their offspring is a common motif in Japanese culture. Although imagined tigers already appear in the oldest collection of poems, *Manyōshū*, tigers are not native to Japan.

As discussed in detail in the conclusion, *bonsai* and *netsuke* are usually referred to as "miniatures" in English. This is quite unfortunate since they are *not* "miniatures" if this word means the proportionate reduction in scale of "real" objects. Neither *bonsai* nor *netsuke* are replicas of reduced scale. Nor are they fractal arts. Like the rock garden, these representations of "nature" are not based on nature and natural beings "objectively out there." It is also significant to notice that these items—*bonsai*, *hakoniwa*, and *netsuke*—are quotidian objects that the folk used and enjoyed in their everyday life.

Once an aristocratic pastime during the Heian period, the hobby of listening to the sounds of insects—the auditory perception of "nature"— became highly commercialized during the Edo period. An occupation of selling insects emerged. The bamboo cages for them were replaced by lacquerware for the warlords and other wealthy people. The singing of caged insects became an important entertainment for the folk as well. The sale of insects became an indispensable feature of open markets, much enjoyed by children. Even right after the end of World War II, the practice continued, only to decline after the economic boom and the intense Americanization/Westernization of entertainment began to take over (Umeya 2005). Listening to insects never expanded in Japan as it did in China, where cricket fighting developed, dating back more than a millennium and involving large financial stakes (Feng 2021). Whether one considers the aesthetic enjoyment of insects' singing in Japan or cricket fights in China, these trends exemplify the way people aggressively bring "nature" into the cultural sphere.

Cultural Nationalism and the Symbols of "Japanese Nature"

With Western colonialism as the global force threatening Japan, the Japanese developed their cultural nationalism by establishing their collective sense of self. The symbols of "Japanese nature" they chose were rice plants, cherry blossoms, and Mount Fuji. These were also the symbols used to counter the intensive process of urbanization taking place in Edo during the mid-nineteenth century.

Rice and Rice Paddies with Pure Water

As introduced earlier, woodblock prints played a major role in identifying and promoting the symbols of the collective self of the Japanese. While urbanization certainly gave birth to the rural, as elsewhere in the world (Berque 1990: 87, 110–12), the symbols chosen to represent Japanese nature in these woodblock prints are not really rural-cum-nature. Travelers are often depicted against the backdrop of rice paddies, suggesting that rice and related activities constitute an unchanging Japan, in contrast to the transient and changing scene epitomized by Edo (Tokyo), to which both roads (Tōkaidō and Kisokaidō) lead. Far from the "reality" of mud, sweat, and fertilizer, rice and rice paddies remind viewers of the beauty of eternal Japan.

Neither the imperial nature with flowers and butterflies nor the warriors' nature with rocks and empty space—representations common in previous periods—included rice and rice paddies as the visual symbols of "Japanese nature." These were created by the Edo artists during this period of unprecedented economic changes, with the rural community fully participating in the rapid developments (Berry 2007; Francks 2009; Gordon 2012). Edo, the urban center, saw the efflorescence of the plebian culture of the merchant class. Merchants and their artists were not rice farmers, and the aristocrats and warriors were not only *not* farmers but also the consumers of rice to whom farmers had to supply rice as tax.

During the Edo period, rice and its cultivation were extolled in other media, such as in poems, and most importantly in nativist philosophy, which "reconstitute[d] agricultural work and valorize[d] its practice as an application of the 'Ancient Way' (*kodōron*)" (Harootunian 1988: 23). The obvious difficulty of rice also being the staple food for the Chinese, let alone the outside origin of wet-rice cultivation, had to be overcome. Hirata Atsutane (1776–1843), a nativist scholar and one of the four major figures in the nativist movement, emphatically celebrated Japanese rice and denigrated Chinese rice. For him, rice production and consumption were equivalent to the worship of Shinto deities and the repayment for their blessings. In his search for the Japanese rice to be the divine rice, he degraded Chinese rice as "inferior" and "begun by the mandate of men"; therefore, "those who eat [it] are weak and enervated" (quoted in Harootunian 1988: 211–12). Since Hirata considered eating and working as religious acts, he demeaned other peoples who quarreled during meals "like dogs" and claimed that others admired the Japanese because of their good eating manners (213). To Hirata, then, humans are to animals as the Japanese are to other peoples. These "other peoples," who ate inferior rice and had bad manners, were non-Japanese Asians, primarily the Chinese.

Important for the theme of this book is that rice paddies in these woodblock prints are "water paddies" (*suiden*)—paddies filled with beautiful transparent water, with no ground showing, where "water ears," that is, succulent ears of rice plants, grow. In the fall, when the plants bear grains, they are depicted as golden ears, moving in the wind like golden waves. That is, rice and rice paddies represent *Japanese nature without dirt*.

Cherry Blossoms

During the ancient period mountain cherries were the only cherry trees for the Japanese, who during later periods actively planted them in their yards, along rivers, and in temples, shrines, schoolyards, and geisha quarters, literally all over Japan. They were planted for their beauty, *not* for fruit to eat. They were planted along the embankments of rivers and aqueducts not only for their flowers and the practical purpose of strengthening the banks, but also to purify the water, since leaves and petals were believed to have antitoxic powers (Smith and Poster [1986] 1988: plate #42).

We saw in chapter 3 how cherry blossoms were chosen to represent Japan at the imperial court during the Heian period. During the Edo period, a number of shoguns, including Tokugawa Ieyasu (1542–1616), Hidetada (1579–1632), Iyemitsu (1604–51), and Yoshimune (1684–1751), ordered the planting of cherry trees in various locations in Edo, whose fertile soil of volcanic ashes was ideal. During this period the shogunate government reinforced the system whereby regional lords and their retainers were required to reside in Edo every other year, and leaving their families behind in Edo when they return to their own domain. It was a policy designed to weaken their financial resources by saddling them with the cost of the elaborate procession of moving back and forth between their territory and Edo. Even more important, the policy of lords' having to leave family behind in Edo was a clever means to curtail any plot for a revolt against the shogun in their own territory. As a byproduct of this system, many regional lords brought cherry trees from their own regions to plant in Edo, resulting in 250 to 260 varieties of cherry trees in Edo alone at that time (Hayashi 1982: 54–55).

The Edo capital was transformed into the land of cherry blossoms, which in turn led to the construction of "Japan as the land of cherry blossoms," since Edo represented Japan. In this construction and representation of Japan, woodblock prints played a powerful role, as they did for rice paddies. The most famous print series was *Meisho Edo Hyakke* (One hundred celebrated places of Edo) by Andō Hiroshige (1797–1858).[3] Hiroshige's work consists of 115 prints of these "places" marked as "famous places" (*meisho*). Among these, twenty-one places were chosen because of the beauty of their cherry blossoms. Plum blossoms appear only four times.[4]

Although the woodblock prints placed Edo at the center stage of "Japan, the land of cherry blossoms," during the Edo period famous places for cherry blossoms were also identified in Kyoto. Most important was Maruyama Park, with the well-known weeping cheery tree.

The Japanese wished cherry trees to belong exclusively to Japan, as the episode involving the aforementioned Kaibara Ekken (1630–1714), who inaugurated the Japanese tradition of *saijiki*, testifies. He declared in 1698 that according to a Chinese person he questioned in Nagasaki, there were no cherry trees in China. In his celebrated *Yamato Honzō*, a book on botanical species of Japan, published in 1709, the Chinese source of this information was identified as Kaseiho, who was from Sichuan province, where cherry trees do not grow, although they grew elsewhere in China. Since Kaibara Ekken was the most revered botanist, his proclamation excited the Japanese, who believed this report to be true (Saitō 1982: 28–29). There has been a long history of the quest for the relationship between Japan's Somei *Yoshino* cherry tree and the king cherry of Jeju Island, South Korea.

Given the Japanese convention in visual arts of representing seasons and months through various flowers, and given that cherry blossoms last only for a very short time, it is remarkable that their beauty played such a powerful role in the choice of celebrated places (*meisho*). *Both in fact and in its self-representation*, Japan became a land of cherry blossoms, with their "unique" beauty.

While there is no question that cherry blossoms are gorgeous in full bloom, it is nonetheless noteworthy that the naturalization of their supremacy involved cultural forces rather than strictly "natural" ones. The timing of full bloom varies across Japan, which stretches from northern Okinawa to Hokkaido—that is, from a subtropical to a subarctic climate. Today, television assiduously predicts and follows the timing of blossoms from their beginning to full bloom, as they do the typhoons. It is also significant to recognize that it is plum blossoms, rather than cherry blossoms, that emerge right after winter, and the Japanese do enjoy plum blossom viewing, but not with the same enthusiasm. The Japanese routinely stress that the cherry petal has a tiny slit in the middle, whereas the plum blossom does not. All visual representations of the blossoms stress the difference. There are only nine wild species, with as many as three hundred cultivated species of cherry (Iwaki 1995). Many do have a slit in the middle of their petal, but not all.

The aesthetic appreciation of blossoms is deeply embedded in the symbolic structure that has persisted throughout history. First and most important is the equation of cherry blossoms with spring as the seasonal counterpart of rice in the fall. Cherry blossoms represented the soul exclusive to the Japanese, just as rice grains contained the soul of deities. It was for this reason that Kaibara Ekken had to establish the "fact" that cherry trees did not grow in China (on the complex symbolism of cherry blossoms, see Ohnuki-Tierney 2002a: 27–58, 106–7).

Mount Fuji

Until the Edo period, when the crossing of territories became easier for the Japanese, Mount Fuji, the tallest mountain in Japan, was not visible to most. At 12,388 feet (3,776 meters), it is a volcano that last erupted in 1707 and is considered active. It stands above the clouds, giving the sense of a sacred aura. *Unjō* (above the clouds) is the space for the celestial beings, as in the "Tale of the Bamboo Cutter" in chapter 3. Those who are allowed to go up to the Imperial Palace floor are called *unjōbito* (people above the clouds). Most Japanese today think of Mount Fuji as looking the same from time immemorial. Yet, even in the Kamakura (1185–1333) and Nanbokuchō periods (1336–92), people thought that dirt from below the earth's surface suddenly erupted overnight and became Mount Fuji during the time of the legendary emperors described in *Nihonshoki* (Torii 1998: 7–8).

According to Torii (Torii et al. 1998: 274–79), in the earlier collections of poems, Mount Fuji does not appear frequently. When it does, the poets find some personal affinity with the mountain but do not use it as a symbol of Japan. In the *Manyōshū*, out of 4,500 poems, 14 refer to the mountain, with 5 referring to it as Fuji (Torii et al. 1998: 274). In the *Kokinshū* (Saeki, ed., [1981] 2020), compiled during the mid-Heian period (905–14), only 6 out of 1,111 poems refer to Mount Fuji, but not as a symbol of Japan. Out of 1,970 poems in the *Shin Kokinwakashū* (Fujiwara no Teika [1439] 1992), only 10 include Mount Fuji, for the poets' personal reasons.

During the Edo period, the Tōkaidō and Kisokaidō, two major roads to Edo made by the Bakufu to promote political unification, provided a much easier way for the folk in western Japan to travel to the regions where they could in fact *see* the mountain.

In a museum catalog entitled *Nihon no Kokoro: Fuji no Bi Ten* (The Spirit of the Japanese: The Beauty of Mt. Fuji) Torii (1998: 2–11) provides a description of the meanings assigned to Fuji in religions and other traditions from the ancient period to the postwar period, with exhaustive visual representations. The mountain's physical characteristics vary depending on the period when it was portrayed. In the first painting of Mount Fuji, dated to 1069 (4–5), it has only one peak, whereas in the Muromachi period (1338–1573) it began to have three peaks.

Beginning with the Azuchi Momoyama period (1573–1603), Mount Fuji appeared as a motif in warriors' attire, helmet, and other accessories. During the Edo period (1603–1868), it appeared on all sorts of objects, including netsuke, combs, ceramic and porcelain wares, lacquerware, kimonos, and mirror holders. (Torii 1998: 91–120).

During the Edo period, Mount Fuji came to represent Japan and Japanese nature. When urbanization was developing at an accelerated pace, Fuji began to represent the unchanging, eternal Japanese self. Numerous visual representations were made, including two series, *Fugaku Sanjūrokkei* (Thirty-six views of Mt. Fuji) and *Fugaku Hyakkei* (One hundred views of Mt. Fuji) by Katsushika Hokusai, and two series, *Fuji Sanjūrokkei* (Thirty-six views of Mt. Fuji) and *Fujimi Hyakuzu* (One hundred views of Mt. Fuji), by Utagawa Hiroshige. Hiroshige also executed another series, *Tōkaidō Gojūsantsugi* (Thirty-six stations along the Tōkaidō) (Torii 1998: 130–33, 162–67, 267–69).

During the Edo period, the sacredness of the mountain led to rapid development of a cult called Fuji-kō, after the death at age 106 of Hasegawa Kakugyō, who climbed the mountain 128 times in the belief that reaching the summit promised healing of various illnesses. The Bakufu perceived its explosive popularity as a threat and prohibited it a number of times (Torii 1998: 7). Toward the end of the Bakufu period in the mid-nineteenth century, Japan went through a number of social upheavals, including the arrival of Commodore Perry in 1853 and 1854, the great earthquake of Edo in 1855, the cholera epidemic of 1858, and serious political turmoil. This turbulence led to the enormous popularity of climbing Mount Fuji to receive the "reward for this world" (*gensei ri'eki*) (Miyata 1975: 148; Torii 1998: 7–8).

In chapter 2, I explained how hunting as a subsistence economic activity ceased, at least in the agrarian section of Japan, when wet-rice agriculture took over. Hunting became a leisure activity for princes, who supervised the hunt by their underlings, usually on horseback from a hilltop. It was entertainment, a sport, a ritual, or, especially, a show of valor on the part of the elite. The method of chasing wild boar and deer by surrounding them from four directions was called *makigari*. The foothills of Mount Fuji became the most important and prestigious field for this mode of hunting, as shown in a number of paintings in Torii (1998: 28–29 on the Muromachi period; 30–31 on the Momoyama period; and 32–33 on the Edo period). They show upper-class warriors on horseback, with their servants chasing the animals with a bow and arrow. In contrast to these portrayals in paintings, hunting scenes never appear in the urbane woodblock prints of the merchant class in Edo.

Summary and Discussion

The Edo period went through epochal developments. First, there was the complete takeover of political power from the emperors by the shogunate, which established the capitol in Edo (Tokyo). Second, this was followed by the closing of the country to the outside world.

During this period, the heightened development of urbanization and consumerism led to a vigorous development of plebian culture, with a far greater number of people participating in cultural activities. For all these developments, "nature" was called to duty more intensively than during the previous periods of history.

The collective identity of a people, including their cultural and political nationalisms, is almost always predicated on the presence of the Other, who prompts further articulation of the Self—of who they are as opposed to the Other (Ohnuki-Tierney 2015: 125–52). Even though Japan was nominally closed to the outside world, this was the time when the Japanese became increasingly aware of the threat of Western colonial power, which propelled the Japanese to reaffirm their own collective identity and develop their cultural nationalism. They chose rice paddies, cherry blossoms, and Mount Fuji as the country's symbols. Rice paddies and cherry blossoms were the symbols of Japan's autochthony, literally demarcating its territory, while Mount Fuji, standing above the clouds, symbolized its eternity. For these historical developments, historical agents were no longer the court elite or the warriors but predominantly the members of the merchant class.

A new scheme of temporality developed with the relocation of the capital to Edo, where everyday activities, such as a diet with more seafood, made the people more acutely aware of the changing seasons. The development of *saijiki*, a collection of terms for seasons, and their mandatory use in the composition of the *haikai* established a new system of temporality. Furthermore, intense urbanization propelled the Japanese to seek their primordial self in rice agriculture, leading to another system of temporality based on the growing stages of rice.

During this period, the Japanese engaged in an intensive culturalization of "nature" through visual arts, landscape architecture, and literature. In addition to rice grains, aestheticized rice paddies with pure water became the dominant motif of representation in woodblock prints and literature. They perfected the gardening technique of reshaping every branch of a tree to be the "perfect shape in nature." They developed *bonsai* and *hakoniwa* to represent "nature" in a very small container. *Netsuke*, a very popular folk item in Edo, follows the same tradition of representations of everyday items reproduced as small-scale objects—like the rock garden of the political elite, but in the everyday lives of the folk.

Although this pattern of the construction of "nature" as the other side of urbanization, which destroys nature, is universal, there are distinctive characteristics of the Japanese version. The process centers on plants, with little emphasis on nonhuman animals. This sharply contrasts with the Western concept of nature, epitomized by the phrase "the king as hunter." The king must subdue and kill wild nature to establish human culture/society under his political leadership. The political power of the Japanese emperor in contrast rests on the management of time, that is, safeguarding the growth of rice plants.

Most important for the theme of this book, "Japanese nature" continued to be portrayed without dirt. Rice is represented by rice paddies with pure water and as golden waves of grain when ripe; cherry blossoms are flowers at the top, not the tree roots in the ground. The single most important feature of Mount Fuji is its height, standing "above the clouds," that is, far above the ground.

Notes

1. They are prints #1, 5, 8, 9, 12, 13, 14, 17, 19, 20, 22, 23, 30, 39, 44, 47, 65, 68, 70, 71, 77, 78, 79, 83, 84, and 90. Picture #13 may illustrate seed planting by women but not necessarily rice. Morse (1989) interprets the women in print #90 as carrying fish in their baskets, but because no figures of fish are drawn and the background looks like rice fields, I interpret the contents of the baskets to be rice. Hokusai started to work on this series at age seventy-six in 1836 and completed prints for only twenty-seven of the hundred poems but also left many line drawings. Eighty-nine of them are reproduced in the collection by Morse.
2. This contrasts with the way the sea and mountains are portrayed in the Hokusai series. The sea appears, but only occasionally with fishermen. It appears twice as background (#20, 21), twice with boats sailing at a distance (#4, 7), four times with people crossing the water in a boat (#27 [sea], 36 [river?], 37 [pond?], 76 [sea]). Others involving the sea include one of a large boat with lovers in hiding peeking through an opening (#18), and another of people digging for clams (#92). One print depicts a salt-making scene (#97) but with no sea in the background, and another shows fixing a boat (#33). There is only one scene with fishermen (#3) and one with abalone divers (*ama*) (#11). In sum, in sharp contrast to the agrarian activities that are common themes in these prints, the sea and activities related to it appear far less frequently.
3. Hiroshige came from a family of the warrior class (Smith and Poster [1986] 1988: 9–10; Miyao 1975: 75). The prints in this series were published from 1856 until his death in 1858, numbering 115 in total (Smith and Poster [1986] 1988: 9–10), although the total number varies depending upon which additional

prints after his death are included. Other famous prints include *Illustrated Book on the Famous Sites in Edo* (*Edo Meisho Zue*) by Hasegawa Settan, published between 1829 and 1836.
4. See plates #11, 14, 15, 16, 17, 19, 22, 23, 24, 25, 28, 29, 31, 35, 37, 38, 40, 41, and 42 in Gotō 1975; and plates #92 and 95 in Gotō 1976. Plum blossoms appear in plates #27, 30, 36 in Gotō 1975; and plate #104 in Gotō 1976.

CHAPTER 6

Nationalization and Militarization of "Japanese Nature"
Modern Period (1868–1945)

Part 3 explores how "Japanese nature" became part of Japan's political identity as a nation-state. Japan was nominally closed to the outside world for over two hundred years (1639–1854), although some scholarship has challenged the received wisdom by, for example, pointing to major trade routes via the Sea of Japan through which Japan remained in contact (e.g., Amino 1994: 122–27). Intellectual elites had been absorbing knowledge from the West, especially from the Dutch, to whom Japan remained open. In 1838, during the late Edo period, Ogata Kōan (1810–63) established the Tekijuku (Tekikeisaijuku), a private school for learning Dutch medicine, and recognized English to be the key international language, inaugurating the beginning of the study of Western scholarship in Japan. It was of "fundamental importance in Japan's modern transformation" (Najita 1998).

Commodore Perry's arrival in 1853 and then again in 1854 became a catalyst for officially opening the country. Once their country was opened, the Japanese, both intellectuals and the folk, began to enthusiastically espouse the Western philosophy of "civilization and enlightenment" (*bunmeikaika*), which they thought was the basis of the West's spectacular achievements in science and technology.

Among the upper-class Japanese, there was a craze for Western ballroom dancing and Western music. Emperor Meiji took the lead in the pro-Western movement by cutting his topknot and adopting a Western-style haircut on 20 March 1873, and growing a Kaiser mustache and wearing a Western-style military uniform (Ohnuki-Tierney 2002a: 62–67). The extreme degree to which the Japanese were ready to absorb Western civilization was portrayed in satires and cartoons from this period that remain quite familiar even today. "If you strike a head with a Western-style haircut, you hear the sound of Civilization and Enlightenment" was a popular saying among the people at the time (Miyatake 1925: 42; see also Kanagaki Robun [1870–76] 1926; 1967).

The geopolitical tidal wave at the time necessitated the building of a strong military, all the institutional apparatus for a modern nation, and the political nationalization of the people. It led to what Mosse (1975) called the "nationalization of the masses." Japan militarized itself in a frenzied manner under the banner of the emperor, who remained invisible and inaudible.

Satō (2002) describes the important role played by the media in the intensive "nationalization" of the Japanese in almost every aspect of their lives. The enormously popular magazine *Kingu* (King) ushered in "the age of the king" (*Kingu no Jidai*), which spanned 1925 to 1957. At its peak in 1941, it sold 44,313,534 copies in a year (Satō 2002: 334). *Kingu* was full of propaganda for "Imperial Japan" and the Japanese soul, covering all the "victories" during the wars while avoiding reports of defeats, such as the Saipan mass suicide and the Midway Battle (369–70).

In 1912 the Japan Travel Bureau Foundation (*kōtsūkōsha*) was established and began to encourage tourism to help the local and national economies (Nihon Kōtsū Kōsha 2013; Satō 1997).[1] Overnight trips for students started in 1886 and became an important tradition for schools, lasting until well after World War II. The program was first called Chōto Ensoku (Extended Excursion) and renamed Shūgaku Ryokō (Educational Travel) in 1888 for students in elementary, middle, and high school. Although it started as part of a military exercise, it became separate and aimed at bringing students to visit national heritage and industrial development sites so that they became impressed by "modern Japan." Although visits to "famous sites" with cultural importance were at times included, they never were the major emphasis. These trips served as an effective way to "nationalize" the youth as Japan was building its modern nation-state (Hoshino 1997; Uchida 1994).

Following the example of the creation of Yellowstone as the first US national park in 1872, the Japanese government issued legislation on its own national parks in 1931. In 1934 it designated the Inland Sea and two locations in Kyūshū—Unzan and Kirishima—as national parks. In 1936 the first four postage stamps bearing the images of the national parks were issued—all with Mount Fuji in the background (Nihon Yūbin Kitte Shōkyōdō Kumiai 2003: 143). The history of the development and codification of the national parks reveals that the aim of the government was far from the pure or idealistic goal of preserving "nature"; rather, it had economic reasons, for which the government promoted and used "Japanese nature" to foster cultural nationalism. The initial proclamation of the law itself was a result of the government's struggle with economic crisis: it was an attempt to promote the tourism industry in the hope of attracting foreigners to Japan (S. Satō 1997). As of 2017, there were thirty-four national parks.

In a decision that revealed that its creation of the national parks was for economic reasons, the government allowed companies to extract sulfur at Akan National Park in Kyūshū (Satō 1997), causing environmental hazards. Similarly, in 1922 Kantō Suiden (now called Kantō Denryoku, TEPCO) acquired the water rights in Oze for the construction of a power plant that would put the entire area under water. The plan was hotly debated, as the mass media aired the problem by asking, "Which is more important, a dragonfly or electricity?" (Nakano and Kobayashi 1967: 192–203). Kantō Denryoku continued its operation until 1966, when it finally gave up the attempt to renew its water rights in Oze. By then a surge of interest in environmental protection among the people had led to the establishment of a large number of rules by the government prohibiting rampant abuse of the environment.

In 1927, two newspapers (*Ōsaka Mainichi* and *Tokyo Nichinichi*), with the approval of the Ministry of Railroads, designated one hundred locations as *Nihon Hyakkei* (One hundred views of Japan), and these national parks became "our Japanese pristine nature," which supposedly represents the Japanese identity. During the period of imperial expansion, the government designated three locations in Taiwan as *Japan's* "national parks" (Satō 1997: 712), even planting cherry trees there.

The government continued to neglect the protection of "nature" even after the designation of national park (*kokuritsu kōen*) was changed to nature park (*shizen kōen*) in 1957. The government also designated certain locations in Japan as tourist destinations and certain insects, land mammals, birds, and flowers as the inhabitants of "Japanese nature" (Satō 1997: 711–12). Many of these came to be featured on postage stamps.

In 1989 the government identified one hundred "hidden realms" of Japan, including Oze. The government, the tourist bureaus, and the mass media deployed such terms as *zekkei* (incomparable view)—that is, they idealized "nature" in order to promote the national economy, thereby destroying nature through tourism. The major architect of "Japanese nature" during this period was the national government, instead of the courtiers, warlords, and merchants during the previous periods in history.

Symbolic Representations of "Japanese Nature"

While the nationalization of the masses was going on, Mount Fuji, rice, and cherry blossoms remained as symbols for the collective self of the Japanese.

Japanese Rice

When the Japanese had to establish their own identity against the Chinese, toward the end of the early modern period, they emphasized domestic rice (*naichimai*) as a metaphor for the Japanese, distinguished from foreign rices (*gaimai*) as a metaphor for other Asians. During the eighteenth and nineteenth centuries, nativist scholars, as discussed earlier, strove to establish the Japanese identity and chose agrarian ideology and rice agriculture to represent the pristine Japanese way. This attitude toward the Chinese and the use of domestic rice as a metaphor for the superior Japanese continued during the Meiji period. In a novel called *Kōfu* (The Miners) by Natsume Sōseki (1867–1916), the most miserable life, as envisioned by the Japanese at that time, was to eat *nankinmai* (Nanking rice) and be bitten by *nankinmushi* (Nanking bugs, that is, bed bugs) (Sōseki [1907] 1984; for details, see Ohnuki-Tierney 1994: 104–5).

As Westerners became the dominant Other, the symbolic opposition took the form of "rice vs. meat" (see Ohnuki-Tierney 1994a: 105–8). A distinctive feature of the Otherness of Westerners during the early period of Japanese encounter with them was their butchering and meat eating, as depicted in the *Yokohama-e* (Prints of Yokohama) and *Kaika-e* (Enlightenment prints). With the pressing need to negotiate the Japanese identity, some opposed imitating the West and claimed that a rice diet and rice agriculture were evidence of Japanese superiority. Others advocated the abandonment of rice agriculture and the adoption of animal domestication. They argued that as long as the Japanese continued to eat only rice, fish, and vegetables, their bodies would never be strong enough to compete with the bodies of meat-eating Westerners (Tsukuba [1969] 1986: 109–12). In December 1871, Emperor Meiji issued an ordinance to eliminate the prohibition on meat eating in the imperial household.

These endorsements of meat eating from above were effective in convincing people to eat meat, which they thought was a symbol of "enlightenment." A collection of humorous essays by Kanagaki Robun (1829–94) describing the eager adoption of meat eating at the time is entitled *Aguranabe*, which means "a dish one eats while sitting cross-legged."[2] The book humorously portrays the mood of the day, when cows were seen to provide the miracle of the smallpox vaccine and their meat was not only nourishment for the body but also the source of "enlightenment." He writes: "Everyone—warriors, farmers, craftsmen, merchants, old and young, men and women, wise and foolish, poor and wealthy—all felt 'uncivilized' unless they ate beef" (Kanagaki [1871–72] 1967: 27, 77). A new dish—sliced beef and vegetables cooked in soy sauce and placed on top of a large bowl of cooked rice—was called *gyūnabe* (beef pot) in eastern

Japan and *sukiyaki* in western Japan—was dubbed the "enlightened bowl" (Endō [1910] 1968: 264; Shinmura [1955] 1990: 381).

This is quite extraordinary. The diet of the original inhabitants of the Japanese archipelago had no doubt consisted of animal meat, fish, and plants, but as the agrarian society and its cosmology, which lay at the base of the ancient imperial system, became hegemonic, meat became officially taboo, as discussed in chapter 1.

While rice paddies with pure water and no mud received attention from artists during this period of nationalization and militarization, rice as the Japanese food-cum-nature seems to have received more emphasis. On one hand, with the West coming into the picture, the Japanese were forced to differentiate themselves from other Asians; on the other hand, they had to establish the Japanese identity as opposed to the West (for details, see Ohnuki-Tierney 1994a: 102–20; Tanaka 1993).

Cherry Blossoms

While Mount Fuji and rice / rice paddies were nationalized and militarized during this period, cherry blossoms were used and abused for Japan's imperial pursuit in a spectacularly tragic way.

Within a few years after opening the country, when the government and the people were thrust into the "modernization" effort, cherry blossoms as a symbol of Japan took center stage in public discourse. Some proponents of "modern Japan" claimed that the hitherto popular expression "Cherry blossoms among flowers and warriors among people" epitomized the undesirable feudal Japan that must be shed (Yamada 1977: 115). Some began chopping down cherry trees and replacing them with more useful and commercially profitable species like camphor trees, which were used to produce mothballs to protect silk, rice papers, and other items from worms. On the other side were enthusiastic supporters of another, equally "modern" Japan, including prominent politicians, who went out of their way to protect cherry trees, claiming that now that Japan had opened its door to foreigners who would be visiting, the country should be kept beautiful (Ohnuki-Tierney 2002a: 103–4; Yamada 1977: 115).

It was a turbulent period when the idea of "enlightenment and civilization" was enthusiastically embraced not only by the elite but also by the folk. Coined by Fukuzawa Yukichi in his 1875 work *Bunmeiron no Gairyaku* (An outline of a theory of civilization), the phrase referred to the wholesale adoption of Western culture in the effort to modernize. An opposite force at work was heightened political nationalism. Shintoism, the only indigenous religion of Japan, was elevated to the national religion in an 1870 decree that purported to eliminate "foreign religions," including Buddhism, which originated in India. Even the most famous temples and their treasures were recklessly destroyed (Saeki 1988),[3] together with many cherry trees famous for their beautiful blossoms in the temple compounds (Kyōtoshi 1975: 274; see also Kyōtoshi 1981: 604–5). During the early Meiji period, then, the state had already begun the politicization of cherry blossoms, and the battle over the flower involved both the ordinary folks and the politicians, all trying to define the new or modern Japan.

In the face of the encroachment by Western colonial powers, which colonized all other nations in the Far East except Japan, building a modern military force was of the utmost priority. *The Rescript to the Soldiers*, written by Nishi Amane, was issued in 1882, before the promulgation of the Constitution of Imperial Japan in 1889. A famous, or infamous, passage in the *Rescript* of 1882 states that soldiers' obligation to the country is as heavy as the mountains, but their own lives are as light as feathers (Yui, Fujiwara and Yoshida [1989] 1996: 174). In a draft of this rescript (149–62), his 1878 lecture "Moral codes of soldiers" ("Heike Tokkō"), Nishi advocated that the newly established Japanese soldiers embrace the Japanese spirit, referring to a very well-known poem by Motoori Norinaga in which he equates the Japanese spirit with "mountain cherry blossoms / that bloom flagrantly in the morning sun" (author's translation).[4] In this poem Motoori Norinaga praises cherry blossoms as a celebration of life (e.g., Saitō [1979] 1985: 54; Toita and Yoshida 1981: 20; Yamada 1977: 117). The military purposely misrepresented Motoori's message and emphasized that young soldiers' deaths are as beautiful as falling cherry blossoms.[5]

An even more explicit connection between the flower and the Japanese was established by Nitobe Inazō (1862–1933) in *Bushido: The Soul of Japan*, published in 1899 in English, with a Japanese translation in 1908 (Nitobe [1899] 1912).[6] Like many Meiji intellectuals, he was a cosmopolitan liberal, opposed to both militarism and imperialism. Between 1919 and 1926, he worked closely with intellectual leaders of the world such as Albert Einstein, Marie Curie, and Henri Bergson at the League of Nations. Nitobe stripped *bushidō* of its militaristic and antimodern elements and presented it as the most admirable aspect of Japanese tradition. As seen in the subtitle, he equated *bushidō*, "chivalry" in his translation, with the "Japanese soul" (*tamashii*) and declared: "Chivalry is a flower no less indigenous to the soil of Japan than its emblem, the cherry blossom; nor is it a dried-up specimen of an antique virtue preserved in the herbarium of our history. It is a living object of power and beauty among us" (1).

By "indigenous," Nitobe meant that the sources of *bushidō* are to be found in Buddhism, Shintoism, and the doctrines of Confucius and Mencius, although he was a Christian himself. Citing the aforementioned poem by Motoori Norinaga, he establishes cherry blossoms as the metaphor for the Japanese soul (*yamato damashii*) (Nitobe [1899] 1912: 150–53).

Nitobe placed *bushidō* in the emperor-centered ideology (Nitobe [1933] 1969: 330), creating a smooth path for the military manipulation of the metaphor. Cherry blossom became the metaphor for the "unique" Japanese soul that did not hesitate when facing death. The Japanese were urged to fight and die for the emperor, like a beautiful cherry blossom, which falls shortly after gorgeously blooming.

In this transformative process, the Yasukuni National Shrine played a decisive role. The shrine was originally constructed to console the souls of the fallen warriors who had fought on the side of the "restoration" of the imperial system after a long reign by the shogunate government. Cherry trees were planted and the shrine became a space for various entertainments, including a French circus in 1871, sumo matches, firecrackers, and horse racing in 1877, 1878, and 1881.[7] It was a public park where people strolled, enjoying cherry blossoms, as depicted in a print by Yōsai Nobukazu (1872–1944) created in 1893 (reproduced in Yasukuni Jinja 1984: n.p.; see also Tsubouchi 1999: 55, 57).

Despite its beginning, the shrine had become the citadel of military ideology by the time Japanese militarism reached its height in the 1930s. In this process cherry blossoms became thoroughly "militarized." As the Japanese adopted the Western military system, they developed military insignia with cherry buds, leaves, and blossoms.[8] The government performed a mass enshrinement ceremony for the souls of the fallen soldiers there (Earhart 2008: 412) and gave their mothers medals with a cherry blossom attached. Between 1933 and 1935, the shrine published a five-volume history, edited by Kamo Momoki, the high priest, together with the offices of the Ministry of Army and the Ministry of Navy (Kamo, Kaigun Daijin Kanbō, and Rikugun Daijin Kanbō 1933–35). The title, *Yasukuni Jinja Chūkonshi* (The history of the loyal souls to the emperor at Yasukuni Shrine), makes evident that the character of the shrine had undergone basic changes. "Falling cherry petals" became the emblem of soldiers' sacrifice for the emperor, and ten pink petals were emblazoned on the book jacket of each volume).[9]

Arguably the most important strategy of the government for its "nationalization" was its proclamation in 1872 that Emperor Jinmu had acceded to the imperial throne on 11 February, 2,600 years earlier. In order to "validate" this invention for the people, the government invented a series of imperial rituals and synchronized their performance at the Imperial Palace with those at the local level, that is, at shrines and schools. The government had undertaken a thorough reorganization of over 170,000 shrines in order to connect them with the imperial rituals.

The most elaborate was the *genshisai*, a ritual to support Article 1 of the new constitution by enacting the mythical descent to earth of the grandson of the Sun Goddess, the first Emperor Jinmu. The annual ritual, to be held on 3 January of every year, was inaugurated in 1870. The next in importance was the *kigensetsu*. First instituted in 1872, it was a ritual to celebrate the accession of Jinmu, the legendary first emperor. The majority of the newly established rituals dealt with the imperial soul, as created in the Pledge of the Constitution of Imperial Japan. Of the twenty-one rituals, thirteen had to be officiated by the emperor himself and the rest by the specialist of rituals at the imperial court (Murakami 1977: 76–98, 132). At the same time, the imperial household began to use the archaic Japanese of the Heian period and became completely shielded from the people (182). The emperor became invisible as well as inaudible (Ohnuki-Tierney 2015: 175–80).

Like other authoritarian states, Japan embarked on the inculcation of the young through the nationalization of the school system. In 1873, the government codified that the school year would start in April, that is, the beginning of spring marked by cherry blossoms. This timing was gradually adopted, beginning in 1892 with elementary school, in 1901 for middle school, in 1919 for high school, and only in 1921 for the university. Since then, the beginning of the school year at all levels has been symbolically associated with full-bloom cherries.[10] The state deployed textbooks and school songs in the effort to nationalize the masses. The Ministry of Education issued a new series of school textbooks for the national language in 1932 that were used from 1933 to 1940.[11] They were commonly known as *Sakura Dokuhon* (The cherry blossom readers) and had a color illustration of full-bloom cherry blossoms on the cover and the first pages. The series ends with volume 12 for sixth graders, in which ten poems equating mountain cherry blossoms with the Japanese soul (*yamato damashii*) by well-known Edo-period intellectuals are cited. The last poem, by Takazaki Masakaze, expresses how lucky a human being is to be born in Japan, the country under the sun (Yamazumi 1970: 8–11).

Music underwent a drastic change during the same period, with an almost complete switch to the Western melodic pattern. In the very first music textbook for elementary schools, published in 1881, cherry blossoms appeared as a symbol of cultural nationalism, without militarism. Later, school songs and other songs became increasingly laden with political, nationalistic, and militaristic propaganda. A kindergarten song published in 1887, "Kazo'e Uta" (Counting song) (Horiuchi and Inoue [1958] 1995: 28–29), had been an innocent children's song in the Tokyo area during the Edo period, with lyrics by an unknown writer. The original text was much altered in the 1887 school song version and includes a blatant die-for-the-emperor ideology: "Mountain cherry blossoms, mountain cherry blossoms, even when they fall, it is for His Majesty." In 1888 the song "Kigensetsu" (the day commemorating the founding of the imperial system) was composed, following the government's 1872 proclamation, noted above, about Emperor Jinmu's accession to the imperial throne (30). The song, which became mandatory for pupils to sing, "portrayed" the Japanese as joyful and grateful for the emperor, the father of all Japanese, even though Jinmu was only a legendary figure.

The state continued to inculcate the people with the idea of falling petals symbolizing sacrifice for the emperor throughout the Taishō period (1912–26), even though more liberal and democratic trends were also developing (Duus 1988). This effort culminated in 1937, when Nobutoki Kiyoshi composed a melody with lyrics from a long poem from the *Manyōshū* by Ōtomo no Yakamochi (716–85), who was in charge of the imperial guards (*sakimori*) in ancient Japan. Although it does not contain references to cherry blossoms, it became the de facto national anthem, encouraging soldiers to die for the emperor:

> In the sea, waterlogged corpses,
> In the mountains, those corpses with grasses growing on them.
> But my desire to die next to our emperor is unflinching.
> I shall not look back. (Omodaka [1967] 1983: 86–91, poem #4094; my translation)

Nobutoki's song was broadcast on the day Japan entered World War II; it was played to accompany the silent prayer for the nine war deities who had perished at Pearl Harbor on 8 December (Japan time), and just before every *tokkōtai* (special attack force, a.k.a., "kamikaze") plane took off. The Imperial Rule Assistance Association (Taisei Yokusankai) (Kisaka 1996), founded in 1940 by Prime Minister Konoe to mobilize people for the war effort, declared that this song was next in importance to the national anthem for its "national subjects." Indeed, this "dirge" was broadcasted far more frequently than the national anthem, "Kimiga yo."

With the abolition of regional lords and the wave of "enlightenment and civilization" sweeping through Japan in early Meiji (1868–1912), castles were seen as useless vestiges of a wicked feudal age, ready to be turned into more useful spaces, such as public parks (Yamada [1941] 1993: 399–401). Having resurrected the "warrior's way" without the warriors, the state established the symbolic association between cherry blossoms and soldiers qua yesteryear's warriors by systematically planting cherry trees in castle compounds, despite protests by the former warriors that pine trees were their symbol (Takagi 1998: 1). Wherever a military unit was established, including at castles, cherry trees were planted. Many trees were planted to commemorate military victories, especially at the end of the Russo-Japanese War. As Sano Tōemon, a third-generation custodian of cherry trees, recollects, "cherry blossoms marched with the military" (Sano 1998: 95–96).

Cherry trees were also planted in the colonies to mark them as the territory of Imperial Japan and to give comfort to and encourage Japanese emigrants to continue the Japanese way of life, including the viewing of cherry blossoms (for Manchuria, see Kawamura 1998: 42–43). For the colonized Koreans, cherry trees planted by the Japanese on their land became the symbol of Japanese colonialism—far from beautiful or sublime. After World War II they chopped down those at the Kyongbok Palace in Seoul in preparation for the fiftieth anniversary of the liberation from Japanese colonialism. Their own king cherry has been emphasized as being distinct from the Japanese *someiyoshino*, as discussed in chapter 5.

The symbolism of falling cherry petals reached its height with the *tokkōtai* operation at the very end of World War II. None of these young men truly volunteered (see Ohnuki-Tierney 2006). When Japan was surrounded by American aircraft carriers whose sophisticated radar system would not allow any Japanese military attacks, the vice admirable of the navy, Ōnishi Takijirō, and his right-hand men thought this was the only solution appealing to the Japanese soul, which was supposed to be able to face death without hesitation. They hoped these soldiers would bring about the miracle of victory, like the time when the *shinpū* (God's wind, pronounced also as *kamikaze*) overturned Mongol ships in 1281, preventing their landing in Japan. The first army corps of *tokkōtai* was named *Shinpū*. The pilots wore white headbands with the rising sun in red and the two characters for "God's wind" (*shinpū*) in black calligraphy. A single cherry blossom in full bloom was painted in pink on the side of each plane, against a white background (Ebina 1977: 219) (figure 6.1). Many of the names chosen for the *tokkōtai* corps bore various Japanese words for cherry blossoms (Hattori 1991: 343; Ohnuki-Tierney 2002a: 163–66).

Cherry blossoms were called to duty to aestheticize the deaths of soldiers on the battlefield, followed by their resurrection at Yasukuni Shrine. Like cherry blossoms, which fall after a brief life, the young men sacrificed their lives for the emperor, but they were promised that they would be reborn as cherry blossoms at the national shrine where the emperor would pay homage. With the refashioning of the warrior's way, the flower was assigned to represent the souls of Japanese soldiers qua warriors, which "mandated" them to die without hesitation. The military construction of blooming cherry blossoms as apotheosized soldiers at the national shrine is most astonishing in that it represents a reversal of the ancient agrarian cosmological scheme in which the flower stood for life and prosperity.

130 | *Representations of "Japanese Nature"*

Figure 6.1. *Tokkōtai* (kamikaze) plane with a cherry petal on the side. Yasukuni Shrine. Courtesy of R. Kenji Tierney.

For Sasaki Hachirō, one of the *tokkōtai* (kamikaze) pilots, explicitly skeptical of the war ideology and both critical of and also sympathetic to Marxism, cherry blossoms first appeared as a sunny symbol of youth, beauty, and his enjoyment of young women passing by. Later the flower became a counterpoint to the prevailing frenzied atmosphere in wartime Japan. Still later, the mountain cherry, which blooms without expectation of praise, became a symbol of an ideal human being with modesty and purity, reminding him of the negative side of himself that sought and enjoyed honor and recognition from others. Ultimately, as the time for his sortie became closer, cherry blossoms became the symbol for pilots, including himself, falling like petals. At this point Sasaki directly linked cherry blossoms and the soldiers' deaths, but not as part of the *pro rege et patria mori* ideology. As their deaths became imminent, these student soldiers desperately tried to rationalize why they had to die in their youth.

While cherry blossoms were involved, as it were, in Japan's raging struggle over cosmopolitanism, modernization, and nationalism, they also became the state gift to other countries. The practice began with Mrs. Eliza Ruhamah Scidmore, who was to become the first woman board member of the National Geographic Society. The blossoms captured her attention during her trip to Japan in 1885. After twenty-four years of unsuccessful effort to persuade the US Army superintendent of the Office of Public Buildings and Grounds to plant Japanese cherry trees along the

Potomac River, in 1909 she wrote to then First Lady Helen Herron Taft to inform her of her intention to buy cherry trees from Japan to donate to the District of Columbia. Mrs. Taft responded that she had "taken the matter up" personally. This led to her acceptance of two thousand trees as a gift from Mayor Ozaki Yukio of Tokyo on 6 January 1910, which, however, the inspection team of the Department of Agriculture judged as diseased. President Taft consented to burn the trees on 28 January. Mr. Ozaki then made another shipment—this time of 3,020 trees—which arrived on 26 March 1912 and were planted at the Tidal Basin. In 1935 the District of Columbia commissioners sponsored a three-day celebration—the beginning of the world-famous Cherry Blossom Festival held annually, except during World War II (National Park Service 2009).

There have been other efforts to use cherry trees to establish friendly relations with other nations. At the request of Ōtani Kōzui, the head monk of Honganji monastery, one hundred thousand seedlings were planted along the Siberian railroad, a multinational endeavor undertaken from 1891 to 1916 in which not only the Russians but also the Japanese, Chinese, and Koreans were involved. The monk's intention was to link the Far East to Europe with cherry blossoms in order to establish peace throughout the world (Sano 1998: 54–55). The practice of offering cherry trees resumed after World War II.[12]

Mount Fuji

During the Edo period, Mount Fuji became a dominant symbol of *cultural* nationalism. During the modern period, it also became a dominant symbol of *political* nationalism, as Japan began its colonial expansion and engage in external wars, ambitious to become an empire. A most revealing part of the militarization of "Japanese nature" was the renaming of the aforementioned popular magazine *Kingu* (King), an English word, to *Fuji* in the March issue of 1943 (Satō 2002: 358–72). Mount Fuji as a symbol of Japanese nature stood for the moral height and the eternal life of the Japanese. By the time the magazine was renamed, it was full of warmongering catchphrases and writings, including anti-American manifestos. Reflecting the underlying awareness that the war was not leading to Japan's victory, the theme of *kessen* (decisive last battle) frequently appeared. One of the 1944 magazine covers reproduced in Satō (2002: 369) has a photo of a kamikaze plane with a young pilot.

Between 1926 and 1947, sixteen postage stamps with a picture of Mount Fuji were issued by the government (Torii et al, eds. 1998: 197). Beginning in 1881 there have been two school songs and four text books contain passages in praise of Mt. Fuji (Torii, et al. 1998: 196).

Mount Fuji even became a pattern on kimonos. In *Wearing Propaganda: Textiles on the Home Front in Japan, Britain, and the United States, 1931–1945* (Atkins, ed. 2005), Fuji appears as the background in a number of kimono designs whose major motifs were fighter planes, soldiers, the Rising Sun flag, and many symbols representing Japan's technological and military advances (plates #3–17, 8–9, 9–5, 9–6, 13–13). In one of them (2005: 8–9) the caption reads, "Mount Fuji looms as an iconic symbol of Japan." And in another plate (no. 13–32) the caption explains, "Empire and modernization . . . Mount Fuji, the anchor of tradition."

Summary

During the modern periods, there was an even more intensive and extensive nationalization of "Japanese nature" under the auspices of the government. Julia Thomas (2002) details how the state exercised power in the process of establishing the image of Japanese love of nature and Japan's unique harmony with nature. The people were told where to go for "stupendous views" (*zekkei*), even though increased tourism undoubtedly had a negative impact on these *zekkei*. Furthermore, Japan expanded "Japanese nature" to its colonies by planting cherry trees. Thus, during this period, it was the government that identified Japanese nature for the people, who had been nationalized far more than during the previous period.

The three dominant symbols of Japanese nature—Mount Fuji, rice, and cherry blossoms—went through a series of changes in their meaning during Japan's periods of intense nationalization and militarization. Mount Fuji became an important symbol of Japan with its eternal life. As the West became Japan's dominant Other, the symbols of opposition were rice versus meat. Cherry blossoms became the symbol of loyal soldiers who offered their lives to the emperor and would be reborn at Yasukuni Shrine, guaranteeing the continuation of the Japanese and Japan.

During this time, there was an even more intensive and extensive nationalization of "Japanese nature" under the auspices of the government, which Thomas (2002) considers a process of "political modernity," pointing out the political uses of "nature" from the nineteenth to the early twentieth century.

Notes

1. The Japan Travel Bureau was created in 1912 for research on tourist recreation and travels. It underwent some changes in its name and operations. In 2008, it became JTB Corp.
2. To eat while squatting signifies a major breach of proper eating manners. To sit on one's legs (*seiza*) was and still is the proper way to eat. Thus, meat eating brought a drastic change in eating manners.
3. For example, the buildings of Kōfukuji, a famous temple in Nara, were destroyed. The five-story pagoda was sold to a person who wanted to melt it down for scrap metal (Murakami, Tsuji and Washio 1970: 103–5, 171–72; Ōta 1979: 164; Saeki 1988: 160–62; Yamada [1941] 1993: 400).
4. Motoori's self-portrait and the poem, written when he was sixty-one years old in 1790, appear on the cover of volume 1 of his collected works (Motoori [1790] 1968).
5. Some consider Motoori Norinaga responsible for establishing a link between cherry blossoms and the Japanese ethos of *monono aware*, the pathos of evanescence. However, in his voluminous work on *Genji* (e.g., Motoori [1790] 1968: esp. 201–42), he could not find any systematic link between cherry blossoms and the ethos of pathos. His major thesis is that *monono aware* constitutes the essence of Japanese literary and visual arts and is not a product either of the Buddhist worldview or of Confucian doctrine (e.g., 25–26).
6. Nitobe's book became a major source for non-Japanese who wished to know the secret of how Japan, a tiny, hitherto unknown Asian country, had gained victory over Russia, a mighty Western nation, in the Russo-Japanese War. Nitobe's text was a major influence on Ruth Benedict's *The Chrysanthemum and the Sword* ([1946] 1967).
7. See Tsubouchi (1999) p. 29 and the book jacket for the circus, and pp. 69 and 73 for horse racing. The circus was also performed at Asakusa Temple (Tōkyō to Edo Tōkyō Hakubutsukan 1993: 106).
8. In the promulgation issued on 20 October 1870, the government (still called Dajōkan) specified the insignia for the navy as a single-petal blossom, leaves, and buds around an anchor, and for the army as a cherry blossom only in the design on the buttons on the uniform for those above the rank of second lieutenant (*shōi*) (Ōta 1980: 49, 131). In later years the army included cherry blossoms in many of its insignias. The buds are also significant because they represented young men, who were told to fall like cherry petals after a beautiful but short life.
9. The front cover of the original cloth edition in indigo has ten falling cherry petals in pink and the title in gold. The back cover has five falling cherry petals. On the spine are the title and "the editors, Yasukuni Shrine, under the supervision of the Ministry of Army and Ministry of Navy" in gold. The falling cherry petals do not appear on all copies. A copy of volume 4 at the Far Eastern Library at the University of Chicago, donated by Yamazaki Tōji, has a cover with a design of falling cherry petals. But no other volumes had this

design. None of the five at the University of California, Berkeley, donated by the Mitsui family, has the cherry petal design.
10. In 2012 the University of Tokyo and eleven other universities proposed to change the beginning of the school year to autumn in an effort to coordinate with academic calendars outside of Japan and promote globalization of Japanese academia, including acceptance of foreign students—a part of the government's policy known as Global 30, which officially ended in 2013–14 (Monbu Kagakushō G30 Uebbu Saito (G30 Website), 2017.
11. The first volume, *Shōgaku Kokugo Dokuhon*, was published in 1932 and the last, volume 12, in 1938 (Kaigo 1964a: 539). An extensive socioeconomic and political context of the history of textbooks is in Kaigo (1964b: 609–14).
12. Today, Japanese newspapers annually report the blooming of these cherry blossoms in the United States, often photographed against the background of the Capitol building. A commemorative stamp issued in 1975, when the emperor and empress visited the United States, depicted an American flag in the center with cherry blossoms clustered beneath it. The Japanese Association for Flowers (Nihon Hana no Kai), a private organization, donated 1,500 seedlings to Bulgaria for the 1,300th anniversary of the country; 5,000 seedlings to Versailles in France; and more seedlings to Iran and Hamburg, Germany (Kawai and Ōta 1982: 93), to Australia in 1987 (*Asahi Shinbun*, 7 November 1997), to Uzbekistan in 2002 (*Asahi Shinbun*, 12 June 2002), and to Beijing in 2003 (*Japan Times*, 19 February 2003). Several Japanese "sister" municipalities and private organizations pledged to plant one thousand cherry trees along the Danube River and in other sections of Vienna by the year 2000 (*Asahi Shinbun*, 30 April 1996).

Part IV
"Nature" Consumed

CHAPTER 7

Domestication/Commodification of "Japanese Nature"
Contemporary Period (after 1945)

While the forces of intensive urbanization, nationalization, and militarization have been pushing "nature" away and replacing it with culturalized "Japanese nature," the enormously powerful force of capitalism has been at work since at least the early seventeenth century, reaching its crescendo during the contemporary period. This chapter outlines the co-prosperity between consumerism and the cosmological principle as it relates to nature. In chapter 8, I will turn to a theoretical understanding of the phenomenon.

"Domestication" of Nonhuman Inhabitants

The term "domestication" is somewhat misleading, since it has been used in the context of plant and animal domestication in history. In this section, I use it to refer to the way the nonhuman inhabitants of Japanese nature are brought into the human sphere as pets. Pets are different from other animals that are loved and cared for by humans but also serve humans, such as horses and cows as farm animals.

In the Japanese use, "pets" include two types: companion animals and "beloved toy animals"—small animals *kept inside* as personal companions. The classifications are more traditional than legal and also somewhat arbitrary. Thus, goldfish and caged insects are enjoyed inside, but they are not really "beloved toy animals," to which only the miniature dogs kept inside belong, even though other dogs are kept outside as pets. In recent years the government has instituted some regulations, such as the Law to Protect Animals, first legislated in 1973.

Goldfish—Fish Not from Nature

The goldfish was an accidental mutation of carp in southern China around the third to fourth century CE. Raising goldfish began during the latter half of the tenth century in China. The name "goldfish" was chosen since it was thought to bring good financial fortune and has been treasured as a "living art"—a *fish that is not from nature*. During the fourteenth through sixteenth centuries, raising them in porcelain bowls and pots became popular. The practice was first introduced to Osaka, Japan, at the end of the Muromachi period (1338–1573) and was brought in a number of times from China during the cyclical conquest era (1477–1573), but the sociopolitical situation was too volatile for people to appreciate the fish. During the Genroku period (1688–1704), shops selling goldfish emerged, but the fish remained expensive. It was a hobby enjoyed only by the elite. In the middle of the Edo period (1603–1868) it became a "beloved toy" for the masses. Consequently, the fish and activities associated with it were depicted in a number of well-known woodblock prints and other visual and literary products. In Yamatokōriyama in Nara Prefecture right after the Meiji Restoration in 1868, which abolished the warrior class, the lower-class warriors who had lost their means for living began the "mass production" of goldfish, lowering the price and making them available for the folk (Ishida 1996; Matsui 1942).

The first book on goldfish was *Kingyo Sodatekusa* (How to raise goldfish) by Adachi Yoshiyuki, published in 1748. It is written on rice paper with a brush, with a number of excellent illustrations of the fish. Andō was from Sakai, Osaka, the commercial hub introduced in chapter 4. Japanese who are old enough still remember the sight of wooden boxes with goldfish swimming in them at open markets where children could scoop goldfish with a little net and buy them. These outdoor markets have become very few in number in recent years.

Insects

As described in chapter 3, by the Heian period the tradition of listening to the sounds of insects was well established among the courtiers at the palace and became popular among the folk during the mid-Edo period, leading to the birth of an occupation of "selling insects." They were usually captured in the countryside and sold in Edo and other cities so that the urbanites would feel reassured of their closeness to "nature." Initially, insects were placed in a small cage, usually made of fine strips of bamboo, but they began to be put in lacquerware containers for daimyo and other wealthy people; insects had also become a standard feature, along with goldfish, at open markets and were much enjoyed by children and adults (Umeya 2005). According to the record kept from the late Meiji period (1868–1912) to the beginning of the Shōwa period (1926–89), of the ninety-three households in the Kamiyachi district in Kanazawa, individuals from some fifty households traveled to cities to sell insects, primarily pine crickets (*matsumushi*) and bell crickets (*suzumushi*). The rest of the households helped capture the insects. In the beginning they captured them in the mountains in the back of the village, but with the construction of the railroad in 1898, they went all the way to the dunes of the Noto peninsula, known for the abundance of pine crickets. They sold the insects in Kyoto to the west, Toyama to the east, and Takayama in Gifu Prefecture to the south. This business from Kamiyauchi was terminated in 1965, primarily due to overharvesting (Daimon 2012). The final blow to the practice was the economic boom of the 1980s, which led to drastic changes in the Japanese lifestyle through intense Americanization/Westernization (Umeya 2005), as the Japanese chose other forms of entertertainmant and hobbies.

Rabbits

As noted in chapter 2, field rabbits (*no-usagi*) were too good not to eat, and therefore the folk circumvented the official prohibition against eating four-legged animals by counting rabbits' legs using the term for birds' legs.

While field rabbits never became pets, imported rabbits became outside pets of warlords and later the wealthy. The "rabbit mania," referred to in Japanese as *usagi babburu* (rabbit bubble), took place in Tokyo for eight years between 1871 and 1879, the very beginning of the Meiji period. It was a time when wealthy people, like the former warriors, lost their fortunes because of their drastic change of status under the Meiji government, and as a result they sold imported rabbits that they had kept as pets. Since rabbits provide meat for food and fur for clothing and rapidly multiply, they became a favorite item for sale, leading to a craze over the purchase and sale of rabbits even by ordinary people. The Tokyo municipal government became concerned and started to require registration, levy taxes, and prohibit auction meetings, leading to the end of this mania in 1879.

An even more dramatic rabbit mania for investment took place in 1930–31 when Japan was in the midst of an economic depression. Referred to as *Angora Kyōran* (Angora craze), it was over the investment in and sale of imported Angora rabbits, favored for their soft and long hair to be used for clothing (Fuji'i 1938).

Dogs

During the hunting-gathering Jomon period, dogs were used for hunting and other activities by the Jomon people, who did not eat them and buried them in graves. During the subsequent periods they became a source of food (Kobayashi 2008: 111–15).

CHIN

The miniature dogs as "beloved toy animals," known in English as the Japanese "chin," are very small dogs with silky long hair. They were artificially bred quite early in history and have gone through artificial breeding a number of times. What we know today as chin date to the Meiji period. They originated in Tibet and came to Japan via China and Korea. The kanji character for this dog had to be invented in Japan since there was no Chinese character for it. It consists of a left radical used to identify it as an animal and a radical on the right meaning "middle" since they were dogs, which should be kept outside the house. Yet chins lived inside, like cats—the only inside pets in early times (Taniguchi 2012: 79, 81, 176) (https://ja.wikipedia.org/wiki/chin).

According to *Shoku Nihonki*, Shilla, an ancient Korean kingdom (57 BCE–935 CE), made a tribute of a dog to the Japanese imperial court in 732 CE. It is quite unlikely that the dog was a chin. There are a number of other early sources in which a dog is mentioned, but none of these was a chin (https://ja.wikipedia.org/wiki/chin).

Perhaps the best source for information about the pets in the lives of the Heian elite is *Makura no Sōshi*, by Sei Shōnagon (2007), who served Empress Consort Teishi during the 990s and early 1000s. The book was likely completed in the year 1000 or 1002. It was the time of Emperor Ichijō (980–1011), who was infamous for his excessive love of his cats. Some of the scenes at the court, such as essay #7 (#9 in some editions), indicate they had cats inside and dogs outside. During the cyclical conquest era large dogs were imported by the Portuguese and became a status symbol for top warriors, symbolizing their power. They were kept outside.

During the Edo period, the fifth shogun, Tokugawa Tsunayoshi, was notorious for protecting animals even to the detriment of people. He issued the infamous Law of Compassion for All Living Beings in 1682, which protected all the animals and imposed severe punishments for people who were not kind to them. He was known as the "Dog Shōgun" because of his obsessive love of dogs. Chins were his favorite, and he ordered two daimyōs to acquire a large number of chins, which were transported in luxurious carriages to the Edo castle, as described in *Sannōgaiki* (Jin Yōshi), an Edo-period historical chronicle of the lives of the three shoguns (Tsunayoshi, Iyenobu, and Iyetsugu) (Taniguchi 2012: 80). They were treated like the Heian aristocrats, always transported in a carriage so that their feet did not have to touch the ground.

MILITARIZATION OF DOGS

Although the practice of having chins and other pets inside the house continued during the later periods, information in the modern period is about dogs used by humans for specific services. For example, "military dogs" were used by the government right after World War I when it imported German shepherds. After the Manchurian Incident in 1931 they became useful as messengers and guard dogs, leading to the celebration of their military uses. However, in later wars modern military technology became too advanced for the use of dogs. Many were left behind when Japan lost the war in 1945 and soldiers returned to Japan proper. There is a monument at Yasukuni Shrine in memory of these dogs.

The story of Hachikō became the model for the idea of dogs as nonhuman animals that serve humans. Professor Ueno Eisaburō in the Department of Agriculture at the Imperial University of Tokyo adopted Hachikō as a puppy. It was shipped to him in January 1924, fifty days after its birth. Hachikō was a purebreed of the highly prized Akita lineage. Professor Ueno took tender care of it. The two left home every morning for the Shibuya rail station, where the professor said goodbye to Hachikō, who came back to the station in the late afternoon to await the professor's return. Only seventeen months later, Professor Ueno unexpectedly passed away while talking to his colleague at the university. During the funeral and the wake, as the story goes, Hachikō stayed near his clothes and fasted for three days. Hachikō then resumed the routine and looked for him in the morning and in the afternoon until he died on 8 March 1935.

Saitō Hirokichi, the foremost scholar of dogs, especially Akita and other Japanese breeds, learned about Hachikō and wrote an article about him in the *Asahi* newspaper that touched the hearts of many people. In 1934, a year before Hachiko's death, a statue was erected at Shibuya station.

Since Hachikō lived during the height of the escalating militarism in Japan, the government seized the opportunity to use the story to demonstrate the importance of *on*, profound gratitude toward someone—for example, gratitude toward the emperor, parents, and teachers. Chapter 26 of volume 2 of the Ministry of Education's textbook on morality was entitled "Do Not Forget *On*" (Monbushō 1934: 74–77). Hachikō became the model for a human who would not forget what he/she received. As World War II accelerated, the government issued an ordinance to collect all metal objects, even rings, to be melted and reused for military purposes. On the day before Japan surrendered, the Hachikō statue was melted down at the Hamamatsu factory of the Japanese railroad. In 1947 sculptor Andō Takeshi created another statue, which stands at Shibuya station today (moved a short distance as the plaza was expanded). It is an important landmark for young dating couples, for many of whom such notions as *on* (gratefulness) and *chū* (loyalty to the emperor) are no longer familiar moral codes. In 1987, a movie, *Hachikō Monogatari* (The story of Hachikō), introduced the phrase "*Chūken* Hachikō" (loyal dog), although it also stressed the love between a human and a nonhuman animal. Saitō Hiroyoshi, who first made Hachikō famous in his newspaper article, pointed out that it was love between Professor Ueno and Hachikō, like a parent and a child, and had nothing to do with the moral of loyalty to the emperor. (Information on Hachikō is in a number of sources, including Oda 2020 and Tōkyō Daigaku 2013.)

Contemporary Pet Boom

In contemporary Japan, there have been several "pet booms," as the Japanese have adopted the English term "boom" to refer to these sudden surges of popularity. They sometimes call it "nekonomics" because *neko* in Japanese means a cat, combined with "economics." The first was in the 1950s when people moved to the suburbs and required watchdogs. For ten years, Spitz was the favorite breed, since it is small enough to be a "beloved toy dog" yet barks loudly to warn of the approach of a stranger. The second pet boom took place with the bubble economy, hitting a peak in the 1980s when affluence set in. Between 1968 and 1984, the highest numbers of registered dogs were Maltese, Pomeranians, and Yorkshire Terriers. The popularity of Siberian Huskies, spurred by the movie *South Pole* in 1983, was short lived.

Beginning in the early 1990s, "companion animals," such as miniature Dachshunds, long-haired Chihuahuas, and toy Poodles became the first choice. They were called "cuddling dogs." These more recently imported dogs reduced the popularity of chin.

The government takes a survey of pet owners every so many years. In 2003, 36.5 percent of the Japanese had a pet or pets; in 2010, 34.3 percent; and in 2020, 30.4 percent. Usually dogs are most numerous, followed by cats, goldfish, tropical fish, and birds, although their popularity fluctuates. Every survey is partial, since there is a great deal of variation, depending on the region and class.

The 2003 survey reports the reasons for having a pet:

1. The family members like animals—46.8 percent (1983); 53.2 percent (1990); 57.2 percent (2000); 60.5 percent (2003).

2. A pet makes you feel relaxed (*kimochi ga yawarageru [magireru] kara*)—19.4 percent (1983); 27.9 percent (1990); 45.2 percent (2000); 47.9 percent (2003).

According to a survey by Pet Food Industry (Pettohūdo Kyōkai), in 2020, there were 8,489,000 dogs and 9,64,4000 cats as pets. It is often said that the need for companionship resulted in part from changes in living arrangements—increasingly older people are living alone, rather than with their children and their families.

However, subsequent or other "pet booms" are different, requiring some other explanation. The pet boom of recent years is among relatively wealthy people for whom pet ownership is a status symbol. Many are quite young—in their twenties and thirties—and they are usually women but also sometimes men, as I observed in the shopping district Azabu-Jūbangai, where there are two pet stores. These women and men have their pets—almost all imported miniature dogs—walk on the street with a leash. More often than not, the owner makes sure to keep the paws of the dog from touching the ground. It started with owners carrying their "inside dog" like a baby, as I observed in Kyoto in 2019. Then, the "pet cart," called *kyarī baggu kāto* (carry bag cart), industries moved. The owner puts his or her dog in the cart and walks on the street so that the pet takes a "walk " while in a cart so that its paws do not touch the ground (figure 7.1; book cover). Almost all these pet dogs are clad in facy attire, including a hat. This practice fueled the pet cart industry. Amazon, Rakuten Ichiba (a Japanese equivalent of Amazon), and other internet sellers featured some twenty to thirty different pet carts with prices from around ¥5,000 ($34.25 in September, 2024) to close to ¥90,000 ($616.52 in September, 2024) in 2021. The prices remained similar in 2024. It is not hard to spot these dogs in a cart in major cities like Tokyo and Kyoto. At Mitsubishi UFUJI Bank at Roppongi, Tokyo, a notice in the elevator states: "Please put your dog, if you have one, in a cart so that it does not bother other customers." That is, pet owners are expected to have pet carts so that the animals do not walk on the floor of the bank.

The governmental rules for carring a pet in a train stipulate that it has to be in a case that is no more than 120 cm in total (length, width, and height) and weighs less than 10 kg, with a ticket for ¥290 per case. Many carry a pet in a special "backpack" carried in the front of the person, with a transparent window on one side so that the dog can see outside.

Other businesses that took advantage of the pet boom include the pet food industry, which eliminated the practice of feeding leftovers from family meals to dogs. Since many dogs are still kept outside, home building companies avidly advertise and urge people to build a "pet friendly" house so that they can keep their pets inside.

144 | *Representations of "Japanese Nature"*

Figure 7.1. An inside dog in a "pet cart." Photo by the author.

Memorial Services and Burials for Pets

While pet cemeteries exist in France, Germany, and several other countries, the arrival of pet memorial services and burials in Japan is recent, as are those for aborted fetuses, which appeared during the period of Japan's economic boom (Ohnuki-Tierney 1984a: 78–81). The reason for the practice, as offered by religious institutions and businesses, is the belief in the soul of all beings of the universe, leading to posthumous care of their souls by creating cemeteries, funeral parlors, and related facilities and activities. There is an expensive posthumous expenditure for the care of pets. The price for cremation depends on the weight and size of the pet, as well as the mode of service, which includes private cremation or cremation together with pets owned by others; the family's attendance during the cremation; and cremation at home, in which case a special truck equipped with the cremation facility comes. In 2021, according to a website, the fee started from ¥12,000 for an animal up to 2 kg, such as a bird, hamster, or chipmunk. If cremated together with the pets of other owners, it cost ¥52,000 for an animal over 40 kg, such as a Tosa dog or St. Bernard. The ashes can be placed in one's yard, in the owner's family tomb, or in a pet cemetery with an expensive tombstone. In Tokyo proper, there are about ten of these pet cemeteries, called *rei'en* (garden for the souls), and the charge for the burial of ashes ranges from ¥50,000 to ¥10,000, depending on the type of burial. They often advertise on the walls of train stations.

Given the premise that all beings of the universe have a soul, memorial services for them are not alien even to contemporary Japanese. The one for whales has a long history and is well known today in part due to mass media reports. A number of temples offer the memorial services for whales and some forty-three temples have a stele in their compound, just like those for humans, although without names, with the oldest dated to 1671 (Freeman 1989: 159). Memorial services are performed also for what we call inanimate objects, of which the best known are the rituals for used needles and for dolls, which have a long tradition. No tax is levied on the income from officiating these services. In 2005, Jimyōin, the Organization of Religious Institutions at Kasugai City in Aichi Prefecture, filed a lawsuit against the tax office, requesting the exemption of ¥670,000, claiming that memorial services for pets are religious acts and should be interpreted the same as the memorial services for needles and dolls. The Nagoya District Court rejected the suit (*Asahi Shinbun*, 24 March 2005). On 12 September 2006, the Japanese Supreme Court also rejected the suit and ruled that taxes must be levied for income from the pet memorial services provided by temples and shrines.

Businesses have come up with everything imaginable that can be sold to grieving owners whose pets have died. They include an alcove for ¥18,000 for the deceased pet, just like those for deceased family members, with special incense for ¥770.[1]

Clean Pets

Although not welcome by the pet food industry, technological advancement introduced two types of "clean pets": Tamagotchi and robot pets. The wildly popular Tamagotchi is a virtual reality pet. Housed in a tiny computer, usually egg shaped (*tamago* in *Tamagotchi* means "egg"), it allows the owner to "nurture" a pet from the time it is an egg to its death, which can occur easily if the owner neglects to care for it (Yokoi 1997). The owner can create a pet that does every conceivable activity, including going to the toilet, eating at restaurants, getting married, and going overseas, while *remaining clean* in a small plastic case. This handheld digital pet was created in Japan by Akihiro Yokoi of WiZ and Aki Maita of Bandai, and released in Japan by Bandai on 23 November 1996; in May 1997 it was introduced to the rest of the world. It became one of the biggest toy fads in the 1990s and early 2000s. By 2019, over eighty-two million Tamagotchis had been sold worldwide. In the summer of 2019, a strong revival of its popularity took place in the United States.

The Tamagotchi is an excellent example of simulacrum or hyperreality. Some consider that it cultivates a nurturing attitude and love of animals in children. Others say that it gives a false sense of relationship between humans and nonhuman animals. The owner must clean the daily mess of the pet without ever handling it. It also simulates the life cycle, including death, without real experiences and associated emotions. In general, this seems to be one more example of the cardinal rule of avoiding ground/dirt while allowing "animals" to come into the human sphere.

Another "clean pet" is the Robot Pet. According to an advertisement from Rakuten Ichiba in December 2024, robot dogs and cats are the most numerous, although there are others, for example, one parrot, one lizard, and one animal-like round cushion made of very soft material with a tail. The prices range from around ¥3,000 to ¥22,000, with much higher prices for other companion robots.[2] Each has special features: to serve as a friend, to talk, to cuddle, to behave like a family member, to *amaeru* (excessively express affection) while wagging its tail, and so on.

The extent of the success, as it were, of the pet boom may be shown by the birth of the "trust" for dogs called "NPO Corporation Pet Life Net," which guarantees the care of the pet even after the death of the owner, at which time the pet goes to the corporation (*Asahi Shinbun*, 23 March 2024). Another indication is the "pet hotels," which began to emerge in the 1960s with a big pet hotel at Narita airport built in 2005 with the cost depending upon the size and weight of the pet. The emergence of pet hotels indicates that the old custom of keeping dogs outside the house has yielded to the practice of keeping them inside the house (*Asahi Shinbun*, 30 March 2024).

"Nature Foods from Purified Ground"

Another important dimension of "nature" in the lives of contemporary Japanese is "natural food." Concern over food safety has been a phenomenal development in many, especially highly industrialized, societies. While meat, poultry, and fish sold in the United States are often labeled with information about where they were caught or how they were raised (cage free, free range, fed only plant food, etc.), most conspicuous is the emphasis on "natural food," which is only loosely conceptualized as food grown, not processed; as food that has not been genetically modified; and as food free from chemical fertilizers, pesticides, preservatives, and artificial ingredients. Psychologist Paul Rozen, in a personal communication, pointed out to me that the lay American concept of "natural" is such that our corn (domesticated, with five to six gene changes by human intervention) is natural, but a wild wolf with one gene inserted that affects its fur thickness is highly unnatural.

In Japan, there were some earlier movements to promote "natural food," such as macrobiotics, by Sakurazawa Nyoichi (1893–1966). His advocacy of natural food was based on yin/yang philosophy and Shintoism, linking animal meat with yin and thus designating it carcinogenic (Sakurazawa 1938). Taking the name George Ohsawa, he traveled overseas widely to propagate his natural food as medical treatment.[3]

Natural food (*shizenshoku*) became enormously popular in the 1980s, driven not only by concerns about health in general but also by the cancer scare. There have been a number of "fads"—various foods were said to be the best for the prevention of cancer. The National Life Bureau was reorganized to become the Consumer Affairs Agency in 2009. They identified two categories of food for the promotion of health: "functional food" and "designated health food."

The former avoids harmful elements, especially fat and sugar. The latter "designates" certain foods and food combinations that positively contribute to health. The makers are required to get governmental permission before selling functional food. For designated health food, the seal of government approval is given and the manufacturers place it on their products.

The current emphasis, at least among some segments of the population in Japan, as in the United States, is on "organic food." In Japan it must carry the government's seal of approval, whose design consists of the sun, a plant in the middle, and a cloud, with the English-alphabet acronym JAS (Japanese Agricultural Standard). "The local," that is, locally grown products, are emphasized in Japan as in the United States. The term means geographically local: a restaurant must use vegetables *grown* in the same area where the store is located. As elsewhere, there is considerable emphasis on *terroir* in Japan—tangerines must be from Kishū and the best Japanese tea is from Shizuoka. On its package, every food item tells where it was produced. Also, the labels for pickles, rice crackers, and a large number of other products specify which company in which city made them. Kyoto is well known for a variety of pickles made from plants grown on the foothills and mountains that surround the city. The practice extends to produce. At supermarkets, every vegetable, such as spinach, potatoes, and asparagus, is sold with a label next to it stating the prefecture of its production and that it is a "domestic product," the term ubiquitous today in Japan guaranteeing consumers that it is "domestic" and thus "safe" for consumption.⁴ Some restaurants, like the one at the International House of Japan, even put on the menu where the ingredients came from. The emphasis, however, is different from the "domestic products" in the United States, which emphasizes "domestic" for economic and political reasons. In Japan, the sole aim is to guarantee the hygienic standard. For this purpose, supermarket ads are meticulous, in the store as well as in their advertisements, in informing where the products they sell are from, including those from abroad.

In Japan today "natural food" is equated with plant food, which leads to "natural therapy" using natural medicine, *shōyaku*, and the Chinese-derived medical system (Ohnuki-Tierney 1984a: 91–122). This comes from the concern about meats as possibly carcinogenic. There are a large number of websites with detailed information about the natural foods and organic foods and where they are sold.

As in the United States, these specially designated foods tend to be more expensive and thus are marketed primarily to the wealthier in urban centers. F & F is a chain natural food store. According to their pamphlet, in 2024 it has twenty-one stores in Tokyo, six in the nearby prefecture of Kanagawa, and three more in other nearby prefectures. They emphasize no chemicals, no additives, and no gluten, including gluten-free bread made from rice, not from wheat. In Tokyo in 2024, there are 164 stores that are not exclusively for "natural foods" but sell organic vegetables and other organic foods. In Kanagawa there are 97; in Saitama 40; in Chiba 36; in Osaka-fu 69; in Kyoto 46; in Hyōgo 50; in Hiroshima 33; in Fukuoka 64; and in Okinawa 33.

In the debate over food, the "chemical" has become the chief villain. It is not only "not natural" but also allegedly kills nature and humans. This has been an important concern for the Japanese for some time. It came to the surface in 1993 when US president Bill Clinton tried to open the Japanese market to American imports, which involved forcing the Japanese to import rice, an act of symbolic importance. By then the consumption of rice had been reduced, with affluence enabling the Japanese to emphasize side dishes. A great quantity of rice with a small number of side dishes came to be regarded as the diet of the poor, leading "haute cuisine" to have only a small amount of rice. Yet, there was an uproar over Clinton's push. Almost all the Japanese—Prime Minister Hosokawa, government officials, farmers' unions, and even consumers—objected to this as a repeat of Commodore Perry's opening of the Japanese market (for details, see Ohnuki-Tierney 1995).

The most telling Japanese concern over foods of "foreign" origin was California rice, which was raised from Japanese seeds and had no apparent difference from Japan's domestic rice, either in appearance or taste.

But the opponents of rice importation argued that foreign rice contained *chemicals* from insecticides and from processing. Consumer groups became intensely involved in checking for chemicals in foreign rice, some voicing their fears in newspapers, which also reported the "presence" of molds and bad odor on Chinese rice and dead mice in Thai rice, "reaffirming" the *impurity* of imported rice.[5]

Not surprisingly, the attack on the impurity—that is, the hazards—of foreign rice was coupled with the argument for the purity of Japanese rice. The Japanese argued that rice paddies are essential for Japanese land, functioning as flood control by serving as dams and promoting soil conservation, preservation of underground water, purification of air and water, and beautification of the land. We see the recurrence here of the spatial metaphor of rice paddies as *our nature*. California rice, in contrast, is grown in American paddies, thus serving *their* land and water. The equation of self-sufficiency (*jikyū jisoku*) with the exclusive reliance on domestic rice was a frequent discursive trope. Other metaphors for rice included: the lifeblood crop, the lifeline (*seimeisen*); the last sacred realm (*saigo no seiiki*); the national life; and the prototype of Japanese culture. According to Inoue (1988: 103), the common sentiment was that "American rice would not clear the air, nor would it adorn the scenery with beautiful green." In short, Japanese rice sustains Japanese nature, which is blessed with clean air and beautiful plants (Ohnuki-Tierney 1995: 234–42).

The Japanese Four Seasons

In contemporary Japan, the "official" view of four seasons, codified during the Nara and Heian periods, is still used. Number 19 (2016) of the magazine *Niponica*, published by the Ministry of Foreign Affairs of Japan, is on "Changing Seasons." In this issue, the "four seasons" are those defined in *Manyōshū* and *Kokinwakashū* of the Nara and Heian periods. As the magazine, entitled "Japanese Nature in Four Seasons," purports to introduce Japan, it promotes "Japanese nature in four seasons" in a number of ways, including through information for tourists.

On the other hand, in 2024, common lament I heard was about climate change. According to many, in Japan there is no more spring and fall as enduring periods, sandwiched between a long winter and long summer. Nevertheless, they were extremely anxious for the cherry blossoms to bloom, since they signal "spring." The Asahi newspaper published on 30 March 2024 a survey of people answering the question "Do you go for cherry blossoms viewing?" Of the 2,816 respondents, 65 percent said "yes," while 35 percent said "no." The reasons for going to the viewing were "to feel spring" (1,504 individuals), "to celebrate spring" (1,173 individuals), "to have the feeling of walking / going for picnic" (728 individuals), and "to take photos" (502 individuals). The predominant reasons for not participating were their dislike/fear of crowds and their preference for viewing the blossoms at home. The survey tells that they have "invented" two new types of viewing: solo viewing (viewing alone) and *e'a* viewing (viewing on "air" [TV]). The responses also indicate the impact of COVID-19, which made them avoid crowds. In Japan in 2024, almost everyone wore a mask.

Perhaps the most enduring example of this temporal division is the rules for writing letters and announcements (see Shirane 2012: 213). Today the rules are online, widely available for consultation. For proper correspondence, each letter or announcement must start with the right reference to nature—the temperature or weather, plants, and (though less obligatory) birds and other animals they see or are supposed to see, but not necessarily the ones assigned during the early periods. Using the Gregorian calendar, a letter written in March, for example, would refer to the early spring and *higanzakura* (whose botanical name is *Prunus itosakura*)—the native cherry trees recorded since the Heian period and the first to bloom before other variety of cherry trees—and to the lovely singing of the Japanese bush warbler, adding, however, a warning about remaining winter coldness. For April, a correspondence would start with a reference to the warm weather, the blooming of mountain cherry trees and the cherry trees of the *someiyoshino* variety (a hybrid cherry, and the most numerous of all cherry trees). It would also refer to hibari (the Eurasian Skylark (*Alauda arvensis*))—one of the three singing birds for the Japanese. Also important is a warning for health with the changing of the seasons.

Foods for Four Seasons

Until recently, every recipe book divided its contents into four sections for the four seasons. Tatsumi Hamako was a highly regarded author of a number of cookbooks. Her 1960 book is divided into five sections, each specializing in a certain cooking method, such as broiling or frying. Each section is divided into four—four seasons, with recipes for the type of cooking for each section. Her 2002 book, entitled *Ryōri Saijiki* (Culinary almanac), featured recipes for each season. While the four-seasons approach to fish is not surprising, a whole book on the four seasons for salad and pickles (Joshi Eiyō Daigaku 1968) shows the importance of the idea of four seasons in the foodways of contemporary Japan. In 2018, a small publishing house, Shibata Shoten, was established. It has a special editorial section on the four seasons. Nevertheless, the tradition has been weakened in the very recent past. For example, *Washoku no Kyōkasho* (The textbook for Japanese cuisine) (Morikawa 2022) is intended to be the textbook for *washoku* (Japanese cuisine) from Gion (the best-known district in Kyoto). Yet in this 223-page book, only pages 202 through 208, each with a photo, have recipes for the four seasons.

Most contemporary cookbooks reflect the massive influence of non-Japanese cuisines; the increased use of meat, especially chicken; and consideration of the fast-paced lifestyle in which it is no longer assumed that someone, usually a woman, has a great deal of time to cook. A book, published in 2021, defines *washoku* (Japanese cuisine) as a dish with rice, with the recipes emulating those of famous chefs but easy to make (Abe 2021). Among the cookbooks in stores, many have a title claiming to show how to quickly make meals.

Food items "in season" (*shun*) are of vital importance in many countries. In Japan, as we saw in chapter 5, when the four seasons were no longer based on Kyoto but on the areas with access to fish, it became the major item of cuisine. Unlike meat, fish must be eaten "in season" (*shun*). Its importance is revealed in the belief that the talent of a chef is based on how she/he procures the freshest fish, for which they go to the market very early in the morning. *Buri* (Japanese amberjack or yellowtail, *Seriola quinqueradiata*) is an excellent example of the Japanese use of fish. Considered the symbol of success, it receives a separate name depending on its stage of growth. The names are different in each region. In eastern Japan (*kantō*), they are *wakashi* (15–30 cm), *inada* (30–50 cm), and *warasa* (50–60 cm). The largest in size—above 60 cm in eastern Japan, and 80 cm in western Japan and the Noto Peninsula—is called *buri* in all regions. The months of the year for the *buri* catch are December, January, and February. The term *hamachi* is used for farm-raised fish.

The notion of *shun* extends to plant foods as well. A sign of spring today is strawberries, introduced from Holland toward the end of the Edo period. It is now featured in many cookbooks and advertisements.

It seems the concept of four seasons has remained more in Kyoto than in Tokyo. In Kyoto, where plant foods have been the staple, plant foods are often labeled or advertised in reference to four seasons. Murakami Jū, a well-known store for pickles, a type of "seaweed" cherished by the Japanese, emphasizes different types of *konbu* for each of the four seasons. Suetomi, a well-known store for sweets, offers an elegantly packaged sweet named Kyōfūsen (Kyoto balloons), since the sweets are very light. Each is daintily colored on top. The brochure explains that the colors replicate the colors of the four seasons which courtiers used for their attire.

The concept of *shun* is highly commercialized, as is the notion of the four seasons. Tourist agencies lure customers to various places so they can appreciate the "Japanese four seasons"; restaurants feature the cuisine of the season; department stores sell eating utensils in the shape of a maple leaf for fall or a cherry blossom for spring; and stores feature *wagashi* (Japanese sweets) for each season, like *sakuramochi* in spring, which is a pink rice cake with red bean paste in the center and wrapped in a pickled cherry leaf.

On the other hand, "the cuisine for four seasons" is becoming difficult to practice, not because of changes in the food supply but due to changes in the lifestyle of the Japanese, who do not have time to engage in home cooking. The cookbooks now promise things like "breakfast in ten minutes." Many say that "chi-n"—the sound of microwaves—dominates their cooking. Also, supermarkets and other stores sell food at very reasonable prices. They are required to indicate when they prepared the dishes, such as sashimi (raw fish), and must reduce the price at certain times. It is not hard to eat adequately in Japan without much cooking.

Pure Nature, Pure Water

Water is a dominant symbol of the purity of nature worldwide—be it from upstream rivers, waterfalls, springs, or other "natural" sources. The foremost choice for "natural food" is "pure water." Yet, it is spectacularly ironic that the quest for pure water led to an extreme culturalization of nature. As Kaplan (2011; see also 2007) tells us, in the United States and elsewhere, drinking water has undergone several transformations. In the early twentieth century, chlorinated public water supplanted bottled spring water, but in the 1990s bottled water returned to the market with vigor. Even though some brands, such as Aquafina and Dasani, are only bottled tap water, bottled water came to be considered the pure water.

The bottled water phenomenon then entered another stage—"pure water from nature" had to be from a far-off place, like Fiji. In Japan, there are several kinds of bottled water available. "Tokyo Water" with English on the label is bottled tap water, with an emphasis on how it is safe to drink tap water in Tokyo. Some "natural water" (*ten'nen mizu*) is from "nature," for example, from Kirishima in Kyushu. The very best is Fiji water, advertised as "the soft water from paradise [*rakuen*], whose mineral, silica, beautifies skin, hair, and nails" (advertisement in March, 2024 on Google in Japanese by a firm, Seiyū Asakusa Rox located in Asakusa, Tokyo). The companies reinforce the importance of what they call *shirikamizu* (water with silica) by listing the names of top chefs and five-star hotels from all over the world that use Fiji water. It is hard not to think of a connection between the "paradise" of silica water and the colonial delusion of "primitives" living in a paradise close to nature, not contaminated by "civilization."

Not only "nature" gets bottled up—another version of a "safe drink" is soft drinks. A succinct phrase, "the germ-free Coke," highlights the global consumerism, from New York to New Guinea, successfully facilitated by brand names for soft drinks (Foster 2008). An Indian photographer, Sharad Haksar, has captured the domination of Coca-Cola in Chennai, India, in well-known photographs, including a twenty-by-thirty-foot "Drink Coca-Cola" billboard, at the base of which he depicted a dry water pump with four empty pots lined up next to it. Japan is no exception. Coca-Cola Bottlers Japan, Inc. dominates the soft drink market, catering to young people, although there are competitors.

With an unprecedented amount of information about health concerns, and equally massive information about environmental hazards, consumerism is heightened, but individuals in almost every society, including Japan, are faced with the dilemma of how to navigate their lives. Their quest for natural foods is one conspicuous development, which entails the danger of unknowingly succumbing to capitalism and its clever reaches.

Avoidance of the Ground (*jimen*) in Daily Life

The avoidance of the ground in the daily lives of the Japanese today is more than obvious. There is no need to point out the well-known practice of taking off one's footwear to go into the interior of *any* building (Ohnuki-Tierney 1984a: 21–31). To be inside with shoes on—"dirt feet" (*dosoku*)—was a cardinal sin in the past and still is today. A sign declaring "Feet with shoes strictly forbidden" (figure 7.2) is all too familiar in shrines, temples, and public buildings.

"Inside" is clearly demarcated from "outside" by the *genkan* (entrance) in individual houses and other buildings.[6] Today it is a space made usually of concrete or tiles, about several inches below the main part of the house. This is where the host would tell the guest, "Please come *up*"—in other words, to go inside the house is not to go in but go *up*, as in the case of *shōden* at the Imperial Palace (chapter 4). Whether family members or guests, all go up and change into slippers before entering the main part of the house (figure 7.3). Visitors then change to slippers on wooden floors in the hallway or rooms, now that more interiors are Western style. One must

Figure 7.2. "Strict taboo for footwear." Photo by the author.

change to another set of slippers for the bathroom. Most Japanese clean/vacuum the floor of the house every morning.

Many car owners have a pair of slippers into which they change as they get into their car. Almost all Japanese taxis have white starched covers on the seats and seatbacks, reminding the customers that the inside of the car is "inside," although they are not expected to change into slippers.

This rule leads to a lucrative business in manufacturing slippers. In November 2021, an advertisement by Rakuten Ichiba featured sixteen sets of slippers, each containing single to multiple pairs of all kinds in terms of colors, materials used, designs for the family, for children, for visitors, and so forth. Some are billed as germ free, odor free, breathable, washable, or soft. They are often in sets of four or more, with a set of four selling from ¥3,190 to ¥3,800, but a single pair can be as inexpensive as ¥980.

In the trains and streetcars, people who are sitting may not cross their legs lest their shoes touch those standing in front of them. If children face the window to look outside, their shoes must be taken off, even if the soles of their shoes would not be touching the seat.[7] Children are taught not to sit on the ground. So the best strategy for them to get adults to pick them up and carry them is to stage a mock tantrum and sit on the ground, upon which an accompanying adult will immediately pick them up. They are told to take their shoes off in the *genkan* no matter how urgently they wish to enter in order to, for example, go to the bathroom. The invention of Velcro was a significant event, and it is used on all kinds of shoes for

Figure 7.3. Taking shoes off at the entrance to an inn. Photo by the author.

children as well as adults, making it much easier and faster to put on and take off shoes.[8]

All restaurants with tables and chairs, instead of tatami (straw mats), provide a basket beneath the table or next to chairs on the floor where a customer can put a purse or other belongings so that they do not touch the "dirty floor."

Since the ground is defiling, the feet are the most vulnerable part, requiring fine distinctions to describe. *Rasoku* or *hadashi* refers to the feet without socks or shoes, when the sole of the foot directly touches the ground. *Suashi* refers to the feet without socks but in some kind of footwear so that the sole is not touching the ground.

Some common expressions also reveal the negative valence assigned to the ground. For example, *Dosoku de agaru* (enter the house with one's shoes on) is an expression for the invasion of someone's privacy. It is also the most effective way to describe undesirable characters. Murakami Haruki uses this expression frequently. For example, in *Hard-Boiled Wonderland and the End of the World*, the phrase "without taking shoes off" appears twice (1993: 178–79, 214–15). A Japanese equivalent of "wash one's hands" in English is "wash one's feet," as when one wishes to get out of an undesirable situation, like leaving a gangster group (for details, see Ohnuki-Tierney 1984a: 21–31).[9]

Purification of Cars

Although the inside of a car can be made into a culturally appropriate "inside," its tires touch the ground and remain "dirty." So, shrines and temples offer purification rites for private cars for the New Year and the lucky days, discussed below. Although the notion of purification and its rites are traditionally Shinto, this practice is now shared by Shinto shrines and Buddhist temples. A Shinto priest performs a rite of waving a branch of *sakaki* (whose botanical name is *Cleyera japonica*, see figure 7.4) and a Buddhist monk reads a passage from a sutra. The character for *sakaki* is not one of the large number of characters the Japanese imported from China but was created during the Heian period and consists of the character for tree on the left and the character for deity on the right (Okimori 2011: 52). It is one of the trees considered to be a *yorishiro*, a temporary "abode" for deities.

These religious institutions advertise the service on the internet themselves, or some business, such as a tire company, does it for them. On 3 February 2018, Toyo Tire, a large tire company chain, created an internet advertisement for the car purification ritual for three shrines (Taniho Tenmangū, Meiji Jingū, and Tsubaki Daijinja) and two temples (Kawasaki Taishi and Narita Fudōson). The advertisement states that annually two hundred thousand cars receive their purification rite at Narita Fudōson. In May 2022 three types of purification rites were offered: standard prayers for ¥5,000 to ¥7,000; special prayers for ¥10,000; and all-year special prayers for ¥20,000, which includes a special bonfire ritual, called *goma*, that guarantees additional power of purification. In 2022 at Kawasaki Daishi in Kanagawa Prefecture, where Kōbdaishi, the founder, is enshrined, one received for ¥5,000 the purification rite, an amulet for traffic safety and *migawari mamori* (amulet on the owner's behalf to protect him/her in case of calamity), a sticker for the car, and special stationery with sacred words written on it. The payment for the purification rite is called *hatsuhoryō*. Its literal meaning is the first crop of rice as fee and refers to the offering of the new crop of rice to the deities at the harvest ritual—the practice since ancient times.

The shrines and temples urge the client to choose the "luckiest days" for the purification rites. In contemporary Japan, the Daoist divination has remained quite popular. Takashima divination is enormously popular. Its booklet details which days of the year are the luckiest and which are calamitous and thus to be avoided. People choose the luckiest days for weddings and other important events (Ohnuki-Tierney 1984a: 131–35). The housecleaning to get ready for the New Year usually takes place at the end of the year, and the car purification is recommended for the first

Figure 7.4. Buddhist monk purifying a car. Courtesy of Carolyn Dodd.

lucky days of the New Year—for 2022, it was 1 January or 10 January—to get rid of all the impurities accumulated on the tires during the previous year, although it is done any time of the year since shrines and temples are eager to offer their service for a fee.[10]

Summary

Francks (2009) located the beginning of this type of consumerism in the Edo period. This development reached its crescendo during the contemporary period through the power of advertising and marketing—two practices to be distinguished (Applbaum 2004: 14–15)—to create needs for new goods and practices.

Pets are not simply "goods" but bring comfort, affection, and companionship. Memorial services and burials for them are not only "goods" to purchase but ways to deal with loss. These are what Simmel refers to as the subjective dimension, although it is not always enjoyable.

The pets in their carts and the purification of cars are successful stories of mutual promotion between the cosmological valence of defiled ground and lucrative businesses.

Another spectacular success story is the meeting of the pet boom and animism in the form of ever more elaborate and expensive care for the souls of pets. Animism thus became a fertile ground for capitalism.

These examples of consumerism in contemporary Japan show not a tug-of-war or struggle between capitalism and the "traditional" cosmology and religious beliefs. On the contrary, the two seem to help each other, thereby strengthening and promoting each other.

I continue to deliberate on these questions in the next chapter.

Notes

1. The "traditional" belief was that unborn fetuses and children who have never committed sins are easily reborn, leading to the relative ease with which the Japanese practiced abortion and the lack of elaborate funeral/memorial services (Yanagita [1920] 1979: 250–51). Yet consumerism has nearly supplanted this belief, as the title of Hardacre's 1997 book, *Marketing the Menacing Fetus in Japan*, shows. It has almost succeeded in creating guilt in mothers and, increasingly, their partners, as indicated in their writings on votive plaques (see photo 17 in Ohnuki-Tierney 1984a; I have examined them on every visit to Japan since then). They write their apologies and pray for the peaceful rest of the fetus (1984a: 80–81, 130, 156–57).
2. For example, "Lovot"—trademarked as "emotional Robotics"—sold by Rakuten for ¥498,800 in December 2022.
3. Kushi Michio (1926–2014) was Sakurazawa's disciple and advocated his primarily vegetarian diet, while locating his headquarters in Boston (Lewin 2015).
4. For example, in 2019 in the Azabu district of Tokyo, Daiei Supermarket's advertisement specified the following: "Beef from Kagoshima is ¥798 for 100 gram, but beef from the US is ¥288 for 100 gram. Pork is from Spain, shrimp from Argentina, avocado from Mexico, orange[s] from the US, Kiwi from New Zealand, [and] melon from Guatemala" (author's translation; not all prices are included).
5. They introduced the English term "post-harvest chemicals" into daily parlance and opposed the government's plan to mix imported rice with domestic rice. For molds and bad odor on Chinese rice, see articles in *Asahi Shinbun*, 26 February 1994, and *Mainichi Shinbun*, 25 and 26 February 1994; for dead mice in Thai rice, see *Asahi Shinbun*, 19 March 1994, and *Mainichi Shinbun*, 19 March 1994. For details, see Ohnuki-Tierney 1995.
6. The opposition of *uchi / soto* (inside / outside), extensively discussed by Hendry [2003] 2013: 42–44), takes on another set of symbolic meanings when applied along the horizontal axis.
7. Once, when my sons were small, they sat on the train seat without taking their shoes off and the ticket master of the train literally ran over to tell us it was forbidden.
8. The traditional footwear of Japan was easy to put on and take off, unlike the Western-style footwear (i.e., shoes) that the Japanese adopted around the turn of the twentieth century.

9. In May of 2018, I twisted my left ankle, which needed to be iced and elevated. I asked a clerk at the International House where I could leave my foot up and work. He told me that it was prohibited anywhere in the I-House. Professor Nicole Coolidge Rousmaniere, research director of the Sainbury Institute for the Study of Japanese Arts and Cultures, told me that in 2006 when she was appointed as visiting professor at the University of Tokyo, she was told of the proper attire, in particular never to wear sandals, which exposed her feet.
10. It is somewhat of an irony to notice a strained effort for purity at the Ise Shrine, where they raise rice in their fields and, they write on their pamphlet, "only use chemical fertilizers" (Jingū Shichō n.d.: 20). In other words, they choose "chemical purity" while avoiding the word "chemical," which is the forbidden item in government-legislated organic food. Also, due to overharvesting of white pebbles for the shrine, the law now prohibits getting white pebbles from the *Shiraishi* River. So they manufacture white pebbles that are even whiter than the natural white pebbles.

CHAPTER 8

Rice as Pure Money
Cultural Bases of Consumerism

Earlier chapters focused on how "Japanese nature" has been represented by elites of various kinds—literary, artistic, intellectual, political, economic, military, and so forth. Chapter 7 portrayed contemporary Japan, where a bewildering mix of magico-religious beliefs and practices coexist with heightened consumerism, which has aggressively domesticated the inhabitants of "Japanese nature," such as dogs. "Japanese seasons," if not the traditional "four seasons," remain a mandatory reference in letters and other correspondence. These developments have sustained or even strengthened the cosmo-spatial principle and remain important for day-to-day activities, like the rule of conduct that one should remove shoes when one "goes up" inside a house or other building. In turn the spatial principle promotes consumerism by helping the sale of slippers and pet carts, for example, which strengthen the principle of avoiding the defiled ground "below."

Magical Practice for Sociality

A major characteristic of consumers in Japan today is their use of "magical practices," which are not supposed to exist in a "modern" society with highly developed science and technology. This assumption derives from the so-called social evolutionary theory, which has been a dominant theory for an understanding of modernity. I show how these magical practices relate to the abstract cosmological principles.

Magic versus Religion in the Social Theory of Modernity

The central claim in social evolutionary theory is that the hallmark of modernity is Rationality, calling for the elimination of magic (e.g., Weber

[1930] 1992: 117). Yet, what constitutes religion and magic is an enormously difficult question. "Religion" has changed over time and been defined differently depending on time period, region, and "religious affiliations," as detailed by Tambiah ([1990] 1991). Asad (1983: 244; 1993: 40) argues that "a universal definition of religion" was made in seventeenth-century Europe and then privileged and widely adopted, but in fact religion is a construct—by power—at a particular historical place and time (1983: 252). As a minimum, the notion of transcendence as the central element of religion has been proposed in Western philosophies and theologies. However, the concept is altogether alien to the Japanese (Ohnuki-Tierney 1991) and to many other peoples who do not practice the Abrahamic religions.

Another important dimension in this debate is Leach's "practical religion," which is "concerned with the life here and now" (Leach 1968: 3). He emphasized that "the components of a religious system are meaningful not only because of internal coherence but because of their practical integration with the secular life of the religious congregation" (3). He refers to Tambiah's work on the village Buddhism of northern Thailand, which is "a cult for the living, not a theology for the dead and dying" (41–121).

The basic thesis of the social evolutionary theory is the movement from the past to the present as unilinear *progress* through the "disenchantment of the world"—a phrase used originally by Friedrich Schiller but made famous by Max Weber. It has been claimed that Western societies have shed magic, which they view as embodying irrationality, thereby getting out of the medieval period and arriving via the Enlightenment at the modern period characterized by science and rationality, as Tambiah, a well-known critic of social evolutionary theory, describes ([1990] 1991: 117–20).

Weber himself did not advocate or support this blanket view of unilinear historical progression or, for that matter, "rationality" as the hallmark of modernity. In the introduction to *The Protestant Ethic and the Spirit of Capitalism*, he describes "the specific and *peculiar* rationalism of Western culture" (Weber [1930] 1992: 26; my emphasis). Comparing Catholicism and Protestantism, he states: "The rationalization of the world, the elimination of magic as a means to salvation, the Catholics had not carried nearly so far as the Puritans (and before them Jews) had done" (117).

Marcel Mauss, who recognizes that the distinction between magic and religion is not clear cut, makes a similar point: "We have one case, extraordinary though it may seem, of the Catholic Church upholding belief in magic as a dogma and maintaining it with sanctions" (Mauss [1950] 1972: 92).

Keith Thomas (1971) documented the "decline of magic" in England in the sixteenth and seventeenth centuries with the development of science and technology, which offered scientific explanations of the universe and its calamities. He chose the word "decline" and not "disappearance," believing that magic will not disappear altogether and will appear whenever effective resolution in modern/scientific terms is not available. Thomas Waters (2019) found that, indeed, black magic and witchcraft survived well into modern times and continue today in Britain.

In Western philosophy, a "rationalist" attitude had existed long before the world of Galileo or Newton, and Aristotle and Cicero are but two examples of rationalist authors of classical antiquity (Thomas 1971: 646). In modern philosophy—defined by thinkers such as Descartes, Kant, and Rousseau—and especially since the rise of modern science, rationality has been viewed as the essence of humanity. However, scholars acknowledge enormous complexity in the notion of rationality. The relationships between rationality and empiricism and between rationality and discursive logic are but two of many complex dimensions to this question. Economic rationality in particular became the core of the argument in various schools of modernity theory, as discussed by Emile Durkheim, Karl Marx, and R. H. Tawney, and in the critical theory of the Frankfurt school (see Gellner 1992; Tambiah [1990] 1991; Wilson 1970). Among historians and social scientists, the relationship between religion and capitalism has been an important point, with some examining specific societies, including Robert Bellah ([1957] 1970) on Tokugawa religion in Japan and Simon Schama (1988) on Dutch Calvinism and capitalism.

Bruno Latour ([1991] 1993) refutes the idea of modernity altogether in his well-known thesis, summed up in the title *We Have Never Been Modern*. He rejects a total and irreversible invention that completely breaks with the past. Denouncing the concept of postmodernism, he advocates using the terms "amodern," "anti-modern," and "non-modern."

In anthropology, the focus has been on the relationship of modernity to magic and religion, but less on their relationship to capitalism. Anthropology began as a comparative sociology specializing in study of the "primitives" by the "civilized," that is, by Western scholars. The term "primitive" was commonly used by earlier anthropologists.[1] Whether in social evolutionary theory or modernity theory, the unfortunate dyads at the time were primitive/civilized, traditional/modern, magic/religion, and irrationality/rationality.

Edmund Leach ([1966] 2000) most effectively buried this series of dyads in his Henry Myers lecture. He pointed out how beliefs and practices of others are called magic, but "our" beliefs, such as the belief in a virgin birth in Christianity, are considered religious phenomena. Tambiah ([1990] 1991) forcefully questioned the magic/religion dyad and the assumption of the unilinear progression of history, with rational modernity as the final destination.

Harry Harootunian (2000b: 13–23, 25–58) emphasizes that what "distinguishes modernity is consciousness of time and how it relates to both past and present." He offers a spirited argument against the imposition of Western models of modernity on other societies, and he faults both Marxism and postcolonialism for their assumption of a homogeneous historical time (34, 62), even though his own scholarly identity is with Marxism.

In contrast to the "West," the concept of rationality entered the Japanese vocabulary only when the Japanese philosophers came under the intense influence of Kant and other modern philosophers. Two characters—*risei*—were assigned to this newly introduced concept. Rather than rationality, the capacity for sociality and emotions, especially sadness, has been the defining characteristic of humans as opposed to nonhuman animals in the Japanese view.

William LaFleur (1983: 34–35) observes that the Japanese during the medieval period "would have known well that one of the perceptual differences between man and animal is that beings in the latter category do not weep; pain or emotional distress brings no tears to their eyes." Given the central theme of the monkey performance—the difference between human and nonhuman animals and between the Japanese and the non-Japanese—an important part of the repertoire today is teaching the monkey how to "cry" by putting a handkerchief to its eyes (Ohnuki-Tierney 1987: 200). The trainer has perfected the act: if the monkey fails to put the handkerchief to its the eyes, he proclaims that, after all, the monkey is not human.

Claude Lévi-Strauss visited Japan five times beginning in 1977. He was fascinated by the way that Japan, in his view, took a different historical path toward modernity, and therefore "challenge[d] the notion that progress occurs in a single direction" (Lévi-Strauss 2013a: 106–7). As another scholar put it, "Japan had played the modernity card differently" (Loyer 2018: 689). Lévi-Strauss's *The Other Face of the Moon* (2013b) starts with his fascination with the vitality of the aesthetics of middle Jomon pottery, which may be compared with art nouveau (19–20). The taste for "rough materials, irregular forms, . . . [and] the 'art of the imperfect'" convinced Lévi-Strauss that the Japanese are the true inventors of "primitivism" (95). He is awed by the literary masterpieces of the Heian and other early periods, such as *The Tale of Genji*, which "prefigures a literary genre that would become current in France only seven centuries later" (23). On every aspect of Japanese culture—kinship, art, architecture, and so on—Lévi-Strauss refuses to measure Japan by the Western yardstick.

Though it may surprise many, I think Lévi-Strauss's (2013a: 106–7) position is extraordinarily radical. Comparing the West with Japan, he states that the two did not "occupy successive positions on a single line of development." Instead, "they followed parallel paths" and at every moment in history "made choices that did not necessarily coincide with each other." Having "the same cards in hand, each had decided to play them in a different order." Furthermore, taking the *longue durée* approach, Lévi-Strauss (86–87) considers that "historical knowledge preserves affinities with myths," and thus, "*scientific thought and mythic thought will one day move closer together*" (my emphasis). This is indeed a very radical view, as is his claim that Japan has taken a different path to modernity and his refusal to compare Japan with the Western model.

Magic as "Practical Religion"

The foundational work in the theoretical treatment of magic was *A General Theory of Magic* by Marcel Mauss ([1950] 1972: 24, 97), in which he states: "Magic as a whole is, therefore, an object *a priori* of belief, a belief which is unanimous and collective. It is the nature of this belief that permits magicians to cross the gulf which separates facts from their conclusions." Magic's rite, Mauss continues, is "*any rite which does not play a part in organized cults*—it is private, secret, mysterious and approaches the limit of a prohibited rite" (emphasis in the original). Therefore, as a minimum definition, magic is meant to be performed by an individual for a specific aim, and its efficacy is assessed at the time, while an officiant of religious ritual represents a social group and performs the religious rite more for the general benefit of the group, without the proof of its verification being assessed immediately.

Magic and Sociality

In the anthropological debates on religion and magic, an important role of magical practices in sociality has been almost completely neglected. Tambiah, however, in his *Magic, Science, Religion, and the Scope of Rationality* ([1990] 1991), highlights sociality as the most important function of magic. He illustrates this point using the case of the Trobrianders' treatment of the yam, showing how it illuminates "the social concerns surrounding the magic rather than technological inadequacies." Tambiah concludes: "Malinowski's discovery of the sociological function of magic is then of far greater import than his psychological theorizing" (72–73).

Sociality is arguably the most important dimension of the Japanese "magical practices," whose primary function is for social relationships. Many write on votive plaques about themselves, for example, praying for success in passing the entrance examination to a university, or finding a good boyfriend, girlfriend, or marriage partner. But, more often than not, people pray for the recovery of a family member from an illness or some other purpose expressing concern for others. Many buy small amulets at temples and shrines to give to family members or friends who are hospitalized or embarking on travel. Thus, these "magical practices" are basically means for establishing, retaining, and strengthening social relationships (Ohnuki-Tierney 1984a: 124–44). It is to be expected that such "magical practices" flourish in a society well known for the mesmerizing frequency with which "gift exchange" is practiced—both pointing to the importance that the Japanese place on sociality.

Another major category of "magical" practices is *ofuda*, widely popular since the Edo period. Kyburz (2011, 2014) offers us quite extensive examples. Paper charms, called *ofuda*, are typically issued by the shrine of the local tutelary deity (*ujigami*), since its power is to protect the members of the local community, the parish (*uji*), from misfortune. Therefore, the practice is not for the benefit of individuals but for the collectivity or the social group. Perhaps the most common one is for the safety of the family by averting calamity. These paper charms are placed on the *kamidana* (shelf for deities) of the house. A charm is received every year for a modest sum: approximately ¥200 in 2021. With the rural population increasingly moving to the cities, this prototype is no longer the dominant practice. However, people who go to the Ise Shrine bring the *ofuda* from their home shrine, which Kyburz (2014: 378) sees as intended to "integrate the household into the extended family of the Japanese nation whose essence it represents."

Magical practices are commonplace in many other countries besides Japan. In Belgium, the church at Scherpenheuvel has a long tradition of blessing people in their cars, with more than five thousand cars per year receiving the service from a priest (Ask 2014). Although now taken down, the ubiquitous metal padlocks attached to the railing of the Pont des Arts in Paris were once hard to miss. Around 2008, a couple in love placed a lock on the railing and threw the key into the Seine below as a symbolic gesture in the hope that they remain locked together ever after—a practice later repeated by thousands of couples (figure 8.1). These are acts of sociality par excellence. A similar practice is found in Cologne, Rome, Budapest, London, and other cities. Likewise, people still throw coins into fountains, like the Trevi Fountain in Rome, for good luck (Rubin 2014).

Consumerism and the Role of Religions

Having visited Japan eight times in the 1980s, Félix Guattari was mesmerized by its high-tech neon hypermodernity, infused with animism and consumerism. He attributes this "madness" to the *machinic eros*, which

166 | *Representations of "Japanese Nature"*

Figure 8.1. "Love locks" on a bridge in Paris in 2019. Photo by the author.

compels the Japanese to be "in the thick of things" (*être dans le coup*), producing phenomena such as the "syndrome of puerile cute culture (*kawaii*), the reading-drug of Manga comics, or the intrusiveness of loukoum music." He calls this music the worst kind of pollution. To explain the alarming consumerism, he argues that even though the Japanese adopted without resistance all the trends of the West that arrived on their shores, "the wave of Judeo-Christian guilt that feeds our 'spirit of capitalism' has never managed to swamp them" (Guattari 2015: 14).[2]

Japan is not an exception to the worldwide phenomenon of consumerism. Nonetheless, the way consumerism is allowed to destroy "nature" begs some explanation, especially because of the widely held view that the Japanese live in harmony with Japanese nature. This chapter is an attempt to address this seemingly puzzling phenomenon by offering "cultural logic" to understand the role of magical practice in sociality and the concept of rice as "pure money."

Animism

Although the differences between polytheism and monotheism are highly complex, polytheism embraces animism more readily. Belief in the soul of the deceased is almost universal, as testified by the importance of funerals and burials, as well as the vision of an afterlife, in most societies. Christianity is based on the idea that "man has an *absolute* value" and that there is "room in God's house for every soul, and every single one, the meanest and the lowest as well as the soul of the hero and the sage" (Simmel 1978: 360–61). The soul became the unique property of humans. This is a sacred religious belief. In contrast, the belief in the souls of beings of the universe other than humans is a "magical belief."

Japan's official religions of Shintoism, with billions of deities, and Buddhism, with a human becoming Buddha, recognize no single Almighty God. Animism has been the core of Japanese religiosity, and still is. Memorial services, burials, the daily care of the ancestral alcove at home, and all other rituals related to the care of the soul of humans have been of crucial importance for survivors. As Robert Smith (1974) tells us, for the contemporary Japanese ancestor worship represents the most important religious beliefs and practices, including a series of memorial services for the deceased that are important occasions for sociality, during which the immediate and extended family members gather, usually over a meal.

Memorial services for pets are a recent phenomenon, propelled by affluence. There are large pet cemeteries in France, Germany, and other countries, as well as in Japan. In all cases, they exist for the same basic reason—people have become attached to their pets. But the newly emerged pet cemeteries in Japan are different from their Western counterparts. The practice is based on animism. Memorial services for animate and inanimate beings of the universe are an old tradition, with the ones for sewing needles and dolls being the best known and widely practiced today in many parts of Japan, as discussed in Chapter 7.

Rice as Pure Money

"Magical practices" relate to the nature of religion and religious practices particularly in regard to money. "Money" is a highly complex matter, with a wealth of symbolic meanings in most societies (Graeber 2001; Gregory 1997). Among many peoples in the world—the Chinese, the Greeks, the Romans, the Vedic Indians, the Samoans, the Tongans—money originated as a sacred object (Hocart [1952] 1970: 97–104). Hocart identifies the origin of money as the fee paid to the priest who represents the god; the priest "is presented with some objects in which the nature of that god abides" (Hocart:103). In Greece, for example, mints were housed in temples, and forgery was considered sacrilege. The word "money" comes from Juno Moneta, a temple on the Capitoline Hill where a mint for silver currency was set up in 269 BCE (Hocart 100). Having originated as an offering, money gave rise to trade, which was also sacred in nature, according to Hocart: "[A] little of it [gold] was given away in exchange for quantities of their stuff because *a few ounces of divinity were worth pounds of gross matter*" (101; my emphasis). Likewise, the origin of taxes is religious in nature, since "the Lord loveth a cheerful giver" (Hocart 202). The notion of "belief" too was originally linked to economics. Benveniste ([1969, 1973] 2016) discusses belief (*la croyance*) under the heading of "economic obligations"; and many others, including Belmont (1982), Herrenschmidt (1982), and Pouillon (1982), follow this line (for an extensive discussion of pure money, see Ohnuki-Tierney 1993: 67–74).

For Aristotle ([1946] 1958: 25), "the exchange of commodities" is "getting a fund of money" and is "unlimited." It is "the unnatural form of acquisition," in contrast to acquisition for the management of the household, which is limited. Thomas Aquinas likewise condemned money. Marx's characterization of money as a commodity fetish par excellence is only too well known. For Mandeville and Adam Smith, on the other hand, money provided the means for the individual pursuit of happiness and prosperity (Parry and Bloch 1989). Simmel ([1907] 1950: 283–354) considers money as an instrument of freedom for the individual on the one hand, and a threat to the moral order of the community on the other hand.

These meanings, however, derive *not* from money in practice. Money *as it is used* determines its meaning everywhere. The coins tossed into the box in front of a Shinto shrine and the money offered during collections in churches in Christian societies is to provide for neither basic needs nor luxuries—the two tasks performed by money, according to Simmel (1978: 251). It is or is supposed to be pure, without moral negativity. Money when offered to God or deities is pure, whereas money as a financial gain is dirty. There is neither innately pure nor impure money. Therefore, consumerism or capitalism in general does not invade, as it were, every society in a uniform way but depends on the people's religious practices and value systems. It follows that there is no historical or other "development" from pure money to impure money.

Rice—a symbolic equivalent of "nature"—has been the offering to the deities and the currency, and it continued to be the preferred medium of exchange, over metallic money, during the medieval and early modern periods, when metallic currency was tinged with impurity.

With profound adoration of Tang culture, the Japanese aristocrats were drawn to metallic money and minted coins already in the last years of the seventh century. In 708, silver and copper coins were minted in Japan. During the Nara period, silver coins were discontinued but copper coins were circulated. However, the money economy was dormant (Toshiya 1993: 434–35). That people were not as comfortable with metallic money as with rice is described in *Hyakurenshō*, dated to 1179: "There is a strange sickness going round the country nowadays. It is called the money disease" (Sansom 1961: 184). During the Edo period, there was a debate among scholars about whether the activity of merchants could be considered "productive" (Ohnuki-Tierney 1993: 87), as opposed to the productivity of farmers. The nativist scholars were in the forefront of this debate (Harootunian 1988). The caste system, established during the medieval period but strongly reinforced during the Edo period, placed the merchants at the bottom of the four castes: warriors, farmers, craftsmen, and merchants.

Metallic currency is equivalent to rice in that both are forms of exchange. But while metallic money can be dirty or clean, rice as an item of exchange has always been "sacred" in the past and has been "clean" even today. Rice as pure money continues, at least symbolically. The payment for the "purification" of cars is named *hatsuhoryō* (payment for the first crop of rice). Ishimori (1984) reports that the "gift" for a funeral in one household in Nagano Prefecture finally switched from rice to money only in 1961. Today, in front of most shrines, there are a number of barrels of sake (rice wine). Though empty, they represent donations to the shrine (figure 8.2).

Equivocal money, however, can be as clean as rice if consecrated in precisely the same way rice is: by offering it to the deities and Buddhas; by prescribing it as a gift from the deities, as in the folktales; by identifying it with rice in a specific way, as in the case of gold coins embossed with a rice motif; or by giving it with new bills at culturally prescribed occasions, such as funerals and weddings.

Figure 8.2. Rice wine offertory. Heian Shrine. Photo by the author.

The crucial difference between money and rice, then, is that money is equivocal while rice is unequivocal. Money thus can be an important unalienated gift or a devilish fetish, while rice as an item of exchange is always an unalienated gift among interdependent individuals; there is no impure rice currency. This is because rice as a medium of exchange retains its originally religious, or, more broadly, cosmological meaning—the soul of rice embodies the peaceful souls of the deities.

One important practice of the Japanese use of money is the tradition of *saisen*—coins tossed into the *saisen* box placed in front of every shrine. People give coins, usually a fairly small amount of money, and pray. When I visited Himeji Castle in 2019, I went up to the top floor where there is a small shrine. I saw a group of people coming behind me. A man in his forties tossed his coins, turned around to address the group, and told them in his western Japanese dialect: "This deity is very effective (*yoku kikihannoya*). Why don't you give some *osaisen* [/o/ is honorific]?" The *saisen* practice originated as offerings—such as papers, cloth, or the first crop of rice—to thank the deities for their protection (Hirai [1985] 1995).

The *saisen* is different from Christian practices of a tithe to the church, alms to the poor, or the basket passed around for the support of church and charity in that *saisen* is literally tossed into a wooden box by an individual for a specific purpose, for example, someone's recovery from an illness or business prosperity. It is similar to the votive plaque but more aggressively done, trusting in and demanding the deity's help, although it is often also done on behalf of others and for their benefit.

The practice of tossing metallic coins in a wooden box, and the term *saisen* itself, are relatively new. But the tradition of offering a new crop of rice to deities, first by the emperor and later by people, has a long history, as early as 796 CE (Hirai [1985] 1995). When metallic currency was introduced, one of its primary uses was as an offering to the deities (Yanagita [1942] 1982: 287). At Tsuruoka Hachimangū, the *saisen* box was installed sometime between 1532 and 1555 (Hirai [1985] 1995). Even today, many shrines do not have a *saisen* box (Yanagita [1942] 1982: 286). On the other hand, some shrines collect a fair amount of currency. For example, at Fushimi Inari Taisha, they gathered about fifty boxes from various branch shrines; on 4 January 2020, several employees from a local bank counted the bills and coins, which included ¥10,000 bills as well as small bills and coins (figure 8.3) (*Kyōto Shinbun*, evening edition, 4 January 2020).

Reward in This World—The Basic Tenet of Religions

As introduced in chapter 3, the Japanese identified their religion as offering benefits while they are alive in this world, rather than salvation after death. Theirs is *practical religion*, as Leach noted.

Figure 8.3. Counting of money offertory. Fushimi Inari Shrine on 4 January 2020. Courtesy of *Kyōto Shinbun*.

Worldly benefits are not only the basic tenet of Japanese Buddhism—folk Shintoism also has plenty of folk deities advocating for worldly benefits. Miyata (1975: 101–20) describes *fukushin shinkō* (beliefs in lucky deities), the tradition of the worship of deities who bring good luck. Among the most popular of these deities are the seven deities of prosperity (*shichifukujin*), who visit people on New Year's in a treasure boat (*takarabune*). Each of these seven deities brings good fortune, personal and financial. The worship of these seven deities developed among the merchant class in Kyoto during the Muromachi period (1338–1573). During the mid-Edo period, paintings with the seven deities arriving in a boat loaded with gold and silver coins and bales of rice were very popular among the merchants. Today, right in Tokyo, the tourist office of Shinjuku district widely advertises tours for pilgrimages to shrines with these seven lucky deities. There are over twenty temples and shrines dedicated to the seven deities in Tokyo.

Th reward for good behavior in the *Noh* drama *Hachinoki* is granting territory to one of the play's characters. In folktales of the late Muromachi period and Edo period, the reward for good behavior was often ōban koban, as in the "Old Man and Cherry Blossoms," introduced in chapter 4. The ōban *koban*, literally "big judgment and small judgment," refers to the large coin created by Hideyoshi in 1588 and the small one by Iyeyasu in 1595, which were made by mixing gold, silver, and copper. They were used from the late Muromachi period to the late Edo period in commercial transactions. Importantly, the term ōban *koban* represents wealth in general, or more likely "treasure," in some aesthetic sense. Another indication that riches were held in high esteem is the term *chōja*—those who are rich and, *therefore*, politically and socially powerful in the local community. In other words, in Japan money or wealth itself has not been regarded as a symbol of evil or moral corruption. (For detailed discussion of the Japanese notion of wealth, see Ohnuki-Tierney 1993: 63–80).

Consumerism

Consumerism is a social and economic process in which people succumb to the forces pushing the acquisition of goods and practices that are not necessities. "Consumerism" is the latest emphasis in the study of capitalism. In addition, "the value of subjective enjoyment" still is not well studied, nor is how the "[e]go, our desires and feelings, continue to live in the objects we own" (Simmel 1978: 388–89). Kelly (1991: 229) expresses this as "not only a love of things and a desire to consume, but a sense of self defined by the possessions, a self that is what it has" (see also Belk 1988).

Be it linguistic, political, or socioeconomic, the structure of unequal power is seldom articulated in the minds of people, as Marx so clearly recognized in his concept of *commodity fetishism*, where the value of commodities is seen as *natural* by people who are not aware of "all the magic and necromancy that surrounds the products of labour as long as they take the form of commodities" (Marx [1867] 1992: 80–81).

The concept of commodity fetishism has an enduring power for understanding the power of capitalism. Lukács ([1923] 1971: 86–88) further advanced this concept through his understanding of *reification*, which showed how "the commodity form" becomes "the dominant form" in

Rice as Pure Money | 173

Figure 8.4. Amulet advertisement for tourism in Tokyo at subway stations. Photo by the author.

capitalist societies; commodities thereby acquire the appearance of objectivity, while a person loses his/her "natural form," and with it their physical and psychic "qualities."

In this chapter, we saw how people in fact willingly participate in this process of commodity fetishism, and that religions play a crucial role in this process, leading to the ease with which the government and capitalistic enterprises like tourist industries lure people into cooperating in this process. Therefore, it is no surprise to see at major subway stations a large advertisement for tourism in Tokyo that features an amulet (figure 8.4)—Tokyo is defined in reference to "magical practice," which raises no eyebrow among the people.

Eisenstadt (1996: 219–63) devotes a whole chapter to explicating how the Japanese transformed Confucianism and Buddhism through those religions' "tendencies to immanentization" and "more this-worldly emphasis," which were then extended to "the general Japanese cultural climate" (234). We saw in chapter 3 that the very reason the imperial court was moved from Nara to Heian (Kyoto) was to get away from Chinese Buddhism and to promote the court's own preferred sects of Buddhism, which advocated reward in this world (*gensei reiki*). Eisenstadt (235) further points out that what he refers to as Japan's pagan and polythetic traditions—their basically "this-worldly religious outlook"—shaped "the tradition of an entire civilization."

In the aptly titled *Pilgrimage in the Marketplace*, Reader (2014) demonstrates how pilgrimages in Japan are thoroughly embedded in the marketplace, including marketing through advertisements, promotional activities by priests and secular interest groups, and consumer goods such as souvenirs. The phenomenon is not unique to Japan but is found in various other parts of the world.

As quoted above, Guattari noted how "Judeo-Christian guilt" in the pursuit of capitalism did not reach the Japanese shore, while almost everything else from Western civilization did. Japan, however, should not be regarded as an exception. Appadurai (2013) points out that in the global era religion and commerce are intimately intertwined. At least in the case of Japan, the two have enjoyed mutual support.

This brief description of some aspects of consumerism and its interconnections with belief in magic and religiosity in contemporary Japan points to the need to examine the different inlets by which capitalism reaches people, and to the need for an understanding of diverse historical paths, without assuming one particular road of development from the past to the present.

Notes

1. The word was used by the founding fathers of anthropology such as J. G. Frazer in *The Golden Bough, A Study in Magic and Religion* ([1890] 1959); Lucien Lévy-Bruhl in *L'âme primitive* (1927) and *La mentalité primitive* (1922); and B. Malinowski in *Magic, Science, and Religion and Other Essays* ([1925] 1954). In *The Invention of Primitive Society: Transformation of an Illusion* (1988: 8–9), Kuper considers the idea of primitive society as an illusion and fantasy. He seeks to explain the genesis of its persistence.
2. Chabal and Daloz (2006: 159) consider that in Japan, even with its strenuous resistance to Western influence, modernity was achieved only by assimilating Western modernity.

Conclusion

The scope of this book is enormously large, almost open-ended, leading me to offer bold historical interpretations of what has been called "Japanese nature." To take on the *longue durée* is an audacious endeavor, inviting many questions. Nevertheless, there are some precious findings that would not have been accessible by selecting only a short period of history for research.

A study of culture over a long period does not have to lose "the richest in humanity," since the real substance of culture is always what individuals do—the day-to-day lives and behavior of people, broadly defined, as long as we have sufficient historical records.

The major task of this book was to learn how a series of representations of nature became "Japanese nature." These representations include the uses of poems and other literary productions, performing and visual arts, and quotidian activities such as letter writing, cuisine, and rituals of viewing certain flowers. The Japanese involved include both the elite and the folk, and influences have come on geopolitical tidal waves, such as capitalism.

The most important finding is the centrality of the symbolic strength of rice in reference to the representation of "Japanese nature," Japanese religion, and Japanese cosmology. The "creation myth" of Japan began as the Sun Goddess sending her grandson to the archipelago to convert the wilderness into the land of beautiful rice paddies with pure water and succulent ears of rice. This is the prototype of "Japanese nature," which has lasted throughout history and endures even today. Equally important is the belief in the soul of rice as the supreme deity, which is at the core of animism—the most important religious belief of the Japanese. In addition, rice has been the "pure money," laying the basis for the positive value given to "wealth" and leading to the ease with which consumerism has penetrated.

The transition from the Nara period (710–94) to the Heian period (794–1185), the subject of chapter 2, signaled a critical time of change. For the Nara period poets, the rice plant was the focal point of "real nature." Its different stages of growth were celebrated in poems by people of all walks of life, not only courtiers. Bush clovers and stags, frequently referred to in the poems, were in fact the signs that the rice was ready to be harvested. The people saw the tiny pink flowers of bush clover and heard the "longing voices" of stags. In contrast, the Heian poets were courtiers, who enjoyed their opulent life within the compound of the Heian palace. They began portraying "their nature" without direct contact with "real nature." Thus, Seishōnagon, the author of the classic *Makura no Sōshi*, did not recognize the plant shown to her as rice, even though the courtiers had been consuming rice all along. In poems from this period, the songs of birds, which the courtiers heard but seldom saw, and sounds of insects in a bamboo cage, are some of the chosen symbols of "nature." This was the beginning of the representation of nature as "Japanese nature."

In later periods of history, ordinary folks as well as the government became active architects of "Japanese nature," while capitalism has played a significant role in this process. It ends with contemporary Japan, where rampant consumerism and religious beliefs and rituals form a friendly relationship.

Cosmological Principles and the Quotidian

In my previous work, I chose quotidian symbols of nature—the monkey, rice, and cherry blossoms—and examined their life courses. I continue to use the "quotidian" (*quotidien*), de Certeau's original term in French. In the past few decades, Heidegger's philosophy has become influential in anthropology, history, and other related fields (Das 2020; Harootunian 2000a: 59–110; Lefebvre 1994). Setting aside the problem of antisemitism of the *Black Notebooks*, published in 2014, we note that Heidegger clearly states how his existential analytic of *Dasein* must be distinguished from anthropology, psychology, and biology (Heidegger 1962 [1927]: 46). In anthropology, terms and concepts such as "everydayness" and "temporality" have lately received much currency. Veena Das foregrounded "the ordinary" in a series of her writings (e.g., 2014, 2020) and urges us to examine everyday life, ethics, expressions, and the like. I follow the anthropological tradition and use the term "quotidian." Ethnography is by definition a study of the quotidian in broader-contexts of economics and politics.

In *Flowers That Kill*, I presented how the Japanese military government, Hitler, and Stalin relied heavily on the use of flowers—cherry blossoms and roses—to persuade and manipulate the general public. The cherished flowers carry multiple meanings, including life and death, and thus are loaded with emotive appeal to the people. The delivery of the dictators' messages would not have been so successful without this mediation.

The research for this book most clearly demonstrated the mutual reinforcement of the cosmological scheme and day-to-day activities. The "imperial cartography," as I call it, created the spatial divisions of the universe and their valances, when the first imperial palaces—Heijōkyō and Heiankyō—were built in 710 CE and 794 CE, respectively. The divisions were made from the vantage point of the seat of the emperor in the north, to which people would "go up," and from which they would "come down" to the south, with the former assigned a positive valence. In other words, the cartography divides and assigns valences for both the horizontal and vertical divisions of space. This construction is replicated in the first myth-history—the *Kojiki* of 712 CE—commissioned by Emperor Tenmu. It firmly establishes the cosmological spatial scheme.

Concrete examples of the spatial divisions include the "going up" in the imperial cartography of the eighth century, which remains important even today, as expressed in the architectural mandate to have an entrance (*genkan*) from which one "goes up" to the inside of a house and all "insides." Above all, avoidance of the defilement of "the below" has been the cardinal rule for conduct, leading to strict rules in regard to the feet, footwear, carriages, and all matters and manners related to the defilement of the ground. Most importantly, among the other inhabitants of the universe, the four-legged animals have remained abominable creatures forbidden for consumption, because having four legs means they have maximum contact with the ground.

We see the beginning of the temporal divisions in *Manyōshū*, compiled in 759, which established the centrality of rice plants, whose stages of growth laid the initial ground for what became the structure of "the four seasons." By that time, wet-rice agriculture had become the foundation of the political economy of the imperial system. These cosmological principles were sustained for such a long period of time precisely because they also became the principles of thought and conduct in the daily lives of the people.

During the ancient (Nara) period, the year was divided into seasons according to the developmental stages of rice, the most important plant. The four seasons then developed into an elaborate scheme, with each season identified by a plant and a bird as well as an activity. The seasons became increasingly "culturalized," rather than the response to environmental changes. The aristocrats praised the four seasons without ever actually seeing "nature." They established the rituals of celebrating plum blossoms, cherry blossoms, and chrysanthemums. They wore the colors and flowers designated for each of the four seasons on their kimonos. The establishment of temporal divisions led to an enormous importance placed on the almanac, *saijiki*. The four seasons were incorporated in the daily lives of the Japanese—cookbooks divided the foods and the cooking methods into four seasons. Even pastries (*wagashi*) are shaped in the form of a cherry blossom in pink or a persimmon in orange in the spring and the fall, respectively.

This process, however, by no means indicates that either the cosmological principle or the daily activities remained the same with the same meanings throughout history. Bush clovers and the call of stags or songs of birds as the sign of the arrival of a season are things of the distant past, since urbanization started quite early in Japan. The planting of rice seedlings and rice harvests are now seen on television, not in person, by most Japanese. In fact, hardly anyone of the younger generation knows the connection between the emperor system and rice.

Unconscious "Power" of Historical Agents

A familiar model in the discussion on cultural change is historical actors who turn into historical agents with the "power" to bring about changes in society. Weber (1947: 324–63, 392–407) made the distinction between *authority*, which is legitimate, and *power*, which is not legitimate.

The notion of power is extremely difficult to define. Clifford Geertz (1980: 134–35) is dubious about the term as defined in most modern political theory, which views power as "the capacity to make decisions by which others are bound, with coercion its expression, violence its foundation, and domination its aim." For the concept of power, "ideology," as defined by Antoine Destutt de Tracy (1754–1836), is integral but, like power, it has been used in many ways (Wolf 1999: 25; Althusser 1971: 158). Wolf (1999: 4) focuses his inquiry on "how ideologies become programs for the development of power," and culture as "a framework of sociopolitical mobilization and ideological strategizing" (2001: 76).

It is widely recognized that the vision of a Julius Caesar, a Napoleon, or other powerful leaders in "heroic histories" as agents wielding power singlehandedly is far from historical reality. From Abraham Lincoln to Martin Luther King Jr. and Barack Obama, their accomplishments have involved a great number of other individuals and historical developments. It is important to discard the notion that a single individual "makes history." The plurality of historical agents and geopolitical and social contexts, including, for example, the rise of capitalism and consumerism, are all significant factors making history move, reproducing itself while transforming itself (see Ohnuki-Tierney 2002a: 292–97 for detailed discussion of historical agents).

There is a long tradition in social theory about the way people misrecognize what Bourdieu emphasized in his work (for the history of misrecognition in social theory, see Ohnuki-Tierney 2002a: 281–92). Bourdieu uses the concept of "symbolic violence" to point out the way the underclass misrecognizes and embraces the cultural capital of the upper class, without either side being conscious of the process (see Bourdieu [1972] 1982: 192; 1990: 84–85; 1991: 51, 209–13). Boudieu's concept of symbolic violence is important for understanding culture as historical process and "nature as representation." Individuals with power are more often than not unconscious of their own power to replicate their habitus, just as artists are not expecting others to reproduce "nature" as they represent it.

The inequality and stratification with which Bourdieu was concerned are not main components in the universal model of a society today, especially in the recent period during which, for example, the power to influence "taste" in quotidian life, such as clothing, has been in the hands of younger people whose power of influence is facilitated by globalization and mass media. Even among them, I predict that unconscious power play exists, since not all youth in every country have equal power—financial, social, or even political.

The whole process of representations of "Japanese nature" has been "naturalized." That is, there has never been an active, overt coercive effort on the part of those who contributed to the representation of Japanese nature to make others subscribe to their representations. A courtier who praised Japanese nature did not even expect that she/he had any influence over other Japanese. Those folks who read the *waka* poems by the elite did not subscribe to the Japanese four seasons concept because they were told to replicate it. Those who produced cuisine for each season were not told to do so. They replicated the originally elite construction of "Japanese nature" and seasons without being told and in the process participated in the retention of these ideas.

At the root of the unconscious nature of symbolic domination is the *absence* of articulation of "meaning" in our statements and behaviors. I have called attention to this in *Flowers That Kill*, whose subtitle is *Communicative Opacity in Political Spaces* (Ohnuki-Tierney 2015). Communicative opacity is a ubiquitous phenomenon. In anthropology, Leach pointed out in 1954 how different individuals draw different meanings from the same symbols and actions: "And just as two readers of a poem may agree about its quality and yet derive from it totally different meanings, so, in the context of ritual action, two individuals or groups of individuals may accept the validity of a set of ritual actions without agreeing at all as to what is expressed in those actions" (Leach [1954] 1965: 86). In a similar vein, Sidney Mintz wrote, "People's agreeing on what something *is* is not the same as their agreeing on what it *means*" (Mintz 1985: 158).

I consider culture to consist of a wide net of symbolic meanings that offers ways for the individual to comprehend his/her environment using the senses, mind (Weltanschauung/ worldview), and affect (ethos) (Ohnuki-Tierney 1981). Geertz (1973: 12; 1980: 135) pointed out that "culture is public because meaning is," that is, culture is "intersubjective." I propose that what is "public," "shared," or "collective" is not a particular signification in a given context of communication, but *the field of meaning*, that is, all the culturally recognized meanings of a given symbol, which are vast in the case of polysemic symbols, those with multiple meanings (Turner 1967: 30, 50; 1975: 155). A particular signification in a given context is often *not* shared among all social actors, and yet communicative opacity is rarely recognized. "Communication" goes on because they share the field of meaning of a symbol, not because they share the same signification. What is shared is communicative *capability*, which represents merely a potential for communication. Also important, symbols include those without material/physical representation, which I call zero signifiers, whose presence and meaning are signaled by the predicates (for details, see Ohnuki-Tierney 1993b, 1994b).

The most articulate proposition on our *unawareness* of the *absence* of communication was by Baudelaire, who became acutely aware that the ground was shaking with the emergence of significant paradigmatic instability during the rise of *modernité*. Baudelaire ([1869] 1951: 201) explained that the world gets by because of misunderstanding, which prevents the realization that people would never come to agreement.

Building on the insights of Baudelaire, Bourdieu, and others, I foreground the importance of recognizing the unawareness of communicative opacity and attempt to identify specific factors responsible for the phenomenon. My interest in communicative opacity is not confined to analyses of power inequality in class structure in a given society, an almost exclusive concern of Bourdieu, but includes broader social spaces, including ordinary social interactions.

Magic, Religions, and Capitalism in Contemporary Japan

In postmodern, high-tech Japan, we witness such a profusion of magical beliefs and practices. I proposed that we abandon the social evolutionary theory that places "magic" at the beginning of the road to modernity with the triumph of rationality. Instead, the behaviors based on magical thinking, such as purchases of amulets, are acts of sociality—offerings to family members, relatives, friends and others to express their concern about their health and other matters.

Another highly visible phenomenon is the quotidian practices of Shintoism and Buddhism, such as memorial services for pets and purification of cars. The extension of the care of the soul to dead pets in contemporary affluent Japan is, I suggest, due to two factors. First, the rationale is an extension of animism, which postulates that every being of the universe has a soul and that it must be treated well upon the death of the owner. A second important factor for the sale of amulets and the memorial service for pets lies in the Japanese view of wealth. Even the very reason for moving the capitol from Nara to Kyoto was in part to promote the sects in Buddhism that advocated reward in this world, which also was the theme of folktales in which good behavior was rewarded with wealth.

The basis of this "worldly" attitude, I suggest, derives from "rice as pure money." Rice has been "sacred" while also serving as currency. Today, all the price tags for offering prayers, amulets, and so forth are labeled as *hatsuhoryō* (payment of the first crop of rice), which originated as the offering to the deity for rice crops. So, it is the pure money that priests and monks receive. Purification of cars derives from the clever extension of the notion that the ground defiles—the cardinal spatial valence of the Japanese universe throughout history. It is an efficient way to receive the "pure money," since it does not involve actual cleaning of tires but simply performing a very brief ritual of waving an exorcism stick.

Representations of the Zero

Lévi-Strauss ([1962] 1966: 16–36), who worked in societies with less emphasis on representations, especially visual representations, proposed his famous concept of *bricoleur*—a craftsman whose tool/means is "whatever is at hand," "defined only by its potential for use." In societies where the tradition of visual, auditory and other types of "representations" has been developed, it is these representations that constitute the source for artistic creation, as emphasized by Gombrich ([1960] 2000: esp. 24–25): "[A]rt is born of art, not of nature," that is, "the grip of conventions and the power of traditions" are the source for artistic creation.

In Japanese representations of nature and its inhabitants, there is a distinct tradition: the absence or the minimum physical presence of the entity—the concept of "zero signifiers," as explained earlier. This emphasis on formlessness and invisibility, I suggest, is related to the Japanese conception of the invisible, nonmaterial soul. Its presence becomes known only when it leaves the body where it temporarily sojourned.

"Nature" is turned into a blank slate on which to inscribe human creation. The inscription uses minimal physicality, leaving the slate with ample zeros. The height of its development is the so-called rock garden, where a few rocks in the sea of white pebbles are present. The viewers are not passive. They are called to be active participants in interpreting the scene, using their memory and imagination. *Wabi-cha*, a type of tea ceremony also developed during the medieval period, is stripped to the bare minimum, using the everyday type of utensils and being performed in *shoinzukuri*, a most simple structure. The master of the tea ceremony described his ceremony in the midst of the busy city of Sakai as creating "nature" in the urban center.

The *on'nagata*—a male actor who specializes in playing the role of a woman in Kabuki—is able to be more "feminine" than a woman can. The Japanese audience, as I personally observed, perceives and appreciates this inscription on "nature" as "natural," unconstrained by biological givens, as Barthes ([1970] 1982) repeatedly stresses.

During the Edo period, with the efflorescence of the merchant culture, a number of different plebeian arts representing "Japanese nature" emerged. The distinct pattern of keeping materiality to the minimum continued. For example, the netsuke are *not* miniature inhabitants of "nature." An insect, a dog, a monkey, a bird, or a frog, with their features dramatically changed, tells a story that the artist wishes to narrate. Or a tigress fiercely protecting her cubs—needless to say, the artist had never seen a tiger, not native to Japan, let alone a tiger with two cubs. Thus, the artist's creation is *not* an imitation of a being of the universe out there, objectively and physically. Also, during the Edo period, bonsai and *hakoniwa* flourished; the artists, often ordinary folk, developed the way to create their nature. What they created was never a fractal. In the literary sphere, the haiku, with only 5/7/5 syllables per line, offered the opportunity for the reader to experience the depth of feeling and the infinity of the universe through only seventeen words. The minimum of physicality in these representations creates a dialogic experience in the Bakhtinian sense, inviting viewers and listeners to participate in the interpretation, using their own memory, experience, and feelings.

In this tradition, the concealment of the role of human hands in re-creating "nature" became imperative. This contrasts markedly with some of the Western traditions. For example, the gardens of palaces in France, like Versailles, are blatantly not replicas or imitations of "nature." The geometric configurations are meant to show human creativity.

It is tempting to interpret the phenomenon as the Mickey Mouse of Benjamin ([1931] 2008). Although Benjamin himself never explicitly explained what his Micky Mouse meant, it no doubt relates to his concern with technology and the human body in relation to modernity (cf. Mourenza 2020). The Japanese case, however, has been a part of the Japanese conceptualization of the "form" in relation to "matter."

References

Abe Tsukasa. 2021. *Abe Gohan: Puro no Tenuki Washoku* [Abe rice recipes: Japanese cuisine by chefs made easy to make]. Tokyo: Tōyō Keizai Shinpōsha.
Adachi Yoshiyuki. 1748. *Kingyo Sodategusa* [Manual for raising goldfish]. Osaka: Tanbaya Rihē, hoka nimei.
Agamben, Giorgio. (1995) 1998. *Homo Sacer: Sovereign Power and Bare Life*. Stanford, CA: Stanford University Press.
Ajia Rekishi Shiryō Sentā. 2016. *Kōbunsho ni Miru Senji to Sengo: Tōji Kikō no Henten* [During and after war in the official documents: Changes in the structure of governance]. Tokyo: Kokuritsu Kōbunshokan.
Althusser, Louis. 1971. *Lenin and Philosophy*. New York: Monthly Review Press.
Akasaka, Norio. 1988. *Ō to Tennō* [King and emperor]. Tokyo: Chikuma Shobō.
Akima Toshio. 1972. "Shisha no Uta: Saimei Tennō no Kayō to Asobibe" [The Songs of the dead: Songs of Emperor Saimei and *Asobibe*). *Bungaku* 40(3): 97–112.
Akita Hiroki. 2002. *Geta: Kami no Hakimono* [Wooden clogs: The footwear of the deities). Tokyo: Hōsei Daigaku Shuppankyoku.
Alley, Kelly E. 2002. *On the Banks of the Gaṅgā: When Wastewater Meets a Sacred River*. Ann Arbor: University of Michigan Press.
Allsen, Thomas T. 2013. *The Royal Hunt in Eurasian History*. Philadelphia: University of Pennsylvania Press.
Amino Yoshihiko. 1994. *Nihon Shakai Saikō: Ama to Retto Bunka* [Rethinking Japanese society: People of the sea and the culture of the archipelago]. Tokyo: Shōgakkan.
Appadurai, Arjun. 2013. *The Future as Cultural Fact: Essays on the Global Condition*. New York: Verso.
Applbaum, Kalman. 1998. "The Sweetness of Salvation: Consumer Marketing and the Liberal-Bourgeois Theory of Needs." *Current Anthropology* 39(2): 323–49.
———. 2004. *The Marketing Era: From Professional Practice to Global Perspective*. New York: Routledge.
Arakawa Hirokazu. 1983. *Netsuke* [Netsuke]. Tokyo: Nihon Zōge-Chōkokukai.
Aristotle. (1946) 1958. *The Politics of Aristotle*, ed. and trans. Ernest Barker. Oxford: Oxford University Press.
Asad, Talal. 1983. "Anthropological Conceptions of Religion: Reflections on Geertz." *Man* 18(2): 237–59.

———. 1993. *Genealogies of Religion: Discipline and Reasons of Power in Christianity and Islam*. Baltimore, MD: Johns Hopkins University Press.
Ask, Mathias. 2014. "For Drivers in Belgium, God Is Their Insurance Agent." *Wall Street Journal*, 12 September.
Asquith, P. J. 1981. "Some Aspects of Anthropomorphism in the Terminology and Philosophy Underlying Western and Japanese Studies of the Social Behavior of Non-Human Primates." DPhil thesis. Oxford: University of Oxford.
Asquith, Pamela. 1984. Reichōruigaku no Yukikata [Directions for primate studies]. *Shishō* 717: 36–51.
Atkins, Jacqueline M. ed. 2005. *Wearing Propaganda: Textiles on the Home Front in Japan, Britain, and the United States, 1931–1945*. New Haven, CT: Yale University Press.
Auerbach, Erich. (1946) 1974. *Mimesis: The Representation of Reality in Western Literature*. Princeton, NJ: Princeton University Press.
Augé, Marc. (1992) 1995. *Non-Places: Introduction to an Anthropology of Supermodernity*. New York: Verso.
Barthes, Roland. (1970) 1982. *Empire of Signs*. New York: Hill and Wang.
Bates, Catherine. 2013. *Masculinity and the Hunt: Wyatt to Spenser*. Oxford: Oxford University Press.
Baudelaire, Charles. (1855) 2001. *The Painter of Modern Life and Other Essays*. London: Phaidon.
———. (1869) 1951. *My Heart Laid Bare and Other Prose Writings*. New York: The Vanguard Press.
Begam, Richard. 2021. "Modernism after Poststructuralism; Or, Does Badiou Save Us from Drowning?" *Modernism/Modernity* 28(1): 117–36.
Belk, Russell W. 1988. "Possessions and the Extended Self." *Journal of Consumer Research* 15(2): 139–68.
Bellah, Robert N. (1957) 1970. *Tokugawa Religion*. New York: Beacon Press.
Belloli, Andrea P. A. 1984. *A Day in the Country: Impressionism and the French Landscape*. Los Angeles: Los Angeles County Museum of Art.
Belmont, Nicole. 1982. "Superstition and Popular Religion in Western Societies." In *Between Belief and Transgression*, ed. Michael Izard and Pierre Smith, 9–23. Chicago: University of Chicago Press.
Benedict, Ruth. (1946) 1967. *The Chrysanthemum and the Sword*. New York: Houghton Mifflin & Co.
Benjamin, Walter. (1931) 2008. "Mickey Mouse." In *The Work of Art in the Age of Mechanical Reproduction and Other Writings on Media*, 338–39. Cambridge, MA: Harvard University Press.
———. (1934) 2006a. "Paris: The Capital of the Nineteenth Century." In *The Writer of Modern Life: Essays on Charles Baudelaire*, 30–45. Cambridge, MA: Harvard University Press.
———. (1934) 2006b. *The Writer of Modern Life: Essays on Charles Baudelaire*. Cambridge, MA: Harvard University Press.
———. (1936) 1968. "The Work of Art in the Age of Mechanical Reproduction." In *Illuminations*, ed. Hannah Arendt, 217–51. New York: Schoken Books.

———. (1955) 1986. "On the Mimetic Faculty." In *Reflections*, ed. Peter Demetz, 333–36. New York: Schoken Books.

———. (1982) 2002. *The Arcades Project*. Cambridge, MA: Harvard University Press.

Benveniste, Émile. (1969, 1973) 2016. *Indo-European Language and Society*, trans. Elizabeth Palmer. London: Faber and Faber. Republished as *Dictionary of Indo-European Concepts and Society*, trans. Elizabeth Palmer. Chicago: HAU Books.

Berlin, Isaiah. (1959) 1992. *The Crooked Timber of Humanity*. New York: Random House.

Bernier, Bernard. 2006. "National Communion: Watsuji Tetsuro's Conception of Ethics, Power, and the Japanese Imperial State." *Philosophy East and West* 56(1): 84–105.

Berque, Augustin. 1990. *Nihon no Fūkei, Seiyō no Keikan, soshite Zōkei no Jidai* [Comparative history of landscape in East Asia and Europe]. Tokyo: Kōdansha.

———. 1994. "Identification of the Self in Relation to the Environment." In *Japanese Sense of Self*, ed. Nancy Rosenberger, 93–104. Cambridge: Cambridge University Press.

Berry, Mary Elizabeth. 1982. *Hideyoshi*. Cambridge, MA: Harvard University Press.

———. 1994. *The Culture of Civil War in Kyoto*. Berkeley: University of California Press.

———. 2007. *Japan in Print: Information and Nation in the Early Modern Period*. Berkeley: University of California Press.

Bertelli, Sergio. (1990) 2001. *The King's Body*, trans. Burr Litchfield. Philadelphia: Pennsylvania State University Press. Originally published as *Il corpo del re: Sacralità del potere nell' Europa Medievale e moderna*. Florence, Italy: Gruppo Editoriale Florentino.

Berthier, François. (1989) 2000. *Reading Zen in the Rocks: The Japanese Dry Landscape Garden*, trans. and with a philosophical essay by Graham Parkes. Chicago: University of Chicago Press.

Billington, James H. (1966) 1970. *The Icon and the Axe: An Interpretive History of Russian Culture*. New York: Random House.

Birukawa Masataka. 2009. "Heian Jidai ni okeru Kegare Kannen no Henyō: Jingi Saigi kara no Bunri" [Changes in the concept of defilement during the Heian period: Its separation from sacred rituals and festivals]. *Nihon Shisōshigaku* 41: 56–73.

Blacker, Carmen. 1975. *The Catalpa Bow: A Study of Shamanistic Practices in Japan*. London: George Allen & Unwin.

Bolitho, Harold. (1989) 1996. "The Tempō Crisis." In *Cambridge History of Japan*, ed. Marius Jansen, 5:117–67. Cambridge: Cambridge University Press.

Bourdieu, Pierre. (1972) 1982. *Outline of a Theory of Practice*. Cambridge, UK: Cambridge University Press.

———. (1979) 1984. *Distinction: A Social Critique of the Judgement of Taste*. Cambridge, MA: Harvard University Press.

———. 1990. *In Other Words: Essays Toward a Reflexive Sociology*. Stanford, CA: Stanford University Press.

———. 1991. *Language and Symbolic Power*. Cambridge & Oxford, UK: Polity.

Braudel, Fernand. (1967) 1973. *Capitalism and Material Life, 1400–1800*. London: Weidenfeld and Nicolson.
———. (1969) 1980. *On History*. Chicago: University of Chicago Press.
Bray, Francesca. 1986. *The Rice Economies: Technology and Development in Asian Societies*. Oxford: Basil Blackwell.
Brettell, Richard R., and Caroline B. Brettell. 1983. *Painters and Peasants in the Nineteenth Century*. New York: Rizzoli International Publications.
Brown, Delmer M. (1993) 1997. Introduction to the *Cambridge History of Japan*, ed. Delmer M. Brown, 1:1–47. Cambridge: Cambridge University Press.
Bulmer, Ralph. 1967. "Why Is the Cassowary Not a Bird? A Problem of Zoological Taxonomy among the Karam of the New Guinea Highlands." *Man* 2(1): 5–25.
Burke, Edmund. (1757) 1998. "A Philosophical Enquiry into the Origin of Our Ideas of the Sublime and Beautiful." In *A Philosophical Enquiry into the Origin of our Ideas of theSublime and Beautiful and Other Pre-Revolutionary Writings*, 49–199. London: Penguin Books.
Candea, Matei. 2010. "Ontology Is Just Another Word for Culture." *Critique of Anthropology* 30(2): 172–79.
Cartmill, Matt. 1993. *A View to a Death in the Morning: Hunting and Nature Through History*. Cambridge, MA: Harvard University Press.
Carrithers, Michael, Matei Candea, Karen Sykes, Martin Holbraad, and Soumhya Venkatesan. 2010. "Ontology Is Just Another Word for Culture." *Critique of Anthropology* 30(2): 152–200.
Cassirer, Ernst. 1955. *The Philosophy of Symbolic Forms*. Vol. 2, *Mythical Thought*. New Haven, CT: Yale University Press.
Chabal, Patrick, and Jean-Pascal Daloz. 2006. *Culture Troubles: Politics and the Interpretation of Meaning*. Chicago: University of Chicago Press.
Chen, Shou. *Gishi-Wajin-Den* (Treatise on the Wa People). Written during the latter half of the 3rd Century, CE. Japanese Translation by Ishihara Michihiro. 1958. Tokyo: Iwanami Shoten.
Clifford, James, and George Marcus, eds. 1986. *Writing Culture*. Berkeley: University of California Press.
Cranston, Edwin A. 1993. "Asuka and Nara Culture: Literacy, Literature, and Music." In *Cambridge History of Japan*, ed. Marius Jansen, 1:453–503. Cambridge: Cambridge University Press.
Damon, Frederick H. 2017. *Trees, Knots, and Outriggers: Environmental Knowledge in the Northeast Kula Ring*. New York: Berghahn Books.
Daimon Satoru. 2012. "Mushi Uru Mura" [The village that sold insects]. *Hito to Shizen* 3: 6.
Dannaud, Sylvie, and Gertrude Dordor. 2009. *À la Cour des signges*. Château de Saint-Rémy-en-l'Eau: Éditions Monelle Hayot.
Darling, Kate. 2021. *The New Breed: How to Think about Robots*. London: Allen Lane.
Das, Veena. 2020. *Textures of the Ordinary: Doing Anthropology After Wittgenstein*. New York: Fordham University Press.
de Certeau, Michel. (1975) 1988. *The Writing of History*. New York: Columbia University Press.

Deleuze, Gilles. (1968) 1994. *Difference and Repetition*, trans. Paul Patton. New York: Columbia University Press.
———. (1988) 1993. *The Fold: Leibniz and the Baroque*. Minneapolis: University of Minnesota Press.
———. (1990) 1995. *Negotiations*. New York: Columbia University Press.
Descola, Philippe. (1986) 1994. *In the Society of Nature: A Native Ecology in Amazonia*, trans. Nora Scott. Cambridge: Cambridge University Press.
———. 2013. *The Ecology of Others*. Chicago: Prickly Paradigm Press.
———. (2005) 2014. *Beyond Nature and Culture*. Chicago: University of Chicago Press.
———. 2014. "Modes of Being and Forms of Predication." *Hau: Journal of Ethnographic Theory* 4(1): 271–80.
Detienne, Marcel, and Jean-Pierre Vernant. (1979) 1986. *The Cuisine of Sacrifice among the Greeks*, trans. Paula Wissing. Chicago: University of Chicago Press.
Durkheim, Emile, and Marcel Mauss. (1901–2) 1963. *Primitive Classification*. Chicago: University of Chicago Press.
Duus, Peter. 1988. "Socialism, Liberalism, and Marxism, 1901–1931." In *Cambridge History of Japan*, ed. Peter Duus, 6:654–710. Cambridge: Cambridge University Press.
Earhart, David C. 2008. *Certain Victory: Images of World War II in Japanese Media*. New York: M. E. Sharp.
Ebersole, Gary. 1989. *Ritual Poetry and the Politics of Death in Early Japan*. Princeton, NJ: Princeton University Press.
Ebina Kenzō. 1977. *Kaigun Yobi-Gakusei* [Navy student reserve]. Tokyo: Tosho Shuppansha.
———. 1983. *Taiheiyō Sensō ni Shisu–Kaigun Hikō Yobi Shōkō no Sei to Shi* [To die in the Pacific War: Life and death of the navy aviation reserve officers). Tokyo: Nishida Shoten.
Eisenstadt, S. N. 1996. *Japanese Civilization: A Comparative View*. Chicago: University of Chicago Press.
Elias, Norbert. (1939) 2000. *The Civilizing Process*. Oxford: Blackwell Publishing.
Elison, George. 1981. "Hideyoshi, the Bountiful Minister." In *Warlords, Artists and Commoners: Japan in the Sixteenth Century*, ed. G. Elison and B. L. Smith, 222–44. Honolulu: University of Press of Hawaii.
Ellen, Roy. (2006) 2008. *The Categorical Impulse: Essays in the Anthropology of Classifying Behavior*. New York: Berghahn Books.
———. 2020. *Nature Wars: Essays around a Contested Concept*. New York: Berghahn Books.
Ellwood, Robert. 1973. *The Feast of Kingship: Accession Ceremonies in Ancient Japan*. Tokyo: Sophia University Press.
Endō Moto'o. (1910) 1968. "Gyūnabe" [Beef bowl]. In *Meiji Jibutsu Kigen Jiten* [Dictionary of the origins of the Meiji objects], ed. Shibundō Henshūbu, 264. Tokyo: Shibundō.
Feng, Emily. 2021. "Inside the Jaw-Clenching World of Cricket Fighting in China." *NPR*, 23 October.

Fiskesjo, Magnus. 2017. "China's Animal Neighbors." In *The Art of Neighboring: Making Relations across China's Borders*, 223–36. Amsterdam: Amsterdam University Press.
Francks, Penelope. 2009. *The Japanese Consumer: An Alternative Economic History of Modern Japan*. Cambridge: Cambridge University Press.
Francks, Penelope, and Janet Hunter. 2012. *The Historical Consumer: Consumption and Everyday Life in Japan, 1850–2000*. New York: Palgrave.
Frazer, James George. (1890) 1959. *The New Golden Bough*. New York: New American Library.
Frye, Northrop. (1957) 1990. *Anatomy of Criticism*. Princeton, NJ: Princeton University Press.
Fuji'i, Jōji. 2011. *Tennō to Tenkabito* [Emperors and shoguns]. Tokyo: Kōdansha.
Fuji'i Takeo. 1938. *Angora Usagi Konjaku Monogatari* [Angola rabbits, past and present]. Tokyo: Ikuseisha.
Fujio Shin'ichirō. 2014. "Nishi Nihon no Yayoi Inasaku Kaishi Nendai" [The time of the beginning of rice cultivation in western Japan]. *Kokuritsu Rekishi Minzoku Hakubutsukan Kenkyū Hōkoku* 183: 113–43.
Fujioka Michio. 1956. *Kyōto Gosho* [Kyoto Imperial Palace]. Tokyo: Shōkokusha.
Fujiwara no Teika, et al. Circa 1439. *Shin Kokinwakashū*, Sasaki Nobutsuna, ed. [1929] 2020. Iwanami Shoten.
Fukuda Yūji. 2009. "Gendai Nihon no Shōhi Bunka ni kansuru Ichi Kōsatsu" [A study on the consumption culture of modern Japan]. *Journal of Atomi University* 7: 149–157.
Fukutō Sanae. 1998. "Mau Warabetachi no Tōjō: Ōken to Warabe" [The emergence of dancing children: Kingship and children]. In *Ōchō no Kenryoku to Hyōshō: Gakugei no Bunkashi* [Expressions of the kingly power: Cultural history], ed. Fukutō Sanae, 209–50. Tokyo: Shinwasha.
Furet, François. 1972. "Quantitative History." In *Historical Studies*, ed. F. Gilbert and S. R. Graubard, 45–61. New York: Norton.
Furugaki Kōichi. (1991) 1996. "Bonsai." In *Kokushi Daijiten*, ed. Kokushi Daijiten Henshū Iinkai, 12:809. Tokyo: Yoshikawa Kōbunkan.
Gates, Hill. 1987. "Money for the Gods." *Modern China* 13(3): 259–77.
———. 1997. *China's Motor: A Thousand Years of Petty Capitalism*. Ithaca, NY: Cornell University Press.
Geertz, Clifford. 1973. *The Interpretation of Cutures*. New York: Basic Books.
1980. *Negara: The Theatre State in Nineteenth-Century Bali*. Princeton, NJ: Princeton University Press.
Gellner, Ernest. 1992. *Reason and Culture*. Oxford: Blackwell.
Geschiere, Peter. 2009. *The Perils of Belonging: Autochthony, Citizenship, and Exclusion in Africa and Europe*. Chicago: University of Chicago Press.
———. 2013. *Witchcraft, Intimacy and Trust: Africa in Comparison*. Chicago: University of Chicago Press.
Gombrich, E. H. (1960) 2000. *Art and Illustion: A Study of the Psychology of Pictorial Representation*. Princeton: Princeton University Press.
Goody, Jack. 1993. *The Culture of Flowers*. Cambridge: Cambridge University Press.

Gordon, Andrew. 2012. "Consumption, Consumerism, and Japanese Modernity." In *Oxford Handbook of the History of Consumption*, ed. Frank Trentmann, 485–504. Oxford: Oxford University Press.

Gotō, Shigeki, ed. 1975. *Tōkaidō Gojū-San Tsugi* [Fifty-three stations along the Tōkaidō]. Tokyo: Shūeisha.

———, ed. 1976. *Kiso Kaidō Rokujū-Kyū Tsugi* [Sixty-nine stations along the Kiso Road). Tokyo: Shūeisha.

Graeber, David. 2001. *Toward an Anthropological Theory of Value: The False Coin of Our Own Dreams*. New York: Palgrave.

———. 2015. "Radical Alterity Is Just Another Way of Saying 'Reality'—A Reply to Eduardo Viveiros de Castro." *Hau* 5(2): 1–41.

Gramsci, Antonio. 1996. *Prison Notebooks*, vol. 2, trans. Joseph Buttigieg. New York: Columbia University Press.

Gregory, Christopher A. 1997. *Savage Money: The Anthropology and Politics of Commodity Exchange*. Reading: Harwood Academic Publishers.

———. 2004. "On Religiosity and Commercial Life: Toward a Critique of Cultural Economy and Posthumanist Value Theory." *Hau: Journal of Ethnographic Theory* 43(3): 45–68.

Griffiths, Mark. (2009) 2010. *The Lotus Quest: In Search for the Sacred Flower*. New York: Vintage.

Guattari, Félix. 2015. *Machinic Eros: Writings on Japan*. Minneapolis, MN: Univocal Publishing.

Habu, Junko. 2004. *Ancient Jomon of Japan*. Cambrdige University Press.

Hall, Edward. (1966) 1969. *The Hidden Dimension*. Garden City, NY: Doubleday Anchor Book.

Hallowell, A. Irving. 1926. *Bear Ceremonialism in the Northern Hemisphere*. Philadelphia: University of Pennsylvania Press.

Hamilakis, Yannis. 2003. "The Sacred Geography of Hunting: Wild Animals, Social Power, and Gender in Early Farming Societies." In *Zooarchaeology in Greece: Recent Advances*, ed. E. Kotjabopoulou, Y. Hamilaki, P. Halstead, C. Gamble, and P. Elefanti, 239–47. British School at Athens Studies 9.

Handelman, Don. 2020. *Moebius Anthropology: Essays on the Forming of Form*. New York: Berghahn Books.

Harada, Nobuo. 1993. *Rekishi no Naka no Kome to Niku* [Rice and meat in history]. Tokyo: Heibonsha.

Hardacre, Helen. 1997. *Marketing the Menacing Fetus in Japan*. Berkeley: University of California Press.

Harootunian, Harry. 1988. *Things Seen and Unseen: Discourse and Ideology in Tokugawa Nativism*. Chicago: University of Chicago Press.

———. (1989) 1996. "Late Tokugawa Culture and Thought." In *Cambridge History of Japan*, ed. Marius Jansen, 5:168–258. Cambridge: Cambridge University Press.

———. 2000a. *Overcome by Modernity: History, Culture and Community in Interwar Japan*. Princeton, NJ: Princeton University Press.

———. 2000b. *History's Disquiet*. New York: Columbia University Press.

———. 2023. *Archaism and Actuality: Japan and the Global Fascist Imaginary*. Durham, NC: Duke University Press.

Harris, Courtney Leigh. 2023. *Tiny Treasures: The Magic of Miniatures*. Boston: Boston Museum of Fine Arts.
Hartley, Janet M. 2021. *The Volga: A History of Russia's Greatest River*. New Haven, CT: Yale University Press.
Hasegawa, Hiroshi. 1987. *Kome Kokka Kokusho* [The black book on the rice nation). Tokyo: Asahi Shinbunsha.
Hashimoto Yoshihiko. 1985. "Jige" [People below]. In *Kokushi Daijiten*, ed. Kokushi Daijiten Henshū Iinkai, 6:719. Tokyo: Yoshikawa Kōbunkan.
Hattori Shōgo. 1991. "Kamikaze Tokkōtai no Kōgeki" (Attacks by kamikaze special attack forces). *Rekishi to Tabi* (Rinji Zōkangō 50: Taiheiyō Senshi Sōran), 342–45.
Hayashi Yasaka. 1982. "Kinsei Saibaishi" [Horticulture in the early modern period]. *Nihon Jishin* 23: 53–55.
Hayashiya, Tatsusaburō. 1981. "Chūsei geinō no shakaiteki kiban" [The social foundation of arts during the medieval period]. In *Yōkyoku Kyōgen* [Yōkyoku and Kyōgen], ed. Nihon Bungaku Kenkyū Shiryō Kankōkai, 201–9. Tokyo: Yūseidō Shuppan.
Heidegger, Martin. (1927) 1962. *Being and Time*, trans. John Macquarrie and Edward Robinson. New York: Harper and Row.
Henare, A., M. Holbraad, and S. Wastell, eds. 2006. *Thinking Through Things: Theorizing Artifacts Ethnographically*. London: Routledge.
Henderson, John S. 1981. *The World of the Ancient Maya*. Ithaca, NY: Cornell University Press.
Hendry, Joy. 2003. *Understanding Japanese Society*, 3rd edn. London: Routledge Curzon.
Herrenschmidt, Olivier. 1982. "Sacrifice: Symbolic or Effective?" In *Between Belief and Transgression*, eds. Michael Izard and Pierre Smith, 24–42. Chicago: University of Chicago Press.
Herzfeld, Michael. 1997. *Cultural Intimacy: Social Poetics in the Nation-State*. New York: Routledge.
Hida Norio. 2002. *Nihon Tei'en no Shokusaishi* [History of plants management for Japanese gardens]. Kyōto: Kyōto Daigaku Gakujutsu Shuppankai.
Higuchi Yuriko and Fujita Suzaku. 2014. *Manyō no Shiki* (The four seasons of Manyō). Kyōto: Tankōsha.
Hirai Naofusa. (1985) 1995. "Saisen" [Offertory]. In *Kokushi Daijiten*, ed. Kokushi Daijiten Henshū Iinkai, 6:177. Tokyo: Yoshikawa Kōbunkan.
Hirono Takashi. 1998. *Shoku no Manyōshū: Kodai no Shokuseikatsu wo Kagaku suru* [Diet in Manyōshū: Scientific study of diet in the ancient period). Tokyo: Chūōkōronsha.
Hirose Shizumu. (1978) 1979. *Saru* [Monkeys]. Tokyo: Hōsei Daigaku Shuppankyoku.
Hoa, Ho Hoang. 2015. "Nihonjin no shizenkan to nihon teien no zen no shibigan" [Japanese concept of nature and Zen aesthetic appreciation of Japanese gardens]. In *Nichi-etsu kōryū ni okeru rekishi, shakai, bunka no shokadai* [Historical, social, and cultural issues in relations between Japan and Vietnam), ed. Jianhui Liu. Kyoto: International Research Center for Japanese Studies.

Hocart, A. M. (1936) 1970. *Kings and Councilors: An Essay in the Comparative Anatomy of Human Society*. Chicago: University of Chicago Press.
———. 1952. *The Life-Giving Myth*, ed. Lord Raglan. London: Methuen.
Holtom, D. C. (1928) 1972. *The Japanese Enthronement Ceremonies*. Tokyo: Monumenta Nipponica.
Hora, Tomio. 1979. *Tennō Fushinsei no Kigen* [Origin of apolitical nature of the emperor system]. Tokyo: Azekura Shobō.
———. 1984. *Tennō Fushinsei no Dentō* [Tradition of apolitical nature of the emperor system]. Tokyo: Shinjusha.
Horace (Quintus Horatius Flaccus). 1999. *Odes and Epodes*, trans. C. E. Bennett. Cambridge, MA: Harvard University Press.
Horiuchi, Keizō, and Inoue Bushi, eds. (1958) 1995. *Nihon Shōkashū* [Collection of Japanese songs]. Tokyo: Iwanami Shoten.
Horton, H. Mack. 2012. *Traversing the Frontier: The Man'yōshū Account of a Japanese Mission to Silla in 736–737*. Cambridge, MA: Harvard University Press.
Hoshino Akira. 1997. *Shūgaku Ryokō no Rekishi: Senzen no Bu* (History of School Trips: Prewar Period). *Chiri Kyōiku* 26: 6–5.
Hunt, Lynn. 1989. "Introduction: History, Culture, and Text." In *The New Cultural History*, ed. Lynn Hunt, 1–22. Berkeley: University of California Press.
Ide Shinryō and Ushiyama Keikō. 2016. "Kodai Nihon ni okeru Kegare no Kan'nen no Keisei" [The development of the concept of defilement in ancient Japan]. *Shinshū Daigaku Kyōikugakubu Kenkyū Ronbunshū* 9: 81–93.
Iida, Michio. 1983. *Mizaru Kikazaru Iwazaru—Sekai Sanzaru Genryūkō* [No see, no hear, no Say—The source(s) of the three monkeys in various cultures of the world]. Tokyo: Sanseidō.
Iinuma Kenji. 2001. "Kankyō Rekishigaku Josetsu: Shōen no Kaihatsu to Shizen Kankyō." [Introduction to environmental history: Development of Shōen and the natural environment]. *Minshūshi Kenkyū* 61: 3–31.
Iiizumi Kenji. 1996. "Harimanokuni Fudoki, Shikama 'Itōshima Dennshō' Kō" [Harima Fudoki / Shikama Itojima oral tradition—Meaning of the emperor's failure of hunting]. *Risshō Daigaku Bungakubu Ronsō* 103: 41–62.
Imae Hiromichi. 1993. "Sakon no Sakura Ukon no Tachibana" [Cherry blossoms on the left and the mandarin orange on the right hand (of the Imperial Palace)]. In *Nihonshi Daijiten*, ed. Shimonaka Hiroshi, 3:614. Tokyo: Heibonsha.
Imanishi Yūichirō. 1994. Miyabi ("Aesthetics of the people in Kyoto" – various understandings of this term). *Nihonshi Daijiten* 6: 529. Tokyo: Heibonsha.
Ingold, Tim. 1993. "The Temporality of the Landscape." *World Archaeology* 25(2): 152–74.
Inoue Hisashi. 1988. "Kome no Hanashi (5)—Amerika no Kome" [Discussion on Rice (5)—American Rice]. *Days Japan* 1(6): 103.
Inoue Kiyoshi. (1953) 1967. *Tennōsei* [The emperor system]. Tokyo: Tōkyō Daigaku Shuppankai.
———. (1963) 1967. *Nihon no Rekishi* [History of Japan]. Vol. 1 Tokyo: Iwanami Shoten.
Inoue, Mitsusada. 1984. *Nihon Kodai Ōken to Saishi* [The kingship and ritual in ancient Japan). Tokyo: Tōkyō Daigaku Shuppankai.

Ishida Sadao. 1996. "Kingyo" [Goldfish]. In *Kokushi Daijiten*, ed. Kokushi Daijiten Henshū Iinka, 4:518–19. Tokyo: Yoshikawa Kōbunkan.

Ishimori, Shūzō. 1984. "Shi to Zōtō—Mimai Junōchō ni yoru Shakai Kankei no Bunseki" [Death and gifts—Analysis of human relations through the records of gifts]. In *Nihonjin no Zōtō* [Gift exchange of the Japanese], eds. Itoh Mikiharu and Kurita Yasuyuki, 269–304. Kyoto: Mineruva Shobō.

Isozaki Arata. 1995. "Ise." In *Ise Jingū* [Ise Shrine], ed. Ishimoto Yasuhiro, Isozaki Arata, and Inagaki Eizō, 7–31. Tokyo: Iwanami Shoten.

Itō Daisuke. 2011. *Shōzōga no Jidai—Chūsei Keiseiki ni okeru Kaiga no Shisōteki Shinsō*. [The age of portraits—Conceptual base of the paintings during the formative period]. Nagoya: Nagoya Daigaku Shuppankai.

Itō, Mikiharu. 1979. "Ta no Kami" [Deity of the rice paddy]. In *Kōza Nihon no Kodai Shinkō* [Belief system in ancient Japan], ed. T. Matsumae, 162–81. Tokyo: Gakuseisha.

Itō Shirō. 2011a. "Matsuno'o Taisha no Shin'ei" [Figures of the deities at Matsuno'o Shrine]. In *Matsuno'o Taisha*, ed. Itō Shirō, 50–83. Kyōto: Matsuno'o Taisha.

———. 2011b. "Kakko Kaisetsu: Matsuno'o Taisha no Shin'ei" [Explanation of each deity: Figures of the deities at Matsuno'o Shrine]. In *Matsuno'o Taisha*, ed. Itō Shirō, 84–87. Kyōto: Matsuno'o Taisha.

Itō Shuntarō. 1995. *Nihonjin no Shizenkan* [View of nature of the Japanese]. Tokyo: Kawade Shobō.

Itō Tomowo. 1992. *Kinu* [Silk], 2 vols. Tokyo: Hōseidaigaku Shuppankyoku.

Iwaki Kunio, et al. eds. 1995. *Shokubutsu no Sekai (The World of Plants)*. No. 52. Asahi Hyakka. Tokyo: Asahi Shinbun Tokyo Honsha.

Iyenaga Saburō. (1959) 1970. *Nihon Bunkashi* [Cultural history of Japan]. Tokyo: Iwanami Shoten.

Jay, Martin. (1993) 1994. *Downcast Eyes: The Denigration of Vision in Twentieth-Century French Thought*. Berkeley: University of California Press.

Jin Yōshi. 1880. *San'ō Gaiki* [Records of the three shōguns]. Hand-written documents. N.p. Some consider Dasai Shundai as the author. Housed in Waseda University Library.

Jingū Shichō. n.d. *Ise no Jingū* [Ise Shrine]. Uji: Jingū Jichō.

Jinja Honchō. 1995. "Gozōei Yōzai no Kyōkyūgen" [Sources of the building materials]. In *Sengū Ronshū*, 473. Uji: Jinja Honchō.

Joshi Eiyō Daigaku. 1968. *Sarada Tsukemono Jūnikagetsu* [Salad, pickles, twelve months]. Tokyo: Joshi Eiyō Daigaku Shuppanbu.

Juntoku Emperor. (1219–22) 1929. *Kinpishō*. In, Hanawa Hoki'ichi, ed. Vol. 26: 367–418. Tokyo: Gunsho Ruijū Kanseikai.

Kadokawa Shoten Henshūbu, ed. 1961. *Hōnen Shōnin Eden* [Illustrated deeds of Hōnen Shōnin]. *Nihon Emakimono Zenshū* [Collection of Japanese scroll paintings], vol. 13. Tokyo: Kadokawa Shoten.

Kageyama Haruki. (1978) 2011. *Shinzō* [Images of deities]. Tokyo: Hōsei Daigaku Shuppankyoku.

Kaigo Tokiomi, ed. 1964a. "Kokugo" [The national language 3]. In *Nihon Kyōkasho Taikei*, vol. 9. Tokyo: Kōdansha.

———. 1964b. "Kokugo" [The national language 6]. In *Nihon Kyōkasho Taikei*, vol. 9. Tokyo: Kōdansha.
Kameda Takashi. (1993) 1996. "Rikuden." In *Kokushi Daijiten*, ed. Kokushi Daijiten Henshū Iinkai, 14:541–42. Tokyo: Yoshikawa Kōbunkan.
———. 1994. "Ren" [Lotus]. In *Kokushi Daijiten*, ed. Kokushi Daijiten Henshū Iinkai, 11:548. Tokyo: Yoshikawa Kōbunkan.
Kamo Momoki, Kaigun Daijin Kanbō, and Rikugun Daijin Kanbō, eds. 1933–35. *Yasukuni Jinja Chūkonshi* [History of the loyal souls at the Yasukuni Shrine], vol. 1 (1935), vol. 2 (1934), vol. 3 (1934), vol. 4 (1935), vol. 5 (1933). Tokyo: Yasukuni Jinja Shamusho.
Kanagaki Robun. (1870–76) 1926. *Seiyōdōchū hizakurige* [Journey on foot to the western sea]. Tokyo: Iwanami Shoten.
———. (1871–72) 1967. *Aguranabe* [Bowls eaten while sitting with legs crossed]. Tokyo: Iwanami Shoten.
Kant, Immanuel. (1781) 1966. *Critique of Pure Reason*. New York: Doubleday & Company.
———. (1790) 2000. *The Critique of Judgment*. Amherst, New York: Prometheus Books.
———. (1793) 2001. "Analytic of the Sublime." In *Basic Writings of Kant*, ed. Allen W. Wood, 306–8. New York: Random House.
Kantorowicz, Ernst H. (1957) 1981. *The King's Two Bodies*. Princeton, NJ: Princeton University Press.
Kaplan, Martha. 2007. "Fijian Water in Fiji and New York: Local Politics and a Global Commodity." *Cultural Anthropology* 22(4): 685–706.
———. 2011. "Lonely Drinking Fountains and Comforting Coolers: Paradoxes of Water Value and Ironies of Water Use." *Cultural Anthropology* 26(4): 514–41.
Kaplan, Steven L. 1976a. *Bread, Politics and Political Economy in the Reign of Louis XV*, vol. 1. The Hague, Netherlands: Martinus Nijhoff.
———. 1976b. *Bread, Politics and Political Economy in the Reign of Louis XV*, vol. 2. The Hague, Netherlands: Martinus Nijhoff.
Katō Hidesachi. (1984) 1996. "Kiku no Mon" [The chrysanthemum crest]. In *Kokushi Daijiten*, ed. Kokushi Daijiten Henshū Iinkai, 4:51. Tokyo: Yoshikawa Kōbunkan.
Kawai Ryōichi, and Ōta Yōai. 1982. "Nihonjin no Kokoro no Furusato: Sakura" [The primordial space for the Japanese soul: Cherry blossoms). *Nihon Jishin* 23: 89–93.
Kawamura Minato. 1998. *Manshū Tetsudō Maboroshi Ryokō* [The dream travel by the Manchurian railroad). Osaka: NESCO.
Kawasoe Taketane. (1978) 1980. *Kojiki no Sekai* [The world of *Kojiki*]. Tokyo: Kyōikusha.
Kelly, John. 2014. "Introduction: The Ontological Turn in French Philosophical Anthropology." *Hau: Journal of Ethnographic Theory* 4(1): 259–69.
Kisaka Jun'ichirō. 1996. "Taisei Yokusankai." In *Kokushi Daijiten*, ed. Kokushi Daijiten Henshū Iinkai. Tokyo: Yoshikawa Kōbunkan.
Kitagawa, Joseph. (1966) 1990. *Religion in Japanese History*. New York: Columbia University Press.

———. 1990. "Some Reflections on Japanese Religion and Its Relationship to the Imperial System." *Japanese Journal of Religious Studies* 17(2–3): 129–78.
Kobayashi Issa. 1929. *Issa Haiku Zenshū* [Collected haiku poems of Issa]. Tokyo: Shunjūsha.
Kobayashi Tatsuo. 2008. *Jōmon no Shikō* [Thought world of Jōmon]. Tokyo: Chikuma Shobō.
———. 2018. *Jōmon Bunka ga Nihonjin no Mirai wo Hiraku* [Jomon culture opening the door for the future of the Japanese]. Tokyo: Tokuma Shoten.
Komatsu Kazuhiko. 1982. *Hyōrei Shinkōron* [Theory on the belief in Hyōrei]. Tokyo: Dentō to Gendaisha.
Koyama, Hiroshi. 1960. *Kyōgenshū (Jō)* [Collection of *Kyōgen*], vol. 1. Tokyo: Iwanami Shoten.
Kubo Noritada. 1961. *Kōshin Shinkō no Kenkyū: Nicchū Shūkyō Bunka Kōshōshi* [Research on Kōshin belief: History of the Japan-China exchange of religious culture]. Tokyo: Nihon Gakujutsu Shinkōkai.
Kubota Jun. 1990. "Nanden no Sakura" [Cherry blossoms in the south garden (of the Imperial Palace)]. *Bungaku* 1(1): 34–48.
Kubota Jun, trans. 2007. *Shin Kokin Wakashū Jyō Ge*. Tokyo: Kadokawa Shoten.
Kumakura Isao. (1990) 1995. *Chanoyu no Rekishi: Sen no Rikyū Made* [A history of the tea ceremony: Up to Sen no Rikyū]. Tokyo: Asahi Shinbun.
———. 2007. *Kobori Enshū* Chayūroku [Friends of Kobori Enshū]. Tokyo: Chūō Kōron.
Kunaichō Kyōto Jimusho. 2019. *Sekai Isan: Moto-rikyū Nijyōjō* [World heritage: Former detached palace]. Kyoto: Kunaichō Kyōto Jimusho.
Kuper, Adam.1988. *The Invention of Primitive Society: Transformation of an Illusion.* New York: Taylor & Frances / Routledge.
Kurano, Kenji, and Takeda Yūkichi, eds. 1958. *Kojiki Norito* [Kojiki and Norito]. Tokyo: Iwanami Shoten.
Kuroda, Toshio. 1972. "Chūsei no mibunsei to hisen kannen" [The social stratification during the medieval period and the concept of baseness]. *Buraku Mondai Kenkyū* 33: 23–57.
Kuroita Katsumi, ed. 1965a. "Nihon Kiryaku" (Chronology of Japanese History). In *Kokushi Taikei*, 10:1–546. Tokyo: Yoshikawa Kōbunkan.
———. 1965b. "Teiō Hennenki." In *Kokushi Taikei*, 12:1–456. Tokyo: Yoshikawa Kōbunkan.
———. 1965c. "Kojidan." In *Kokushi Taikei*, 18:1–132. Tokyo: Yoshikawa Kōbunkan.
———. 1966. "Shoku Nihon Kōki." In *Kokushi Taikei*, 3:1–246. Tokyo: Yoshikawa Kōbunkan.
Kyburz, Josef A. 2011. "The Talisman of Ise: A Certificate of Being Japanese." *Kokusai Nihon Kenkyū Sōsho* 17: 107–23.
———. 2014. "Ofuda—An Overview." In *Ofuda: Amulettes et talismans du Japon* [Ofuda: On Japanese charms], ed. Josef Kyburz, 349–97. Paris: Institut des Hautes Études Japonaises, Collège de France.
Kyōto Kokuritsu Hakubutsukan, ed. 2012. *Ōchō Bunka no Hana* [The flower of the ancient imperial culture]. Kyōto: Kyōto Kokuritsu Hakubutsukan.

Kyōto-shi, ed. 1975. *Kyōto no Kindai* [Kyōto during the modern period]. Vol. 8, *Kyōto no Rekishi*. Kyōto: Gakugei Shorin.
———. 1981. *Shigai Seigyō* [Streets and livelihood]. Vol. 4, *Shiryō Kyōto no Rekishi*. Tokyo: Heibonsha.
LaFleur, William R. 1983. *The Karma of Words: Buddhism and the Literary Arts in Medieval Japan*. Berkeley: University of California Press.
Latour, Bruno. (1991) 1993. *We Have Never Been Modern*. Cambridge, MA: Harvard University Press.
———. 2004. *Politics of Nature*. Cambridge, MA: Harvard University Press.
———. 2005. *Reassembling the Social: An Introduction to Actor-Network-Theory*. Oxford: Oxford University Press.
———. 2010. *On the Modern Cult of the Factish Gods*. Durham, NC: Duke University Press.
Leach, Edmund. (1953) 1961. "Cronus and Chronos." In *The Essential Edmund Leach*, ed. Stephen Hugh-Jones and James Laidlaw, 1:174–81. New Haven, CT: Yale University Press.
———. (1954) 1965. *Political Systems of Highland Burma*. Boston: Beacon Press.
———. (1955) 1961. "Time and False Noses." In *The Essential Edmund Leach*, ed. Stephen Hugh-Jones and James Laidlaw, 1:182–85. New Haven, CT: Yale University Press.
———. (1966) 2000. "Virgin Birth." The Henry Myers Lecture 1966. *Proceedings of the Royal Anthropological Institute of Great Britain and Ireland*: 39–49.
———. 1968. Introduction to *Dialectic in Practical Religion*, ed. Edmund Leach, 1–6. Cambridge: Cambridge University Press.
Lee, Richard. 1968. "What Hunters Do for a Living, or, How to Make Out on Scarce Resources." In *Man the Hunter*, ed. Richard B. Lee and Irven DeVore, 30–48. Chicago: Aldine/Atherton.
Lefebvre, Henri. 1994. *Everyday Life in the Modern World*. New Brunswick, NJ: Transactions Publishers.
Le Goff, Jacques. 1972. "Is Politics Still the Backbone of History?" In *Historical Studies Today*, ed. F. Gilbert and S. R. Graubard, 337–55. New York: Norton.
Lévy-Bruhl, Lucien. 1922. *La mentalité primitive*. Oxford: Clarendon.
———. 1927. *L'âme primitive*. Paris: Alcan.
———. 1928. *The Soul of the Primitive*. New York: Macmillan.
Lévi-Strauss, Claude. (1962) 1966. *The Savage Mind*. Chicago: University of Chicago Press.
———. (1949) 1969. *The Elementary Structures of Kinship*. Boston: Beacon Press.
———. 1992. *The View from Afar*, trans. Joachim Neugroschel and Phoebe Hoss. Chicago: University of Chicago Press.
———. 2013a. *Anthropology Confronts the Problems of the Modern World*. Cambridge, MA: Harvard University Press.
———. 2013b. *The Other Face of the Moon*. Cambridge, MA: Harvard University Press.
Lewin. Tamar. 2015. "Michio Kushi, Advocate of Natural Foods in the U.S., Dies at 88." *New York Times*, 4 January.

Limbourg brothers. 1412, 1416. *Très Riches Heures du Duc de Berry*. Reproduced in 1485–89. MS 65, Chantilly, France, Musée Condé.
Longinus. 1985. *On the Sublime*, trans. J. A. Arieti and J. M. Crossett. Lewiston, NY: Edwin Mellen Press.
Loyer, Emmanuelle. 2015. *Lévi-Strauss*. Paris: Flammarion.
———. 2018. *Lévi-Strauss: A Biography*. Medford, MA: Polity Press.
Lukács, György. (1923) 1971. "Reification and the Consciousness of the Proletariat." In *History and Class Consciousness*, trans. R. Livingstone, 83–222. Cambridge, MA: MIT Press.
Macé, François. 1982. "Mogari Kaishaku no Ichishiron: 'Kanashimi,' 'Shizume,' 'Asobi' no Sankyoku Kōzō" [An interpretation of mogari]. *Ehime Daigaku Kyōyōbu Kiyō* 15: 607–19.
———. 1985. *Genmei Tajō Tennō no Sōgiga Imisuru Maisō Gireishijō no Danzetsuten* [The break in the history of the funeral rituals as indicated by the funeral for Empress Genmei]. *Shūkyō Kenkyū* 266: 55–77.
———. 1989. "The Funerals of the Japanese Emperors." *Nanzan Bulletin* 13: 26–37.
Maeda Ujō. 1980. *Iro: Some to Shikisai* [Colors: Dyeing and colors]. Tokyo: Hōseidaigaku Shuppankyoku.
Malinowski, Bronislaw. (1925) 1954. *Magic, Science and Religion and Other Essays*. New York: The Free Press.
Marra, Michele. 1993. *Representations of Power: The Literary Politics of Medieval Japan*. Manoa: University of Hawaii Press.
Marx, Karl, and Frederick Engels. (1852) 1989. "Manifesto of the Communist Party." In *Basic Writings on Politics and Philosophy: Karl Marx and Friedrich Engels*, ed. Lewis S. Feuer, 1–41. New York: Doubleday.
Matsui Yoshi'ichi. 1942. *Kingyo no Kenkyū* [Research on goldfish]. Tokyo: Kawade Shobō.
Matsumae Takeshi. 1977. *Nihon no Kamigami* [Japanese deities]. Tokyo: Chūōkōronsha.
———. (1988) 1990a. "Inari Myōjin no Genzō" [The original figure for Inari deity]. In *Inari Myōjin*, ed. Matsumae Takeshi, 3–40. Tokyo: Chikuma Shobō.
———. (1988) 1990b. "Inari Myōjin to Kitsune" [Inari deity and the fox]. In *Inari Myōjin*, ed. Matsumae Takeshi, 73–90. Tokyo: Chikuma Shobō.
———. 1993. "Early Kami Worship." In *Cambridge History of Japan*, ed. Delmer M. Brown, 1: 317–58. Cambridge: Cambridge University Press.
Matsumoto Shinpachirō. 1981. "Kyōgen no Omokage" [Images in Kyōgen]. In *Yōkyoku Kyōgen* [Yōkyoku and Kyōgen], ed. Nihon Bungaku Kenkyū Shiryō Kankōkai, 190–200. Tokyo: Yūseidō Shuppan.
Matsuno'o Taisha Shrine. 2011. *Matsuno'o Taisha no Shinei* [Sacred figures at Matsuno'o Taisha]. Kyōto: Matsuno'o Taisha.
Mauss, Marcel. (1925) 1950. *Essai sur le don, forme archaïque de l'échange*. Paris: Universitaires de France.
———. (1950) 1972. *A General Theory of Magic*. New York: Routledge & Kegan Paul.
Mayer, Adrian C. 1991. "Recent Succession Ceremonies of the Emperor of Japan." *Japan Review* 2: 35–61.

Mayuzumi, Hiromichi. 1982. *Ritsuryō Kokka Seiritsushi no Kennkyū* [Research on the history of the development of the nation with penal and administrative laws]. Tokyo: Yoshikawa Kōbunkan.
McCullough, Helen Craig. 1985. *Brocade by Night: "Kokin Wakashu" and the Court Style in Japanese Classical Poetry*. Stanford, CA: Stanford University Press.
McCullough, William. 1999. "The Capital and Its Society." In *Cambridge History of Japan*, ed. Donald H. Shively and William H. McCullough, 2:97–182. Cambridge: Cambridge University Press.
McCullough, William H., and Helen Craig McCullough, trans. 1980. *A Tale of Flowering Fortunes* [*Eiga Monogatari*]. Vol. 2. Stanford: Stanford University Press.
Mennell, Stephen. 1985. *All Manners of Food: Eating and Taste in England and France from the Middle Ages to the Present*. Oxford: Basil Blackwell.
Mezaki Tokue. 1969. *Heian Ōchō* [Heian Imperial Court]. *Nihon Rekishi Zenshū*. Vol. 4. Tokyo: Kōdansha.
Minakata, Kumagusu. (1971) 1972. *Minakata Kumakusu Zenshū* [Collected essays by Minakata Kumakusu]. Vol. 1. Tokyo: Heibonsha.
Minamoto-no-Akikane. 1965. *Kojidan* [Ancient tales]. In *Kokushi Taikei*, vol. 18, ed. Kuroita Katsumi and Kokushi Taikei Henshūkai. Tokyo: Yoshikawa Kōbunkan.
Ministry of Foreign Affairs. 2015. *Niponica* 16. Tokyo: Ministry of Foreign Affairs.
———. 2015. *Niponica* 17. Tokyo: Ministry of Foreign Affairs.
Mintz, Sidney W. 1985. *Sweetness and Power: The Place of Sugar in Modern History*. New York: Vikings.
———. 1994. "Crops and Human Culture." Address to the Third Annual Conference of the Society for the Study of Local and Regional History. Marshall, MN: Southwest State University.
Minzokugaku Kenkyūjo, ed. 1951. *Minzokugaku Jiten*. Tokyo: Tōkyōdō Shuppan.
Miura, Shūgyō. 1988. "Tairei Seido no Enkaku" [Outline of the Tairei (imperial ritual) System]. In *Zusetsu Tennō no Sokuirei to Ōnamesai*, ed. H. Yamamoto, M. Satō, and staff, 142–46. Tokyo: Shinjinbutsu Ōraisha.
Miyake Hitoshi. (1989) 1992. *Shūkyō Minzokugaku* [Folklore study of religions]. Tokyo: Tōkyō Daigaku Shuppankai.
———. 1995. "Nihon no Minzoku Shūkyō ni Okeru Shizenkan" [Concept of nature in Japanese folk religion]. *Shūkyō Kenkyū* 69(1): 91–111.
Miyamoto, Tsuneichi. 1981. *Emakimono ni Miru Nihon Shomin Seikatsushi* [Life of common people in Japan as depicted in picture scrolls]. Tokyo: Chūōkōronsha.
Miyao Shigeo. 1975. "Hiroshige to Meisho Edo Hyakkei" [Hiroshige and the one hundred famous places in Edo]. In *Meisho Edo Hyakkei*, ed. Gotō Shigeki. *Ukiyoe Taikei* 16: 74–80. Tokyo: Shūeisha.
Miyao Tōru. 2018. "Doki Bunka no Hajimari" (The Beginning of Pottery Culture). Heisei 30nendo Niigata Kōkogaku Kōenkai Yōshishū (Lectures at the Niigata Archaeological Society in 2018), pp. 1–12.
Miyata Noboru. 1975. *Kinsei no Hayarigami* [Popular deities during the early modern period]. Tokyo: Hyōronsha.
———. 1988. *Rēkon no Minzokugaku* [Folklore study of the soul]. Tokyo: Nihon Editā Sukūru Shuppan.

———. 1989. "Nihon Ōken no Minzokuteki Kiso" [Ethnographic basis of the Japanese kingship]. *Shikyō* 18: 25–30.

———. 1992. *Hiyorimi: Nihon Ōkenron no Kokoromi* [Weather forecasting: An attempt for an interpretation of the Japanese emperor's power]. Tokyo: Heibonsha.

———. 1993. *Yama to Sato no Shinkōshi* [History of the belief about the mountains and the homestead]. Tokyo: Yoshikawa Kōbunkan.

———. 1994a. "Mizuko Kuyō" [Memorial service for aborted fetus]. In *Taishū Bunka Jiten*, ed. Ishikawa Hiroyoshi et al., 763. Tokyo: Kōbundō.

———. 1994b. "Shiro no Fōkuroa" [Folklore of whiteness]. In Tokyo: Heihonsha.

———. 1995. *Kūkō no tonari machi Haneda* [Town next to the Haneda Airport]. Tokyo: Iwanami Shoten.

Miyatake Gaikotsu, ed. 1925. *Meiji Kibun* [Reports about the Meiji period). Vol. 2. Tokyo: Hankyōdō.

Monbushō (Ministry of Education). 1934. "Nijyūroku: On wo Wasureruna" [Lesson no. 26, Do not forget indebtedness]. In *Jinjō Shōgaku Shūshinsho* Kan 2. [Vol. 2, Textbook on morality], 74–77. Tokyo: Monbushō.

Moore, Sally Falk. 1986. *Social Facts and Fabrications: "Customary" Law on Kilmanjaro, 1880–1980*. Cambridge: Cambridge University Press.

Morikawa Hiroyuki. 2022. *Washoku no Kyōkasho: Gion Kondatechō* [The textbook for Japanese cuisine: Recipes from Gion]. Tokyo: Sekaibunkasha.

Morse, Peter. 1989. *Hokusai: One Hundred Poets*. New York: George Braziller.

Mosko, Mark S. 2017. *Ways of Baloma: Rethinking Magic and Kinship from the Trobriands*. Chicago: Hau Books.

Mosse, George L. 1975. *The Nationalization of the Masses: Political Symbolism and Mass Movements in Germany from the Napoleonic Wars through the Third Reich*. Ithaca: Cornell University Press.

Mostow, Joshua S. 1999. "Nihon no Bijutsushi Gensetsu to 'Miyabi'" [Art historical discourse in Japan and "courtliness"]. In *Ima, Nihon no Bijutsushigaku wo Furikaeru* [Today, we reflect on art history of Japan], eds. Tokyo Kokuritsu Bunkazai Kenkyūjo, 232–38. Tokyo: Heibonsha.

Motoori Norinaga. (1790) 1968. *Motoori Norinaga Zenshū* [Complete works by Motoori Norinaga], vol. 1, ed. Ōno Susumu. Tokyo: Chikuma Shobō.

Mourenza, Daniel. 2020. "Mickey Mouse: Utopian and Barbarian." In *Walter Benjamin and the Aesthetics of Film*, 195–234. Amsterdam: Amsterdam University Press.

Murai, Yasuhiko. 2004. "Tennō, Kuge, to Buke" [Emperor, courtiers, and warriors]. In *Kuge to Buke* [Courtiers and warriors], ed. Kasaya Kazuhiko, 3–8. Kyoto: Kokusai Nihon Bunka Kenkyū Sentā.

Murakami Haruki. 1993. *Sekai no Owari to Hādo Boirudo Wandārando* [Hard-Boiled Wonderland and the End of the World]. In *Murakami Haruki Zenshū* [Collected works of Murakami Haruko], vol. 4. Tokyo: Kōdansha.

Murakami Senjō, Tsuji Zennosuke, and Washio Junkei, eds. 1970. *Meiji Ishin Shinbutsu Bunri Shiryō* [Records on the separation between Buddhas and deities at the time of Meiji Restoration], vol. 2. Tokyo: Meicho Shuppan.

Murakami Shigeyoshi. 1977. *Tennō no Saishi* [Imperial rituals]. Tokyo: Iwanami Shoten.

———. 1986. *Tennō to Nihon Bunka* [The emperor and Japanese culture]. Tokyo: Kōdansha.
Murasaki Shikibu. (1000) 2019. "Suzumushi" [Pine cricket]. In *Genji Monogatari*, vol. 6, ed. Yahai Shigeshi et al., 163–202. Tokyo: Iwanami Shoten.
———. (1000) 2020a. "Tamakazura." In *Genji Monogatari*, vol. 4, ed. Yahai Shigeshi et al., 11–125. Tokyo: Iwanami Shoten.
———. (1000) 2020b. "Kotefu" [Butterflies]. In *Genji Monogatari*, vol. 4, ed. Yahai Shigeshi et al., 167–220. Tokyo: Iwanami Shoten.
Murasaki Yoshimasa. 1980. *Sarumawashi Fukkatsu* [The revival of monkey performances]. Kyoto: Buraku Mondai Kenkyūsho Shuppanbu.
Nagasawa Kikuya, ed. 1990. *Sanseidō Kanwajiten*. Tokyo: Sanseidō.
Naikakufu Seifu Kōhōshitsu. 2003. *"Dōbutsu Aigo ni kansuru Yoron Chōsano Gaiyō"* [Outline of the survey on the loving care of animals]. Tokyo: Naikakufu Seifu Kōhōshitsu.
Nakamura Hiroshi. 1982. "Sakura no Gogen" [The etymology of cherry blossoms]. *Nihon Jishin* 23: 59–61.
Nakamura, Teiri. 1984. *Nihonjin no Dōbutsukan—Henshintan no Rekishi* [Japanese views of animals—History of tales about metamorphoses]. Tokyo: Kaimeisha.
Nakanishi Susumu. 1995. *Hana no Katachi: Nihonjin to Sakura* [The forms of the flower: Cherry blossoms of the Japanese). Vol. 1, *Jō, Koten*. Vol. 2, *Chū, Kindai*. Tokyo: Kadokawa Shoten.
Nakano Takamasa and Kobayashi Kunio. 1967. *Nihon no Shizen* [Japanese nature]. Tokyo: Iwanami Shoten.
Nakao Sasuke. 1986. *Hana to Ki no Bunkashi* [Cultural history of flowers and trees]. Tokyo: Iwanami Shoten.
National Park Service. 2009. "Cherry Blossom Festival: History of the Cherry Trees." National Parks Service, US Department of the Interior, Washington, DC. Last updated 1 March 2023, www.nps.gov/cherry/.
Natsume Sōseki. (1907) 1984. "Kōfu" [The miners]. In *Sōseki Zenshū* [Complete works of Sōseki], vol. 3. Tokyo: Iwanami Shoten. Originally published as a daily newspaper column, beginning 1 January 1907.
Newby, Howard. 1979. *Green and Pleasant Land?* London: Hutchinson.
Nihiname Kenkyūkai, ed. 1955. *Nihiname no Kenkyū* [Research on the Nihiname]. Tokyo: Yoshikawa Kōbunkan.
Nihon Hōsō Kyōkai, ed. 1988. *Nihon no Bi: Sakura* [Beauty of Japan: Cherry blossoms]. Tokyo: NHK Shuppan.
Nihon Kōtsūkōsha (Japan Travel Agency). 2013. Sōgyō 1912nen kara Ichiseiki Sōhatsuteki Shinnka he Mukete – Chōsa Senmon Kikan 50nen no Rekishi (Since its Establishment in 1912, the Creative Progress for One Century – History of 50 years of Investigation and Research). Tokyo: Nihon Kōtsū Kōsha.
Nihon Yūbinkitte Shōkyōdō Kumiai. 2003. *Nihon Yūbinkitte Katarogu* [Catalog of Japanese postal stamps]. Tokyo: Nihon Yūbinkitte Shōkyōdō Kumiai.
Nishida Kitarō. 1965a. "Hatarakumono kara Mirumono he" [From that which acts to that which sees]. In *Nishida Kitarō Zenshū* [Collected works of Nishida Kitarō], 4:3–6. Tokyo: Iwanami Shoten.

———. 1965b. "Mu no Jikakuteki Gentei" [The limit of intelligibility of nothingness]. In *Nishida Kitarō Zenshū* [Collected works of Nishida Kitarō], vol. 6. Tokyo: Iwanami Shoten.
Nishiyachi Seibi. 2009. "Mizuhonokuni no Henkan to Tōji Rinen" (Conversion of the Characters for Mizuho-no-Kuni and the Principle of Governance [sic.]). Vol. 190: 330–56.
Nitobe Inazō. (1899) 1912. *Bushidō: The Soul of Japan*. Philadelphia: Leeds and Biddle.
Nitobe Inazō. (1933) 1969. "Bushidō to Shōnindō" [The way of warriors and the way of merchants]. In *Nitobe Inazō Zenshū*, 6:324–36. Tokyo: Kyōbunkan.
Niunoya Tetsuichi. 1993. *Nihon Chūsei no Mibun to Shakai* [Status and society in medieval Japan]. Tokyo: Hanawa Shoten.
Nonomura, Kaizō, ed. (1953) 1968. *Kyōgenshū (Jō)* [Collection of Kyōgen], vol. 1. Tokyo: Asahi Shinbunsha.
Nonomura, Kaizō, and Andō Tsunejirō, eds. 1974. *Kyōgen Shūsei* [Collection of *Kyōgen*). Tokyo: Nōrin Shoin.
Normile, Dennis. 1997. "Yangtze Seen as Earliest Rice Site." *Science* 275: 309.
Nova, Alessandro. 2011. *The Book of the Wind: The Representation of the Invisible*. Montreal: McGill-Queen's University Press.
Nukada, Iwao. 1972. *Musubi* [Knots]. Tokyo: Hōsei Daigaku Shuppankyoku.
Oda Kōji. 1980. "Suō ni okeru sarumawashi" [Monkey performance at Suō]. In *Suō Sarumawashi Kinkyū Chōsa Hōkokusho* [Report on urgent investigation on monkey performances at Suō], ed. Yamaguchiken Kyōiku Iinkai Bunkaka, 3–29. Yamaguchi Prefecture: Yamaguchiken Kyōiku Iinkai.
———. 2020. "Igai to Shirarete inai Chūken Hachikō no Saigo" [The last days of Hachikō—A not well-known story]. *Dime*, 15 August. https://dime.jp/genre/968088.
Ohnuki-Tierney, Emiko. 1974. *The Ainu of the Northwest Coast of Southern Sakhalin*. Tokyo: Holt, Rinehart and Winston.
———. 1977. "An Octopus Headache? A Lamprey Boil? Multisensory Perception of 'Habitual Illnesses' and World View of the Ainu." *Journal of Anthropological Research* 33(3): 245–57.
———. 1981. "Phases in Human Perception/Conception/Symbolization Process—Cognitive Anthropology and Symbolic Classification." *American Ethnologist* 8(3): 451–67.
———. 1984a. *Illness and Culture in Contemporary Japan: An Anthropological View*. Cambridge: Cambridge University Press.
———. 1984b. "Monkey Performances—A Multiple Structure of Meaning and Reflexivity in Japanese Culture." In *Text, Play and Story*, ed. E. Bruner, 278–314. Washington, DC: American Ethnological Society.
———. 1987. *The Monkey as Mirror: Symbolic Transformations in Japanese History and Ritual*. Princeton, NJ: Princeton University Press.
———. 1990a. "Introduction: The Historicization of Anthropology." In *Culture through Time*, ed. E. Ohnuki-Tierney. Stanford, CA: Stanford University Press.
———. 1990b. "Monkey as Metaphor? Transformations of a Polytropic Symbol in Japanese Culture." *Man*, n.s., 25: 399–416.

———. ed. 1990c. *Culture through Time: Anthropological Approaches*. Stanford, CA: Stanford University Press.

———. 1991. "The Emperor of Japan as Deity (*Kami*): An Anthropology of the Imperial System in Historical Perspective." *Ethnology* 30(3): 1–17.

———. 1993a. "Nature, pureté et soi primordial: La nature japonaise dans une perspective comparative." *Géographie et Cultures* 7: 75–92.

———. 1993b Presence of the Absence: Zero Signifiers and Zero Meanings. *Semiotic* 96 (3/4): 301-08.

———. 1994. *Rice as Self: Japanese Identities through Time*. Princeton, NJ: Princeton University Press.

———. 1995. "Structure, Event and Historical Metaphor: Rice and Identities in Japanese History." *Journal of Royal Anthropological Institute* 30(2): 227–53.

———. 1997. "The Reduction of Personhood to Brain and Rationality? Japanese Contestation of Medical High Technology." In *Western Medicine as Contested Knowledge*, eds. A. Cunningham and B. Andrews, 212–40. Manchester: Manchester University Press.

———. 1999. "Ainu Sociality." In *Ainu: Spirit of a Northern People*, ed. W. W. Fitzhugh and C. O. Dubreuil, 240–45. Washington, DC: National Museum of Natural History, Smithsonian Institution.

———. 2001. Historicization of the Culture Concept. *History and Anthropology* 12 (3): 213-54.

———. 2002a. *Kamikaze, Cherry Blossoms, and Nationalisms: The Militarization of Aesthetics in Japanese History*. Chicago: University of Chicago Press.

———. 2002b. "Ōnamesai to Ōken" [The imperial accession ritual and the kingship]. In *Ten'nō to Ōken wo Kangaeru* [The emperor and the kingship], vol. 5, *Ōken to Girei* [The kingship and ritual], ed. Amino Yoshihiko et al. Tokyo: Iwanami Shoten.

———. 2006. *Kamikaze Diaries: Reflections of Japanese Student Soldiers*. Chicago: University of Chicago Press.

———. 2015. *Flowers That Kill: Communicative Opacity in Political Spaces*. Stanford, CA: Stanford University Press.

———. 2021. *Karafuto Ainu Minzokushi—Sono Seikatsu to Sekaikan* [Ethnography of the Sakhalin Ainu—Their life and worldview], trans. Sakaguchi Ryō. Tokyo: Seidosha.

Okada, Seishi. 1970. *Kodai Ōken no Saishi to Shinwa* [The ritual and myth of the ancient emperor system]. Tokyo: Hanawa Shōbō.

Okimori Takuya, , Sasahara Hiroyuki, Tokiwa Tomoko, Yamamoto Shingo, eds. 2011. *Zukai Nihon no Moji* [Illustrated Japanese characters]. Tokyo: Sanseidō.

Omodaka Hisataka. (1967) 1983. Man'yōshū Chūshaku [Interpretation and annotation of Man'yōshū], vol. 8. Tokyo: Chūōkōronsha.

Ong, Walter. (1982) 2002. *Orality and Literacy*. New York: Routledge.

Orikuchi, Shinobu. (1924) 1983. "Kokubungaku no Hassei (Dai Ni Kō)." [The birth of Japanese literature (2nd edn.)]. In *Orikuchi Shinobu Zenshū* [Collected work of Orikuchi Shinobu], 1:76–123. Tokyo: Chūōkōronsha.

———. (1927) 1983. "Kokubungaku no Hassei (Dai Yon Kō)." [The birth of Japanese literature, (4th edn.)]. In *Orikuchi Shinobu Zenshū* [Collected work of Orikuchi Shinobu], 1:124–216. Tokyo: Chūōkōronsha.

———. (1928) 1975a. "Shindō ni Arawareta Minzoku Ronri" [Ethnographic interpretation of Shitoism]. In *Orikuchi Shinobu Zenshū* [Collected work of Orikuchi Shinobu], 3:145–73. Tokyo: Chūōkōronsha.

———. (1928) 1975b. "Ōnamesai no Hongi" [True meaning of the Ōnamesai]. In *Orikuchi Shinobu Zenshū* [Collected work of Orikuchi Shinobu], 3:174–240. Tokyo: Chūōkōronsha.

———. (1943) 1976. "Kotodama Shinkō" [Belief in the soul of words]. In *Orikuchi Shinobu Zenshū* [Collected work of Orikuchi Shinobu], 20:245–52. Tokyo: Chūōkōronsha.

———. (1947) 1983. "Matsuri no Hanashi" [On the festivals]. In *Orikuchi Shinob Zenshū* [Collected work of Orikuchi Shinobu], 15:271–80. Tokyo: Chūōkōronsha.

———. 1976. "Jōsei Nihon no Bunngaku" [Japanese literature during the ancient period]. In *Orikuchi Shinobu Zenshū* [Collected work of Orikuchi Shinobu], 12:323–509. Tokyo: Chūōkōronsha.

Ōta Rin'ichirō. 1980. *Nihon no Gunpuku* [Japanese army uniforms]. Tokyo: Kokusho Kankōkai.

Ouwehand, Cornelis. 1964. *Namazu-e and Their Themes: An Interpretive Approach to Some Aspects of Japanese Folk Religions*. Leiden: E. J. Brill.

Ozawa Hiroshi. 1987. "Minshū Shūkyō no Shinsō" [The thought structure of the folk religions]. In *Nihon no Shakaishi*, ed. Asao Naohiro et al., 8:296–332. Tokyo: Iwanami Shoten.

Parry, J., and M. Bloch, eds. 1989. *Money and the Morality of Exchange*. Cambridge: Cambridge University Press.

Parry, Jonathan. 1985. "Death and Digestion: The Symbolism of Food and Eating in North Indian Mortuary Rite." *Man*, n.s., 20: 612–30.

Pet Food Cooperation. 2020. *Zenkoku Inu Neko Shiiku Jittai Chōsa Kekka* [Report of the national survey of the dogs and cats as pets]. Ippan Shadan Hōjin Petto Hūdo Kyōkai. https://petfood.or.jp.

Piłsudski, Bronisław. 1914. "Na medvedž'em prazdnik ajnov o. Sachalina." *Žhivaia Starina* 23(1–2): 67–162.

Plato. (1935) 2000. *Republic, Books 6–10*, trans. Paul Shorey. Cambridge, MA: Harvard University Press.

Pollack, David. 1986. *The Fracture of Meaning: Japan's Synthesis of China from the Eighth through the Eighteenth Centuries*. Princeton, NJ: Princeton University Press.

Ponsonby-Fane. R. A. B. 1956. *Kyoto*. Kyoto: Ponsonby Memorial Society.

Pouillon, Jean. 1982. "Remarks on the Verb 'To Believe.'" In *Between Belief and Transgression*, ed. Michael Izard and Pierre Smith, 1–8. Chicago: University of Chicago Press.

Ramos, Alcida Rita. 2012. "The Politics of Perspectivism." *Annual Review of Anthropology* 41: 481–94.

Reader, Ian. 2015. *Pilgrimage in the Marketplace*. New York: Routledge.

Rhee, Song-nai, C. Melvin Aikens, and Gina Barnes. 2021. *Archaeology and History of Toraijin*. Oxford: Archaeopress.

Rich, Nathaniel. 2021. *Second Nature: Scenes from a World Remade*. New York: Farrar, Strauss and Giroux.

Richards, Gladys A. (1963) 2016. *Navajo Religion: A Study of Symbolism*. Princeton, NJ: Princeton University Press.

Ricoeur, Paul. 1980. *The Contribution of French Historiography to the Theory of History*. Oxford: Clarendon Press.
Rogers, A. K. 1935. "Plato's Theory of Forms." *The Philosophical Review* 44(6): 515–33.
Rubin, Alissa. J. 2014. "On Bridges in Paris, Clanking with Love." *New York Times*, 28 April.
Ruch, Barbara. 1997. "The Other Side of Culture in Medieval Japan." In *The Cambridge History of Japan*, vol. 3, *Medieval Japan*, 500–43. Cambridge: Cambridge University Press.
Saeki Arikiyo. (1990) 1995. *Himeko. Nihon Kokushi Daijiten*, ed. Kokushi Daijiten Henshū Iinkai, 11:986. Tokyo: Yoshikawa Kōbunkan.
Saeki Etatsu. 1988. *Haibutsu Kishaku Hyakunen* [One hundred years of Expulsion of Buddhism and Destruction of Shākyamuni]. Miyazaki: Kōmyakusha.
Saeki Umetomo, ed. (1981) 2020. *Kokinwakashū*. Tokyo: Iwanami Shoten.
Saigō, Nobutsuna. (1967) 1984. *Kojiki no Sekai* [The world of the *Kojiki*]. Tokyo: Iwanami Shoten.
Saitō Shōji. 1977. *Hana no Shisōshi* [History of concepts associated with flowers]. Tokyo: Gyōsei.
———. (1979) 1985. *Shokubutsu to Nihon Bunka* [Plants and Japanese culture]. Tokyo: Yasaka Shobō.
———. 1982. "Futatabi Sekai no Sakura e" [Once again cherry blossoms of the world]. *Nihon Jishin* 23: 25–30.
Sakakura Atsuyoshi, ed. 1970. *Taketori Monogatari* [The story of the bamboo cutter]. Tokyo: Iwanami Shoten.
Sakamoto Tarō, Ienaga Saburō, and Ōno Susumu, eds. 1965. *Nihonshoki (Ge)*, vol. 2. Tokyo: Iwanami Shoten.
———. 1967. *Nihonshoki (Jō)*, vols. 1 and 2. Tokyo: Iwanamai Shoten.
Sakamoto Yūji. 1977. *Hasu* [Lotus]. Tokyo: Hōsei Daigaku Shuppankyoku.
Sakurai Haruo. 1986. "Okibiki to Shira'ishi Mochi" [Pulling of trees and brining white pebbles]. In *Ise no Jingū to Shikinen Sengū*, 82–121. Tokyo: Kōgakkan Daigaku Shuppanbu.
Sakurai, Katsunoshin. 1988. "Ōnamesai to Kannamesai" [Ōnamesai and Kannamesai]. In *Zusetsu Tennō no Sokuirei to Ōnamesai*, ed. H. Yamamoto, M. Satō, and staff, 32–34. Tokyo: Shinjinbutsu Ōraisha.
Sakurai Tokutarō. 1976. *Minkan Shinkō to Sangaku Shūkyō* [Folk beliefs and the belief in the mountains]. Tokyo: Meicho Shuppan.
Sakurai Yoshiaki. 2011. *Koshi* [Carriages]. Tokyo: Hōsei Daigaku Shuppankyoku.
Sakurazawa Yukikazu. 1938. *Shizen Igaku* [Natural medical practice]. Tokyo: Shokuyōkai.
Sanders, Todd. 2003. "Reconsidering Witchcraft: Postcolonial Africa and Analytic (Un-) certainties." *American Anthropologist* 105(2): 338–52.
Sano Tōemon. 1998. *Sakura no Inochi Niwa no Kokoro* [The life of cherry blossoms, the soul of the garden]. Tokyo: Sōshisha.
Sansom, George. 1958. *A History of Japan to 1334*. Stanford, CA: Stanford University Press.

———. 1961. *A History of Japan, 1334–1615*. Stanford, CA: Stanford University Press.
———. 1978. *A Short Cultural History*. Stanford, CA: Stanford University Press.
Sasaki Hachirō. 1981. *Seishun no Isho* (The Will of the Youth). Ed. by Fujishiro Hajime. Tokyo: Shōwa Shuppan.
Sasaki Kōmei. (1991) 1992. *Nihonshi Tanjō* [The birth of Japanese history]. Tokyo: Shūeisha.
Sasaki Nobutsuna, ed. (1929) 2020. *Shin Kokin Wakashū*. Tokyo: Iwanami Shoten.
Satake Akihiro. (1967) 1970. *Gekokujō no Bungaku* [Literature of the *Gekokujō* (the below conquering the above)]. Tokyo: Chikuma Shobō.
Satake Akihiro, Yamada Hideo, Kudō Riki'o, Ōtani Masao, and Yamazaki Yoshiyuki, eds. (2013) 2019. Manyōshū (Vol. 8). Vol. 2 of Satake, et al. Tokyo: Iwanami Shoten.
———. (2014) 2019. Manyōshū (Vol. 10). Vol. 3 of Satake, et al. Tokyo: Iwanami Shoten.
Satō Kazuhiko. 1995[1985]. Godaigo Tennō. In *Kokushi Daijiten* 5: 859–860. Tokyo: Yoshikawa Kōbunkan.
Satō Kenji. 1994. "Petto (Aigan Dōbutsu)" [Pet—Lovable toy animals]. In *Taishū Bunka Jiten*, ed. Ishikawa Hiroshi et al., 706–7. Tokyo: Kōbundō.
Satō Takumi. 2002. "'*Kingu no Jidai: Kokumin Taishū Zasshi no Kōkyōsei*." [The age of king: Mass communication through popular magazines]. Tokyo: Iwanami Shoten.
Schama, Simon. 1988. *The Embarrassment of the Riches*. Berkeley: University of California Press.
Sei Shōnagon. (1000) 2007. *Makura no Sōshi* [The pillow book], vol. 18, *Shinpen Nihon Koten Bungaku Zenshū*, ed. Matsuo Satoshi and Nagai Kazuko. Tokyo: Shōgakukan.
Seki Keigo. 1978a. "Hanasakajiji'i." [Old man and cherry blossoms]. In *Nihon Mukashibanashi Taisei*, 4:207–28. Tokyo: Kadokawa Shoten.
———. 1978b. "Shitakiri Suzume." [A sparrow whose tongue is cut off]. In *Nihon Mukashibanashi Taisei*, 4:239–48. Tokyo: Kadokawa Shoten.
———. 1981. "Bunbuku Chagama." In *Nihon Mukashibanashi Taisei*, 6:113–19. Tokyo: Kadokawa Shoten.
Seki, Yukihiko. 1991a. "Bushi" [Warriors]. In *Kokushi Daijiten*: 12: 127-28. Kokushi Daijiten Henshū Iinkai, ed. Tokyo: Yoshikawa Kōbunkan.
———. 1991b. "Bushidan" [Stories about warriors]. In *Kokushi Daijiten*: 12: 149-50. Kokushi Daijiten Henshū Iinkai, ed. 12:149–50. Tokyo: Yoshikawa Kōbunkan.
Shields, Christopher. 2020. "Aristotle." *Stanford Encyclopedia of Philosophy*. Last updated 25 August, https://plato.stanford.edu/entries/aristotle/.
Shimura Kunihiro, trans. 1980. *Kojidan* [The stories of ancient times: The origin of the medieval *setsuwa* stories], vol. 58. Tokyo: Kyōikusha.
Shinmura Izuru. (1955) 1990. *Kōjien* [Dictionary], 3rd edn. Tokyo: Iwanami Shoten.
Shinbo Tōru, ed. 1982. *Yamato-e no Shiki: Heian Kamakura no Kachou* [The four seasons of the *Yamato-e* style of paintings: Flowers and birds during the Heian and Kamakura periods]. Tokyo: Gakushū Kenkyūsha.

Shinoda Masahiro. 2019. *Himeko Shūwo Madowasu* [Himeko—Fools people]. Tokyo: Gengi Shobō.
Shirahata Yōbaburō. 2012. *Niwa wo Yomitoku—Kyōto no Koji* [Interpreting the gardens—Ancient temples in Kyoto]. Kyoto: Tankōsha.
Shirane, Haruo. 2012. *Japan and the Culture of the Four Seasons.* New York: Columbia University Press.
Shōji Katsuya. 2014. "Nihon ni okeru Shizen nit suite no Shōkō" [An essay on Japanese nature]. *Nijū-Isseiki Shakai Dezain Kenkyū* 13: 81–90.
Shōzō Satō. 1997. "Kokuritsu Kōen" [National parks]. In *Kokushi Daijiten*, ed. Kokushi Daijiten, 5:711–12. Tokyo: Yoshikawa Kōbunkan.
Shweder, Richard A. 2022. "The Illusions of 'Magical Thinking': Whose Chimera, Ours or Theirs?" *HAU: Journal of Ethnographic Theory* 12(1): 319–25.
Simmel, Georg. (1907) 1950. *The Sociology of Georg Simmel.* New York: The Free Press.
———. 1978. *The Philosophy of Money.* trans. Tom Bottomore and David Frisby. London: Routledge and Kegan Paul.
Smith, Henry D., and Amy G. Poster. (1986) 1988. *Hiroshige: One Hundred Famous Views of Edo.* New York: George Braziller.
Smith, Robert J. 1974. *Ancestor Worship in Contemporary Japan.* Palo Alto: Stanford University Press.
Smith, Robertson. (1889) 1972. *The Religion of the Semites.* New York: Schocken Books.
Soper, Kate. 1995. *What Is Nature? Culture, Politics, and the Non-Human.* Oxford: Blackwell.
Sotomura Ataru. 1992. "'Sakuteiki' ni Iu Karesansui no Genryū." [The origin of Karesansui according to *Sakuteiki*]. *Zōen Zasshi* 56(1): 1–14.
Squatriti, Paolo. 2024. "A Tale of Two Breads: The Eucharistic and the Everyday Loaf in Early Medieval Europe." Public lecture delivered at Downtown Ann Arbor District Library, 18 February.
Sugiura Minpei. 1965. *Sengoku Ransei no Bungaku* [Literature of the turbulent world during the cyclical conquest era]. Tokyo: Iwanami Shoten.
Suzuki Keizō. 1984. "Gissha" [Ox-drawn carriage]. In *Kokushi Daijiten*, ed. Kokushi Daijiten Henshū Iinkai, 4:156–58. Tokyo: Yoshikawa Kōbunkan.
———. (1986) 1994. "Jūni hitoe" [Twelve-layered kimono]. In *Kokushi Daijiten*, ed. Kokushi Daijiten Henshū Iinkai, 7:294. Tokyo: Yoshikawa Kōbunkan.
———. (1991) 1996. "Hōren" [Imperial carriage]. In *Kokushi Daijiten*, ed. Kokushi Daijiten Henshū Iinkai, 12:781. Tokyo: Yoshikawa Kōbunkan.
Suzuki Masamune. 1991. *Yama to Kami to Hito* [Mountains, deities, and humans]. Tokyo: Tankōsha.
Takada Hirohiko, ed. 2009. *Kokin Wakashū.* Tokyo: Kadokawa Shoten.
Takagi Hiroshi. 1998. "Sakura to Nashonarizumu" [Cherry blossoms and nationalism]. In *Seiki Tenkanki ni okeru Kokusai Chitsujo no Keisei to Kokumin Bunka no Hen'yō*, ed. Nishikawa Nagao and Watanabe Kōzō, 1–15. Tokyo: Kashiwa Shobō.
———. 2017. "Taishō Shōwa Senzenki no Gakumon to Ryōbo Mondai." [Problems in regard to the imperial tombs during the prewar periods of Taishō and

Shōwa]. In *Sekai Isan to Tennōryō Kofun wo Tou*, ed. Iwao Fumiaki and Takagi Hiroshi, 129–56. Kyōto: Shibunkaku.
Takashima, Yūzaburō. 1975. *Matsu* (Pine Tree). Tokyo: Hōseidaigaku Shuppankyoku.
Takeda Yūkichi and Nakamura Hirotoshi, eds. (1977) 1982. *Shintei Kojiki*. Tokyo: Kadokawa Shoten.
Tambiah, S. J. 1968. "The Ideology of Merit and the Social Correlates of Buddhism in a Thai Village." In *Dialectic in Practical Religion*, ed. E. R. Leach, 41–121. Cambridge: Cambridge University Press.
———. 1970. *Buddhism and the Spirit of Cults in North-East Thailand*. Cambridge: Cambridge University Press.
———. (1990) 1991. *Magic, Science, Religion and the Scope of Rationality*. Cambridge: Cambridge University Press.
Tanaka, Kōji. 2002. "Crop-Raising Techniques in Asian Rice Culture: Resemblances to Root and Tuber Crop Cultivation." In *Vegeculture in Eastern Asia and Oceania*, ed. Yoshida Shūji and Peter J. Mathews, 45–58. Osaka: National Museum of Ethnology.
Tanaka, Takashi. 1988. "Niiname kara Ōname' e [From the Niiname to the Ōname]. In *Zusetsu Tennō no Sokuirei to Ōnamesai* [Illustrated history of the imperial enthronement rituals and Ōnamesai], ed. H. Yamamoto, M. Satō, and staff, 28–30. Tokyo: Shinjinbutsu Ōraisha.
Taniguchi Kengo. 2012. *Inu to Nihonshi: Ningen to tomo ni Ayunda Ichiman-nen no Monogatari* [Japanese history of dogs: The story for ten thousand years for humans and dogs]. Tokyo: Yoshikawa Kōbunkan.
Tatsumi Hamako. 1966. *Teshio ni Kaketa Watakushi no Ryōri* [My home cooking] Tokyo: Shufuno Tomosha.
———. 2002 *Ryōri Saijiki* [Culinary almanac]. Tokyo: Chūkōbunko.
Tatsumi Masaaki. 1993. *Manyōshu to Chūgoku Bungaku (Dai Ni)* [*Manyōshū* and Chinese literature, No. 2]. Tokyo: Kasama Shoin.
Taube, Karl A. (1983) 1985. "The Classic Maize God: A Reappraisal." In *Fifth Palenque Round Table, 1983*, ed. Merle Greene Robertson. San Francisco: Pre-Columbian Art Research Institute.
Taussig, Michael. 1993. *Mimesis and Alterity: A Particular History of the Senses*. New York: Routledge.
Thomas, Julia. 2002. *Reconfiguring Modernity: Concepts of Nature in Japanese Political Ideology*. Berkeley: University of California Press.
Thomas, Keith. 1971. *Religion and the Decline of Magic: Studies in Popular Beliefs in Sixteenth and Seventeenth Century England*. New York: Charles Scribner's Sons.
Tierney, Kenji. 2023. "Knots in Sumo Wrestling and Japan." In *Knots: Ethnography of the Moral in Culture and Society*, ed. David Lipset and Eric K. Silverman, 23–40. New York: Routledge.
Toda, Teiyū. 1978. *Bokkei, Gyokan* [Bokkei and Gyokan]. Tokyo: Kōdansha.
Toita Yasuji and Yoshida Chiaki. 1981. *Shashin Kabuki Saijiki* [Photo illustrations of the seasons in the Kabuki plays). Tokyo: Kōdansha.
Tokida Kunihiko. 2016. *Nihon no Shuryō oyobi Chōjū Hogoseido no Henka to 2014nen no Chōjū Hogohō Kaisei* [Changes in the hunting and birds and animal protection

system and the 2014 revision of the Law of the Protection of Birds and Animals]. Tokyo: Kankyōshō Nihonseifu.

Tokinoya Shigeru. (1990) 1995. "Baikan" [Sale of ranks]. In *Kokushi Daijiten*, ed. Kokushi Daijiten Henshū Iinkai, 11:452–53. Tokyo: Yoshikawa Kōbunkan.

Tōkyō to Edo Tōkyō Hakubutsukan. 1993. *Edo Tōkyō Hakubutsukan Sōgō Annai* [Introduction to the Edo-Tokyo Museum].Tokyo: Tōkyō to Edo Tōkyō Hakubutsukan.

Tōkyō Daigaku Daigakuin Nōgaku Seimeikagaku Kenkyūka. 2013. *Tōdai Hachikō Monogatari* [Tokyo University story about *Hachikō*.] Tokyo: Tokyo Daigaku Nōgakubu.

Torii Kazushi. 1998. *Nihon no Kokoro: Fuji no Biten* (The Exhibition on the soul of Japan: The beauty of Fuji). Nagoya: NHK Nagoya Hōsōkyoku.

———.1998. "Nihon no Kokoro: Fuji no Bi" [The Soul of Japan: The Beauty of Fuji]. In *Nihon no Kokoro: Fuji no Biten* [The exhibition on the soul of Japan: The beauty of Fuji], ed. Torii Kazushi, et al., 2–11. Nagoya: NHK Nagoya Hōsōkyoku.

Toriiminami Masatoshi. (1988) 1990. "Inarikō no Konnjaku" [Inari cult past and present]. In *Inari Myōjin*, ed. Matsumae Takeshi, 165–90. Tokyo: Chikuma Shobō.

Toshiya, Torao. 1993. "Nara Economic and Social Institutions." In *The Cambridge History of Japan*, ed. Marius Jansen, 1:415–52. Cambridge: Cambridge University Press.

Tsuboi, Hirofumi. (1982) 1984. *Ine o Eranda Nihonjin* [The Japanese who chose rice plant]. Tokyo: Miraisha.

Tsubouchi Yūzō. 1999. *Yasukuni*. Tokyo: Shinchōsha.

Tsukuba, Tsuneharu. (1969) 1986. *Beishoku, Nikushoku no Bunmei* [Civilizations based on rice consumption and meat consumption]. Tokyo: Nihon Hōsō Shuppankai.

Tsumura, Masayoshi. (1917) 1970. *Tankai* [The ocean of stories]. Tokyo: Kokusho Kankōkai.

Tsunoda Ryūsaku and L. Carrington Goodrich. 1968. *Japan in the Chinese Dynastic Histories*. Kyoto: Perkins Oriental Books.

Tsunoda Bun'ei. (1991) 1996. "Hei'an-kyō." In *Kokushi Daijiten*, ed. Kokushi Daijiten Henshū Iinkai, 12:434–38. Tokyo: Yoshikawa Kōbunkan.

Tuan, Yi-Fu. 1984. *Dominance and Affection: The Making of Pets*. New Haven, CT: Yale University Press.

———. 1986. *The Good Life*. Madison: University of Wisconsin Press.

Turner, Victor. 1967. *The Forest of Symbols: Aspects of Ndembu Ritual*. Ithaca, NY: Cornell University Press.

———. 1975. Symbolic Studies. *Annual Review of Anthropology* 4:145-61.

Turner, Terence S. (2009) 2017. "The Crisis of Late Structuralism. Perspectivism and Animism: Rethinking Culture, Nature, Spirit, and Bodiliness." In *The Fire of the Jaguar*, ed. Jane Fajans, 205–43. Chicago: HAU.

Uchida, Kuniaki. 1994. Shūgaku Ryokō (School Trip). Taishū Bunka Jiten (Dictionary of Popular Culture). P. 339. Ishikawa Hiroyoshi, et al. eds. Tokyo: Kōbundō.

Ueda, Kenji. 1988. "Ōnamesai Seiritsu no Haikei" [The background of the establishment of the Ōnamesai]. In *Zusetsu Tennō no Sokuirei to Ōnamesai* [Illustrated history of the imperial enthronement rituals and Ōnamesai]. Pp. 31-32, ed. Yamamoto Hikaru et al., Tokyo: Shinjinbutsu Ōraisha.
Uegaki Setsuya. 1991⌋1996. Fudoki. *Kokushi Daijiten*. Vol. 12: 306. Tokyo: Yoshikawa Kōbunkan.
Umeya Kenji. 2005. "Mushi o Kiku Bunnka" [Culture that listens to insects]. *Hitotoki* 5(8).
Vansina, Jan. 1970. "Culture through Time." In *A Handbook of Method in Cultural Anthropology*, ed. R. Naroll and R. Cohen, 165–79. Washington, D.C.: Natural History Press.
———. 1978. *The Children of Woot: A History of the Kuba Peoples*. Madison: University of Wisconsin Press.
———. 1985. *Oral Tradition as History*. Madison: University of Wisconsin Press.
Varley, H. Paul. 1990. "Cultural Life in Medieval Japan." In *The Cambridge History of Japan*, 3:447–99. Cambridge: Cambridge University Press.
Viveiros de Castro, Eduardo. 1998. "Cosmological Deixis and Amerindian Perspectivism." *Journal of Royal Anthropological Institute*, n.s. 4(3): 469–88.
von Uexküll, Jakob. (1934) 1956. *Streifzüge durch die Umwelten von Tieren und Menschen. Bedeutungslehre*. Hamburg: Rowohlt.
———. 2010. *A Foray into the Worlds of Animals and Humans: With a Theory of Meaning*, trans. Joseph D. O'Neil. Minneapolis: University of Minnesota Press.
Wada Kiyoshi and Ishihara Michihiro, eds. 1952. *Zuisho Wakokuden* [The official history of the Sui dynasty].:Tokyo: Iwanami Shoten.
Wakamori Tarō. 1975. *Hana to Nihonjin* [Cherry blossoms and the Japanese].Tokyo: Sōgetsu Shuppan.
Watanabe Hiroshi. 1973. *The Ainu Ecosystem*. Seattle: University of Washington Press.
Watanabe Minoru. (1964) 1967. *Nihon Shoku Seikatsushi* [History of Japanese diet]. Tokyo: Yoshikawa Kōbunkan.
Watanabe Satomi. 1994. "Hasu no Kanshō no Rekishiteki Hensen ni tsuite" [The historical transition of the appreciation of lotuses[sic]]. *Zōen Zasshi* 57(5): 19–24.
Waters, Thomas. 2019. *Cursed Britain: A History of Witchcraft and Black Magic in Modern Times*. New Haven, CT: Yale University Press.
Watsuji Tetsurō. (1935) 1967. *Fūdo: Ningengakuteki Kōsatsu* [Fūdo: Interpretation from the perspective of the study of humans].Tokyo: Iwanami Shoten.
———. (1937, 1942) 1962. *Watsuji Tetsurō Zenshū Dai Jūkan*. Vol. 10, *Rinrigaku* [Ethics]. Tokyo: Iwanami Shoten.
———. (1949) 1962. *Watsuji Tetsurō Zenshū Dai Jūichikan*. Vol.11, *Rinrigaku* [Ethics]. Tokyo: Iwanami Shoten.
Weber, Max. (1930) 1992. *The Protestant Ethic and the Spirit of Capitalism*. New York: Routledge.
———. 1947. *The Theory of Social and Economic Organization*. New York: The Free Press.
Williams, Raymond. 1973. *The Country and the City*. Oxford: Oxford University Press.

Wilson, Brian R., ed. 1970. *Rationality*. Oxford: Blackwell.
Wolf, Eric R. 1999. *Envisioning Power*. Berkeley: University of California Press.
———. 2001. *Pathways of Power: Building an Anthropology of the Modern World*. Berkeley: University of California Press.
Yamada Munemutsu. 1977. *Hana no Bunkashi* [The cultural history of flowers]. Tokyo: Yomiuri Shinbunsha.
Yamada Takuzō and Nakajima Shintarō. 1995. *Manyō Shokubutsu Jiten* [Dictionary of plants in *Manyō*]. Tokyo: Hokuryūkan.
Yamada Takao. (1941) 1993. *Ōshi* [History of flowering cherry], ed. Yamada Tadao. Tokyo: Kōdansha.
Yamagishi Tokuhei, ed. 1958. *Genji Monogatari* [*The Tale of Genji*]. Vol. 1, *Nihon Koten Bungaku Taikei*. Vol. 14. Tokyo: Iwanami Shoten.
———, ed. 1959. *Genji Monogatari* [*The Tale of Genji*]. Vol. 2, *Nihon Koten Bungaku Taikei*. Tokyo: Iwanami Shoten.
———, ed. 1962. *Genji Monogatari* [*The Tale of Genji*]. Vol. 4, *Nihon Koten Bungaku Taikei*. Vol. 17. Tokyo: Iwanami Shoten.
Yamaguchi Osamu. 1996. "Yūbinkitte" [Postal stamps]. In *Kokushi Daijiten*, ed. Kokushi Daijiten Henshū Iinkai, 14:285. Tokyo: Yoshikawa Kōbunkan.
Yamamoto, H., M. Satō, and staff, eds. 1988. *Zusetsu Tennō no Sokuirei to Ōnamesai* [Illustrated history of the imperial enthronement rituals and Ōnamesai]. Tokyo: Shinjinbutsu Ōraisha.
Yamaori, Tetsuo. 1978. *Tennō no Shūkyōteki Ken'i towa Nanika* [What is the religious authority of the emperor]. Tokyo: Sanichi Shobō.
———. 1990a. "Kakureta Tennōrei Keizoku no Dorama: Daijōsai no Bunka Hikaku" [A hidden drama of the succession of the imperial soul: Cultural comparison of the Daijōsai] *Gekkan Asahi*, February: 80–85.
———. 1990b. *Shi no Minzokugaku* [Ethnography of death]. Tokyo: Iwanami Shoten.
Yamashita Kazu'umi. (1984) 1996. "Kidai" [Seasonal topics]. In *Kokushi Daijiten*, ed. Kokushi Daijiten Henshū Iinkai, 4:106. Tokyo: Yoshikawa Kōbunkan.
Yamazumi Masami. 1970. *Kyōkasho* [School textbooks]. Tokyo: Iwanami Shoten.
Yanagita, Kunio. (1920) 1979. "Akagozuka no Hanashi" [The memorial for the newborn]. In *Yanagita Kunio-shū* [Collected work of Yanagita Kunio], 12:214–51. Tokyo: Chikuma Shobō.
———. (1920) 1982. "Saru Mawashi no Hanashi" [The tale of monkey performance]. In *Yanagita Kunio-shū* [Collected work of Yanagita Kunio], 27:336–40. Tokyo: Chikuma Shobō.
———. (1942) 1982. "Nihon no Matsuri" [Japanese festivals]. In *Yanagita Kunioshū* [Collected writings of Kunio Yanagita], 10:153–314. Tokyo: Chikuma Shobō.
———. (1947) 1982. "Sannō no saru" [Mountain deity and the monkey]. In *Yanagita Kunio-shū* [Collected work of Yanagita Kunio], 11:333–337. Tokyo: Chikuma Shobō.
———. (1948) 1982. "Kitsunezuka no Hanashi" [The story about the fox den]. In *Yanagita Kunio-shū* [Collected work of Yanagita Kunio], 13:356–61. Tokyo: Chikuma Shobō.

———. 1951a. "Ta no Kami" [Deity of rice paddies]. In *Minzokugaku Jiten* [Ethnographic dictionary], ed. Minzokugaku Kenkyūjō, 357–60. Tokyo: Tōkyōdō Shuppan.

———. 1951b. "Ningyō" [Dolls]. In *Minzokugaku Jiten* [Ethnographic dictionary], ed. Minzokugaku Kenkyūjō, 435–36. Tokyo: Tōkyōdō Shuppan.

———. (1952) 1981. "Kaijō no Michi" [Sea route]. In *Yanagita Kunio-shū* [Collected work of Yanagita Kunio], 1:3–209. Tokyo: Chikuma Shobō.

———. 1963. "Sakai no Kami ni Ko wo Inoru Fūshū" [The tradition of praying to the deity of the border line for a child]. In *Yanagita Kunio-shū* [Collected work of Yanagita Kunio], 12:250–51. Tokyo: Chikuma Shobō.

———. (1968) 1981a. "Tōno Monogatari" [The stories from Tōno]. In *Yanagita Kunio-shū* [Collected work of Yanagita Kunio], 4:1–54. Tokyo: Chikuma Shobō.

———. (1968) 1981b. "Yōkai Dangi" [Discussion on the monsters/ghosts]. In *Yanagita Kunio-shū* [Collected work of Yanagita Kunio], 4:285–438. Tokyo: Chikuma Shobō.

———. (1970) 1982. "Nihon no Jinkō Mondai" [Population problems of Japan]. In *Yanagita Kunio-shū* [Collected work of Yanagita Kunio], 29:94–114. Tokyo: Chikuma Shobō.

Yasukuni Jinja. 1983–84. *Yasukuni Jinja Hyakunenshi* (History of one hundred years of Yasukuni Shrine), vol. 1 (1983), vol. 2 (1984). Tokyo: Yasukuni Jinja.

Yoda Tōru. 2015. *Bonsai.* Tokyo: Kadokawashoten.

Yokoi Akihiro. 1997. *Tamagocchi Tanjōki: Chō Hitto Shōhin ha Kōshite Tsukurareta!* [Record on the birth of Tamagocchi : How the Super-Hit Merchandize was Made]. Tokyo: Besutosera-zu.

Yokota, Ken'ichi. 1988. "Ōnamesai Seiritsu Jidai Hosetsu" [Additional explanation for the age of the establishment of the Ōnamesai]. In *Zusetsu Tennō no Sokuirei to Ōnamesai*, ed. H. Yamamoto, M. Satō, and staff, 27–29. Tokyo: Shinjinbutsu Ōraisha.

Yoshida Tadanori. 2017. "Naze Suiden de Renkon?" [Why the lotus roots in rice paddies?]. *Nikkei Bijinesu,* 13 January.

Yoshida Teigo. (1972) 1978. *Nihon no Tsukimono* [Possessions in Japanese society]. Tokyo: Chūōkōronsha.

Yoshimura Takehiko. 1998. *Kodai Tennō no Tanjō* (The Birth of Emperors during the Ancient Period.. Tokyo: Kadokawa Shoten.

Yoshino, Hiroko. 1980. *Kitsune—Onyō Gogyō to Inari Shinkō* [Fox and Fox Cult]. Tokyo: Hōsei Daigaku Shuppankyoku.

Yoshioka Masayuki. 1992. "Mogari." In *Kokushi Daijiten*, ed. Kokushi Daijiten Henshū Iinkai, 3:810. Tokyo: Yoshikawa Kōbunkan.

Young, Crawford. 2012. *The Postcolonial State in Africa: Fifty Years of Independence, 1960–2010.* Madison: University of Wisconsin Press.

Index

"above and the below", 14, 15, 16, 18, 31, 47, 58, 59, 60, 76, 77, 79, 80, 100n2
aesthetics, 67, 70, 73–76, 87–90, 94, 99, 108
Agamben, Giorgio, 41
Akita Hiroki, 76–77, 141
Amaterasu Ōmikami (Sun Goddess), 24, 30, 32, 36, 51, 53, 58
amulets, 43n10, 156, 165, 173, 181
Anamori Inari Shrine, Tokyo, 35–36
ancestors, with other deceased humans, 28–30
Andō (Utagawa) Hiroshige (1797–1858), 107, 113, 116, 118n3
Andō Takeshi, 141–42
animals, 4–7, 16, 21, 33–35, 39, 48, 56, 163. *See also* meat eating; nonhuman animals; *specific animals*
animism, 21, 34, 40–41, 158, 165–67, 175, 181
Appadurai, Arjun, 174
Aquinas, Thomas, 28, 168
Aristotle, 7, 12, 19, 41, 162, 168
Asad, Talal, 161
Asquith, Pamela, 36
Augé, Marc, 14

Bandai, 145
Barthes, Roland, 182
Baudelaire, Charles (1821–67), 14, 180
Belmont, Nicole, 168
below, See the "above"

Benedict, Ruth, 133n6
Benjamin, Walter, 10–11, 183
Benveniste, Émile, 168
Bernier, Bernard, 80n1
Berque, Augustin, 64
Bertelli, Sergio, 7
Billington, James H., 5–6
birds, 31, 57, 60, 66, 69, 73, 106
    robot, 146
    twelve months defined by, 17, 72, 88
Bloch, Marc, 13
bonsai, 12, 17, 19, 109, 111, 117, 182
boundary crossing, 30–31, 33–40
Bourdieu, Pierre, 179–80
Braudel, Fernand, 9, 13
Bray, Francesca, 49
Brueghel the Younger, Jan, 39, 43n11
bush clover, 65, 66, 67, 68, 72, 88, 89

Candea, Matei, 20n1
capitalism, 17–18, 137, 153, 158, 161–62, 174–76, 180–81
carriages, 16, 70–71, 76–80, 140–41, 177
cars, 156–58, 165, 169, 181
cartography, 47, 59–60, 79, 177
carts, for pets, 143, 144, 158, 160
Cassirer, Ernst, 23
Chabal, Patrick, 174n2
cherry blossoms, 66–68, 80nn2–3, 133n5, 134n12, 149, 177
    in Heian period, 18, 69, 72, 74, 113, 150
    military and, 12, 18, 125–26, 128–30, 133nn8–9, 176

as symbol of "Japanese nature," 111, 113–15, 117, 122, 124–31, 132
cherry trees, 70, 81–82nn6–7, 98–99, 130–32, 134n12
China, 22–23, 64–65, 67–68, 70, 76, 81n4, 112
chin dogs, 140–41
Christianity, 10, 27, 28, 103, 166–68, 170, 174
chrysanthemums, 71–72, 81n4, 89, 177
circus, 126, 133n7
Clinton, Bill, 148
comic play (*kyōgen*), 94–96, 100n2
Confucianism, 28, 133n5, 173
consumerism, 148, 152–54, 156, 158n1, 158n4, 178
    magical practice for sociality, 160–65
    pets, 143–46, 157–58, 158n2, 160
    religions and, 165–74
Contemporary period (after 1945)
    "domestication" of nonhuman inhabitants, 137–46
    foods, 146–52
    ground and avoidance in daily life, 153–55, 159n7
    Japanese four seasons, 149–50
    pet boom, 142–46, 157–58
    pure nature, pure water, 152–53
    purification of cars, 156–57, 158
cookbooks, 150–52, 178
cosmogony/cosmology, 14–15, 47, 52–56, 58–60, 79–80, 176–78
counting systems, 32, 42n7
countryside (*inaka*), 8–9, 72–73, 138
cows, 36–37, 41, 56–57, 66, 123, 137
creation myth, 52–54, 175
Culinary almanac (*Ryōri Saijiki*) (Tatsumi), 150
culturalization, 97, 108–11, 117, 152
cultural nationalism, 17, 76, 103, 105, 111–17, 121, 127, 131
culture, 4, 7, 12–15, 16, 19n1, 40, 175, 177, 180
    with four seasons and Heian period, 69–80, 149

merchants in Edo period with plebeian, 17, 104, 105, 112, 117, 182
cyclical conquest era (1477–1573), 85, 90, 138, 140

Daloz, Jean-Pascal, 174n2
Das, Veena, 176
Dasein, 63, 176
de Certeau, Michel, 176
deer, 34, 36, 41, 48, 50, 56, 66
deities (*kami*), 22, 25, 43n10, 50, 79, 156, 171–72
    Amaterasu Ōmikami, 24, 30, 32, 36, 51, 53, 58
    as inhabitants of universe, 21, 24, 26–28, 36, 41–42
    soul of rice-cum-, 52–55, 60–61n2
Deleuze, Gilles, 20n3
Descola, Philippe, 4–5, 6–7, 19n1, 40, 43n12
Destutt de Tracy, Antoine (1754–1836), 178
divine title (*shingō*), 27, 86
divinity, few ounces of, 54–55, 167
dogs, 7, 43n12, 48, 56, 140–44, 146, 182
Dōkyō (700–772), 70–71
dolls, 26, 82n7, 145
domestication, of nonhuman inhabitants, 140–46
Durkheim, Emile, 3, 4, 162
Durkheim, Emile and Maus, 3

Early Modern period (1603–1867), 8–9, 38–39, 43, 43n10, 95, 168
eating manners, 112, 133n2
Ebersole, Gary, 23
Edo period (1603–1867), 12, 34, 63, 118, 119n3, 138, 168–69, 172
    consumerism in, 157
    culturalization of "nature," 108–11, 117
    cultural nationalism and symbols of "Japanese nature," 111–17, 121, 127, 131

plebeian schemes of temporality, 105–8
Eisenstadt, S. N., 42n4, 173–74
Ellen, Roy, 4
Engishiki (record of laws and customs), 68
environment (*kankyō*), 6, 7, 18, 41, 63, 64, 106, 122, 153
    anthropological studies on nature and, 3–5
    culture and, 16, 177, 180

fashion, 74, 76, 132, 139, 177–78
festivals, 26, 29, 55, 68, 71, 78, 82n7, 107, 131
a few ounces of divinity, 54–55, 167
fires, 81n5, 82n6, 86
fish, 26, 31, 48, 50, 57, 64, 105–6
    cooking and use of, 151
    goldfish, 137, 138, 139, 142
flowers, 4–5, 29–30, 33, 69, 80n3, 134n12, 176. *See also* bush clover, cherry blossoms
    chrysanthemums, 71–72, 81n4, 89, 133n6, 177
    plum blossoms, 65–67, 70, 80n2, 81n6, 114, 119n4, 177
    twelve months defined by, 17, 72, 88, 114
Flowers That Kill (Ohnuki-Tierney), 176–77, 179
folk, 32–33, 59, 78–79, 118
folktales, 33, 39, 64, 80, 83n10, 110, 115, 169
    Medieval period, 98–99
    rewards in, 78, 172, 181
foods, 8, 31, 42n3, 49, 53–55, 57, 66, 112, 147, 178. *See also* meat eating; rice
    chemicals on, 146, 148–49, 158n5, 159n10
    for four seasons, 150–52
    plant, 28, 42, 106, 148, 151, 158n3
footwear, 16, 96, 159n9, 160, 177
    with avoidance of ground, 76, 93, 99, 153–55, 159n7
    traditional, 77, 159n8
foxes, 16, 33–36, 39, 41, 48
Francks, Penelope, 157
Frazer, James George, 23, 40, 174n1
Fudoki, 49–50, 64, 66
Fujii Jōji, 86
Fujiwara no Teika (1162–1241), 87–88, 106
Fukuzawa Yukichi, 124
funerals, 51, 57, 60n1, 62n5, 141, 158n1, 166, 169

Geertz, Clifford, 178, 180
gekokujō (lower conquering the upper), 16–17, 85, 93, 95, 103
Genmei (Empress) (r. 707–15), 50, 60n1, 64, 77
Genshin (1476–1559), 83n8
Geschiere, Peter, 20n1
Gishi Wajinden, 51
The Golden Bough (Frazer), 40, 174n1
goldfish, 137, 138, 139, 142
Gombrich, E. H., 181
Gomizuo (Emperor) (1596–1680), 86–87, 93–94
Goody, Jack, 4
Gotoba (Emperor) (1180–1239), 71, 85, 87
Goyōuzei (Emperor) (1571–1617), 27, 86, 94
Graeber, David, 20n1
grafting (*tsugiki*), 108
Gregory, Christopher A., 49
ground, avoidance of, 16, 76, 80, 93, 99, 143, 153–55, 159n7
    see also "the below"
Guattari, Félix, 165–66, 174

Hachikō statue, 141–42
haikai/haiku, 17, 105, 107–8, 182
Haksar, Sharad, 153
Hall, Edward, 90
Handelman, Don, 20n3
Haneda Airport, 35–36
Harada, Nobuo, 57

Hardacre, Helen, 158n1
Harootunian, Harry, 9, 30, 57, 163
Hasegawa Kakugyō, 116
Hasegawa Settan, 119n3
Hasegawa Tōhaku (1539–1610), 39–40
Heian period (794–1185), 35, 43n10, 52, 57, 83n9, 88, 91, 99, 109, 156
    carriages, 70–71, 76–78
    cherry blossoms and, 18, 69, 72, 74, 113, 150
    culturally defined four seasons and, 69–80, 149
    with insects "singing," 73–74, 111, 138, 176
    rituals, 24, 62n5, 68, 127
    women in elite class, 71–74, 140, 141
Heidegger, Martin, 62n6, 63, 176
Hendry, Joy, 159n6
Herrenschmidt, Olivier, 168
Hidari Jingorō, 104
Hirata Atsutane (1776–1843), 29–30, 57, 112
Hirono Takashi, 50
historical agents, 117, 178–80
history, culture as process of, 12–15
Hoa, Ho Hoang, 90
Hocart, A. M., 167–68
Horton, H. Mack, 22–23, 68–69, 89
Hosokawa Katsumoto (1430–73), 90
Hosokawa Morihiro, 148
Huet, Christophe, 39, 43n11
humans, 4–7, 27, 40–41, 43n12, 63, 163–64. *See also* nonhuman animals
    ancestors and other deceased, 21, 28–30
    metamorphosis of animals into, 33–35
hunting, 6–8, 10, 41, 49, 50–51
hunting-gathering, 3, 6, 32, 48, 49, 56, 140, 163

Ichijō (Emperor) (980–1011), 72, 140
Ichirō, Ōga, 67
Iizumi, Kenji, 36, 50
Imae Hiromichi, 82n6
inanimate objects, 26, 145, 167

Inari shrines, 34–36, 170, 171
India, 7, 28, 68, 125, 153, 167
Ingold, Tim, 4
inhabitants of the universe, 31–32, 41–42
    boundary crossing, 33–40
    domestication of nonhuman, 137–46
    without physical form, 21–30
Inoue Hisashi, 149
insects, 16, 25, 39, 64, 80, 89, 112
    domestication of, 137, 138–39
    "singing" of, 73–74, 111, 138, 176
invisible inhabitants, of universe, 21, 28–30
Ise Shrine, 24, 30, 61n5, 74, 94, 159n10, 165
Isozaki Arata, 24
Itō Jakuchū (1716–1800), 83n8

Japanese four seasons, 11, 75, 79–80, 105–6, 149–50, 152, 179
Japanese nature (*Nihon no shizen*), 10, 16–18, 47, 175–76, 179
    Edo period with cultural nationalism and symbols of, 111–17, 121, 127, 131
    Modern period with symbols of, 122–32
Jay, Martin, 5
Jinmu (Emperor), 53–54, 77, 126–28
Jōmon hunting-gathering period (14,500–3,000 BCE), 32, 48, 49, 56, 140, 163

Kaibara Ekken (1630–1714), 105, 114–15
Kakinomoto-no-Hitomaro, 22–23, 50
kamikaze (*tokkōtai*) plane, 128–31
Kamo Momoki, 126
Kamo-no-Mabuchi (1697–1769), 75
Kanagaki Robun (1829–94), 123
Kanmu (Emperor) (r. 781–806), 61–62n5, 70–72, 81–82n6
Kanō Eiō Fujiwara Katsunobu (1731–1805), 107
Kanō Harukawain Osanobu (1796–1846), 107

Kanō Tokuei (1543–90), 83n8
Kant, Immanuel, 6, 20n3, 162, 163
Kantorowicz, Ernst H., 27, 85
Kaplan, Martha, 152
Katsushika Hokusai (1760–1849), 106–7, 116, 118nn1–2
Kelly, John, 20n1, 157, 172
Kingu (magazine), 121, 131
Kitagawa, Joseph, 42n4, 84
Kobayashi Issa (1763–1827), 107–8
Kobori Enshū (1579–1647), 108
Kojiki, 32–33, 37, 50, 69, 79, 89
    rice and, 42, 52–54, 61n2
    space and, 30, 58, 177
Kōninshiki, 56, 93
Konoe Fumimaro, 128
Korea, 15, 18, 51–52, 62n5, 86, 114, 129
kōshin belief and practice, 42–43n10
Kubota Jun, 82n6
Kumakura Isao, 93
Kuper, Adam, 174n1
Kusumi Morikage (1688–1704), 107
Kyburz, Josef A., 165

LaFleur, William, 100n2, 163
Lao Tzu, 63
Latour, Bruno, 11, 20n1, 162
Leach, Edmund, 62n6, 161–62, 170, 179–80
Le Roy Ladurie, Emmanuel, 13
Lévi-Strauss, Claude, 4, 163–64, 181
Lévy-Bruhl, Lucien, 40, 174n1
lives of the folk, 59, 78–79, 118
loneliness. See *sabi* aesthetics
love locks, in Paris, 165, 166
lower conquering the upper. See *gekokujō*
Lukács, György, 11, 172–73

Macé, François, 60n1
magical practice, 18–19, 160–65, 180–81
Malinowski, Bronislaw, 164, 174n1
Manyōshū, 22, 36, 50, 63, 70, 73, 77, 111, 115, 128
    rice in, 16, 66–67, 177
    seasons in, 65–69, 75, 79, 89, 149

marriage, 34, 40, 43n12, 71, 93–94, 164
Marx, Karl, 11, 162, 168, 172
Marxism, 55, 100n2, 130, 163
Matsunoo Taisha Shrine, 24, 25, 31
Mauss, Marcel, 3, 4, 62n6, 161, 164
McCullough, Helen Craig, 68–69
McCullough, W. and McCullough H., 77-78, 181n4
meat eating, 9, 31–33, 42, 42n9, 124, 133n2
    political power with hunting and, 41, 49, 50–51
    prohibitions, 56–57, 123
Medieval period (1185–1603), 34, 57, 163
    monkey in, 37–38, 40, 95–98, 100n2
    rock garden
    social structure unhinged, 16–17, 84–87
    tea ceremony, 87, 90–94, 99
    transformations of "nature," 87–90
Meiji (Emperor), 57, 120, 123
memorial services, 24, 26, 144–45, 157–58, 167, 181
metamorphosis, boundary crossing and, 33–35
militarization, 121, 124, 126, 131–32, 137, 141–42
military, 51, 84, 91, 103, 120. See also shogunate
    cherry blossoms and, 12, 18, 125–26, 128–30, 133nn8–9, 176
    power, 7, 17, 85, 93, 125
Millet, Jean-François (1814–75), 8
mimesis, 3, 10–12, 17, 19
Mintz, Sidney, 13, 180
Mitsuya Shigematsu, 55
miyabi aesthetics, 75–76
Miyake Hitoshi, 21, 42n5
Miyasaka Hakui, 110–11
Miyata Noboru, 10, 27, 59, 171
modernity, 11, 14, 160–64
Modern period (1868–1945).
    cherry blossoms, 122, 124–31, 132
    Japanese rice, 123–24
    military dogs, 141–42

Mount Fuji, 131–32
  symbols of "Japanese nature" in, 122–32
Monet, Claude (1840–1926), 8
money, 11, 15, 19, 166–70, 172, 175, 181
monkeys, 25–26, 33–34, 41, 43nn11–12, 56–57, 68, 100n2, 103–4
  kōshin and, 42–43n10
  netsuke, 110
  performance, 37–39, 95–98, 163
  as sacred messenger, 36–40
Monmu (Emperor) (r. 697–707), 50–51, 60n1
months, twelve, 17, 72–73, 75, 80, 88, 114, 151
moon, 39–40, 68, 78, 107, 163–64
Moore, Sally, 13
Mōri Motonari, 85
Mori Sosen (1747–1821), 95
Morse, Peter, 118n1
Mosko, Mark, 40
Mosse, George L., 121
Mostow, Joshua S., 75–76
Motoori Norinaga (1730–1801), 75, 125–26, 133n4–5
Mount Fuji, 17, 43n10, 83n9, 111, 115–17, 121, 131–32
multisensory perception, of environment, 5–6
Murakami Haruki, 55, 155
Murasaki Shikibu, 16, 70–75, 77, 78, 81n4, 163
Murata Jukō (1422/1423–1502), 92
Muromachi period (1338–1603), 43n10, 83n9, 85, 90–92, 94–96, 98, 115–16, 138, 171–72
Myers, Henry, 162
Myōan Eisai (1141–1215), 91

Nakajima Shintarō, 67, 80n2
Nakamura, Teiri, 33–34
Nakamura Hiroshi, 82n6
Nakanishi Susumu, 63
Nakao Sasuke, 80n2
Nanbokuchō (1336–92), 85, 94, 115

Nara period (646–794 CE), 22, 51–52, 64–69, 77, 149, 168, 176
nationalization, 106–8, 121–22, 124, 126–27, 132, 137
national parks, 18, 121–22, 131
Natsume Sōseki (1867–1916), 123
nature, 3–15, 40, 118, 122. See also Japanese nature, seasons,
  culturalization of, 108–11, 117, 152
  pure water 152–53
  "real," 3, 11, 18, 75, 106, 176
  representations of, 3, 4, 10–11, 14–15, 175, 181
  rock garden, as 17, 89–90, 109–11, 182
  twelve months with culturally defined, 17, 75, 80
  of *yūgen*, *sabi* and *wabi*, 87–89
netsuke, 12, 17, 19, 110–11, 116–18, 182
Newby, Howard, 8
Nihongi, 33, 37, 42, 50, 69, 79, 89
Nihonshoki, 52, 56, 61n2, 68, 77, 115
Nishi Amane, 125
Nishida Kitarō (1870–1945), 12, 23
Nishiyachi Seibi, 58
Nitobe Inazō (1862–1933), 125–26, 133n6
Nobutoki Kiyoshi, 128
noh drama, 87, 94, 99, 172
nonhuman animals, 30–32, 34–41, 137–46
Nukata (Princess) (630?–690?), 69, 89

object where the soul of a deity sojourns. See *yorishiro*
Oda Nobunaga (1534–82), 86, 91–92
Ogata Kōan (1810–63), 105, 120
Ōgimachi (Emperor) (1517–93), 85–86, 103
Ong, Walter, 23
Ōnishi Takijirō, 129
ontology, 14, 19n1, 24, 40–41, 52, 54–56
Orikuchi, Shinobu, 9, 22, 55, 59, 61nn4–5
Ōtani Kōzui, 131

the Other, 64–65, 103, 112, 123
Ōtomo no Yakamochi (716–85), 128

paintings, 39–40, 75, 82n8, 83n9, 107
pathos (*monono aware*), 75, 133n5
Perry, Matthew (Commodore), 105, 116, 120, 148
pets, 137, 139, 158n2, 160
    boom, 142–46, 157–58
    memorial services and burials for, 26, 144–45, 157–58, 167, 181
physical form, universe inhabitants without, 21–30
plants, 4, 5, 21, 30, 41, 48. *See also* flowers; rice; trees
    foods, 28, 42, 106, 148, 151, 158n3
    twelve months defined by, 17, 72, 88, 114
Plato (429?–347 BCE), 3, 7, 10–12, 19
plum blossoms, 65–67, 70, 80n2, 81n6, 114, 119n4, 177
plum trees, 72, 81–82n6
Ponsonby-Fane, R. A. B., 82n6
Portuguese, 103, 140
pottery, 48, 163
power, 7, 14, 38, 95, 97
    historical agents and unconscious, 178–80
    political, 27, 41, 49–55, 59–60, 64, 70, 79, 84–85, 92–94, 99, 103, 117–18
Primitive Classification (Durkheim and Maus), 3
purification, 146–49, 156–58, 169, 181

Ramos, Alcida Rita, 20n1
rationality, 9, 19, 90, 160–64, 181
Reader, Ian, 174
"real nature," 3, 11, 18, 75, 106, 176
religions, 3, 5–6, 9–10, 41–42, 145, 174n1
    consumerism and, 165–74
    with magic and capitalism in Japan today, 180–81
    reward in this world as basic tenet of, 170–72

    in social theory of modernity versus magic, 160–64
    reward in this world (*gensei ri'eki*), 71, 78–79, 99, 116, 170–73, 181
rice, 16, 29–31, 55, 59, 61n5, 66–67, 148
    Japanese, 112, 123–24, 149
    Kojiki and, 42, 52–54, 61n2
    paddies, 47, 56, 60, 112–13, 117–18, 124, 175
    as pure money, 11, 15, 19, 166–70, 175, 181
    the soul of, 9–10, 21, 61nn3–4
    "temporality," 105, 106–8
    wet-rice agriculture, 9, 15, 47, 49, 51, 60, 116, 177
Rich, Nathaniel, 11
Ricoeur, Paul, 13
Robot Pet, 146, 158n2
rock garden (*karesansui*), 12, 87, 91, 99, 118
    as "nature", 17, 89–90, 109–11, 182
    as representation of zero, 19, 182
rope for, with sacred space, 30, 31, 42n6
Rousmaniere, Nicole Coolidge, 159n9
Rozen, Paul, 147
Ruch, Barbara, 85

sabi (loneliness) aesthetics, 80, 87–89
sacredness, 6, 30–31, 34–40, 42n6, 43n10, 95
Saga (Emperor) (786–842, r. 809–23), 71, 72, 81n6
Saitō Hirokjichi, 141, 142
Saitō Shōji, 80nn2–3
Sakurazawa Nyoichi (1893–1966), 147, 158n3
Sano Tōemon, 129
Sansom, George, 85
Sasaki Hachirō, 130
Satō Takumi, 121, 131
Schiller, Friedrich, 161
Scidmore, Eliza Ruhamah, 130–31
seasons, four, 16, 74, 89, 151, 177–78
    Heian period and culturally defined, 69–80, 149

Japanese, 11, 75, 79–80, 105–6, 149–50, 152, 179
Nara period and agrarian, 64–69, 149
Seiji, Andō, 55
Sei Shōnagon (966–1025), 71, 72, 140, 176
Seki Keigo, 83n10
Sen-no-Rikyū, 92–93, 99
shaman, 51, 55, 59, 60n1
Shinkokinshū, 87–88
Shintoism, 21, 28, 52, 124–25, 147, 167, 171, 181
Shirahata Yōbaburō, 100n1
Shirane, Haruo, 11, 74, 88
Shōgaku Kokugo Dokuhon (Elementary School Reader), 134n11
shogunate, 17, 27, 33, 62n5, 77, 85, 86–87, 93–95, 99, 103,104, 108, 113, 117, 126, 172
    chin dogs and, 140–41
Shōwa period (1926–89), 57, 139
Simmel, Georg, 158, 168
Smith, Adam, 168
Smith, Robert, 167
sociality, magical practice for, 160–65
social structure, Medieval period, 16–17, 84–87
    animism and, 21, 34, 40–41, 158, 165–67, 175, 181
    as inhabitant of universe, 21–28, 30, 34, 36, 40–41
    without physical form, 21–26
    of rice, 9–10, 21, 61nn3–4
    of rice-cum-deity, 52–55, 60–61n2
space, 14, 20n3, 30–31, 42n6, 58–59, 177
Squatriti, Paolo, 28
stamps, postage, 131, 134n12
state formation, 49, 51–52
Sugaharain Tenmangū Jinja, 37
Sun Goddess. *See* Amaterasu Ōmikami
surmodernité (supermodernity), 14
symbols, of "Japanese nature," 111–17, 121–32

Taft, Helen Herron, 131

Takagi Hiroshi, 52
Takazaki Masakaze, 127
"The Tale of the Bamboo Cutter," 78–79, 115
Tamagotchi, 145–46
Tanka, Koji, 49
Tatsumi Hamako, 150
Tatsumi Masaaki, 89
Taussig, Michael, 11
taxes, 49, 58, 112, 139, 145, 167–68
tea ceremony (*chanoyu*), 17, 87, 90–94, 99, 182
temporality, 10, 13, 20n3, 105–8, 164, 175
Tenmu (Emperor) (r.672–86), 56, 62n5, 69, 77, 89, 177
Thomas, Julia, 132
Thomas, Keith, 161–62
Tierney, R. Kenji, 42n8
Tokugawa Hidetada (1579–1632), 27, 86–87, 93–94, 104, 113
Tokugawa Iyemitsu (1604–51), 113
Tokugawa Iyeyasu (1542–1616), 27, 86–87, 93–94, 103–4, 113, 172
Tokugawa Tsunayoshi, 33, 140
Tokugawa Yoshimune (1684–1751), 113
Tomb period (250–646), 49, 52, 67, 77
Torii Kazushi, 115–16
Torii Kiyonaga, 109
tourism, 18, 121–22, 132, 133n1, 149, 152, 172–74
Toyotomi Hideyoshi (1536–98), 17, 27, 40, 85–86, 91–93, 99, 172
trees, 30, 64, 69, 108, 156. See also specific trees
Turner, Terence S., 20n1

Ueno Eisaburō, 141, 142
Ukemochi no Kami, 42n3, 53
United States, 35, 105, 121, 130–32, 134n12, 146–49, 152
University of Tokyo, 67, 134n10, 141, 159n9
Up and down – see the "above" and the "below"
Utagawa Toyokuni, 109

Vansina, Jan, 12–13
Varley, H. Paul, 87–88
velcro, 154–55
Viveiros de Castro, Eduardo, 19n1, 40
von Uexküll, Jakob, 41, 64

wabi (plain and humble) aesthetics, 87–89, 90
Wakamori Tarō, 80n3
waka poems, 16–17, 65, 67, 72, 74–75, 84, 87–88, 106, 179
Wang Yi, 69
water, 58, 122
    pure, 47, 60, 112–13, 117–18, 124, 152–53, 175
water field (*suiden*) and land field (*rikuden*), 47, 58
Waters, Thomas, 162
Watsuji Tetsurō, 63, 80n1
Ways of Baloma (Mosko), 40
Weber, Max, 161, 178
Westerners, 103–5, 111, 116, 120–21, 123–25, 162, 174n2
wet-rice agriculture, 9, 15, 47, 49, 51, 60, 116, 177

Whitten, Norman, 12
Williams, Raymond, 8
Wolf, Eric R., 178
woodblock prints, 104, 107, 109, 112–14, 116–17, 138

Yamabe Akahito, 50
Yamada Takuzō, 67, 80n2
Yamanoue no Okura, 23, 42n2
Yamatai federation of kingdoms, 51
Yamazaki Tōji, 133n9
Yanagita Kunio, 9, 21, 30, 54
Yayoi period (800 BCE–250 CE), 48–51, 62n5
yorishiro (object where the soul of a deity sojourns), 22, 30, 79, 156
Yōsai Nobukazu (1872–1944), 126
Yoshida, Chiaki, 125
Yoshida, Teigo, 25
Yoshimura Takehiko, 51
yūgen (mystery and depth) aesthetics, 87–89, 94

zero, 19, 180–83
"zero-time fiction," 12

www.ingramcontent.com/pod-product-compliance
Lightning Source LLC
Chambersburg PA
CBHW051539020426
42333CB00016B/2005